THE LATER LACAN

SUNY series in Psychoanalysis and Culture
_____
Henry Sussman, editor

The Later Lacan

An Introduction

Edited by
Véronique Voruz
and Bogdan Wolf

STATE UNIVERSITY OF NEW YORK PRESS

Published by
State University of New York Press
Albany

For information, address
State University of New York Press,
194 Washington Avenue, Suite 305, Albany, NY 12210-2384

Production and book design, Kelli Williams
Marketing, Fran Keneston

Library of Congress Cataloging-in-Publication Data

The later Lacan : an introduction / edited by Véronique Voruz,
Bogdan Wolf.
    p.   cm. — (SUNY series in psychoanalysis and culture)
  Includes bibliographical references and index.
  ISBN-13: 978-0-7914-6997-2 (hardcover : alk. paper)
  ISBN-13: 978-0-7914-6998-9 (pbk. : alk. paper) 1. Lacan,
Jacques, 1901-1981. 2. Psychoanalysis. I. Voruz, Véronique.
II. Wolf, Bogdan. III. Series.
BF109.L23L38 2007
150.19'5092--dc22   2006012825

10 9 8 7 6 5 4 3 2 1

Contents

Part IV
Jouissance, the Object, Anxiety

Part V
Sexuation

Preface

Véronique Voruz
Bogdan Wolf

An introduction to the *later* Lacan needs to address a few preliminary questions. Why isolate a given phase in Lacan's teaching? Why not simply speak of a more or less gradual evolution over thirty years of seminars and writing? And if there is a distinction to be made, a distinction that cuts through Lacan's teaching, how do we determine the coordinates of this break? Finally, what characterizes Lacan's later work, making it stand out even against his own corpus of earlier writing? The texts assembled in this volume will substantiate the identification of a later Lacan as they work through Lacan's rearticulation of the classic concepts of psychoanalysis and his enunciation of new ones to name the impasses and paradoxes produced by his earlier engagement with both psychoanalytic theory and praxis.

It is a constant feature of the analytic clinic that it rapidly encounters the limits of its theoretical framework: a case of the real catching up. Thus, Lacan's persistent reworking of psychoanalysis—in which his approach resembles that of Freud—has as much or more to do with the practical need to address impasses encountered in the consulting room as it does with theoretical difficulties. And indeed, throughout his teaching Lacan tirelessly introduces new concepts to overcome both the obstacles encountered by Freud and the ones produced by his own framework. Each new cycle of thought enables psychoanalytic practice to retain and renew its clinical efficacy; it is a thought that cannot rest. For instance, Freud grew so accustomed to the rapidity with which his own advances encountered their limits in practice that in the end he named the clinical manifestation of this phenomenon "negative therapeutic reaction." Freud, and Lacan in his wake, eventually had to acknowledge the impossibility of fully 'draining' the unconscious with the signifier. This recognition produces what can be called a 'push-to-the-real' in their work—or an orientation on what, in the unconscious, insists beyond truth. And it is the deep imprint of the real that characterizes, above all, the later teaching.

In this preface we will situate the later teaching in Lacan's work in a preliminary manner, before moving on to introduce the volume itself. We will then conclude by delineating the clinical areas that currently draw most on the later Lacan.

The seminar of Jacques Lacan can be divided into three periods, each lasting for approximately a decade. Roughly speaking, and as developed by Jacques-Alain Miller in his ongoing Paris seminar, each of these periods is characterized by the prevalence of one of the three registers of the analytic experience that Lacan named imaginary, symbolic, and real,[1] and in that order. Clearly, though, it is not because Lacan treats one register of psychical life as somehow predominant over the other two at a given time that all three orders are not elaborated contemporaneously, and with as much attention. For example, the third phase, oriented on the real, also sees a rehabilitation of the imaginary, a register that had previously been regarded as an obstacle to the movement implicit in the 'symbolic' concepts of 'truth', desire, and transference.

The first phase of Lacan's teaching is concerned with the mirror stage, narcissism, identification—and so the formation of the ego. In this phase, Lacan engages in a passionate debate with IPA analysts, seminal psychiatrists, and contemporary philosophers (Kris, Hartmann, Lagache, Jaspers, Ey, Kraepelin, Balint, Winnicott, Bernfeld, Klein, Deutsch, Horney, Macalpine, Anna Freud, etc.). In the course of this often heated debate, Lacan reformulates the clinical questions posed by the ego in terms of the rivalry between symmetrical others, the obstacles posed by the three imaginary passions of love, hatred, and ignorance, the reversibility of ego libido on the imaginary axis, and the intrusion of the imaginary axis in the analytic transference.[2] Lacan's work on the imaginary is informed by the observation of various characteristics of animal behavior: for example, that members of a same species recognize one another through a shared physical feature: certain mating rituals. For speaking beings, however, the signifier disrupts the 'natural' that parades as real. And the alliance of ego and other is both disrupted and propped up by the symbolic.

At this stage, Lacan sought to instrumentalize the symbolic axis to displace the imaginary as *resistance*. This focus on the imaginary culminated in Lacan's work on anxiety in his tenth seminar,[3] in which the many Freudian definitions of angst are taken up by Lacan, who reaches the following 'resolution' of the Freudian problematic: the affect of anxiety alerts the subject to his or her imaginary fragility. In this seminar Lacan also argues that this affect is caused by the proximity of the object. And it is his recognition of the centrality of the object—as irruption of the real—that leads Lacan to formalize the object of anxiety as object *a,* a central concept in Seminar XI, in which the second phase of Lacan's teaching is truly initiated.

With the concept of object *a*—a logical supplement figuring a real caught in the symbolic order—at his disposal, Lacan sets out to articulate various ways in which this real can be circumscribed. Thus, from Seminar XI onward, Lacan works consistently on the parameters of subjective positioning in the Other, or symbolic order. The symbolic coordinates of the subject, already combined with his or her imaginary constructs, are now also articulated with this residual real. With this focus on structure and positioning, Lacan comes up with the very useful logical operations of alienation and separation, which he correlates to the concepts of symptom and fantasy.[4] Lacan's efforts to absorb, treat, or at least account for the residual real caught in the symbolic culminates with his invention of the four discourses, each proposing different articulations of the social bond according to what occupies the position of agent: S_1 (master signifier), S_2 (knowledge), *a* (surplus-enjoyment), or $barred{S}$ (barred subject). Arguably, Lacan's attempts to subsume the real in discourse come to an end with Seminar XX, which just about begins with the following words: "With the passage of time, I learned that I could say a little bit more about it. And then I realised that what constituted my course was a sort of 'I don't want to know anything about it.'"[5]

So the period we refer to as the later Lacan starts with Seminar XX. Following on from Lacan's recognition of the irreducibility of the real, the later teaching is characterized by a concern with the real as immovable; insistent, but also intimately bound up with language in its entirety. In this phase, jouissance characterizes human existence.[6] Not only does jouissance deregulate and upset the pleasure principle of symbolic balance and proportion, it also becomes specific and integral to speech, now conceived as a carrier of jouissance. The symbolic function of speech does not reduce jouissance but produces it. Speech no longer thwarts the external threat of the real or pacifies its influx but deploys it by revolving around the object, by enveloping it symbolically into the symptom. Gradually, it becomes clear that this is where Lacan is taking us—toward the opacity of jouissance ciphered by the signifier in the symptom.

Situating the coordinates of this epistemic break with more precision, Seminar XX initiates the last stage of Lacan's lifelong formalization of psychoanalytic theory: from then on, the unconscious is seen as an apparatus of jouissance, and meaning—as a treatment of jouissance—is seen as a means of enjoyment. Or, as Lacan puts it in Seminar XX, on the one hand "reality is approached with apparatuses of jouissance . . . we focus, of course, on the fact that there's no other apparatus than language"; [7] and on the other, "the unconscious is the fact that being, by speaking, enjoys."[8] Seminar XX is thus host to an uncompromising staging of jouissance as the key concept of psychoanalysis, and it is in this sense that the phase described here as the "later Lacan" is inaugurated.

Although Seminar XX is but a transition seminar to this last phase, from that point on language is primarily, and unequivocally, envisaged in a dual and rather pragmatic manner: language is a means of treating jouissance *and* a means of enjoyment. And in this seminar Lacan begins to draw out the clinical consequences of these propositions. In this pragmatic perspective, the unconscious no longer appears as a repository of repressed truths but as an enjoying apparatus whose main purpose is to preserve the subject's elective mode of jouissance. This, of course, makes the business of analysis more complicated as the analyst has to proceed against the grain of the subject's enjoyment. As such, it is clear that only a strong transferential bond to the analyst will secure the patient's willingness to separate him- or herself from the enjoyment procured by the unconscious.

This recasting of the unconscious as the "accomplice of jouissance," as Miller once put it, evidently presents a momentous challenge to psychoanalysis as invented by Freud. From this point on, Lacan downplays the Oedipus complex, seen as a mythical—and so imaginarized—version of unconscious organization. And it is with the des-imaginarization of the Oedipus that the deciphering of the unconscious becomes less central in the analytic treatment. The relation to meaning and truth is less valued, and for the Lacan of the later period the analytic treatment is oriented on a reduction of the symptom. The *symptom* has to be emptied of the jouissance procured through its articulation with the fantasy so that the subject can make use of his *sinthome* to love, work, and desire.

Though deciphering is less central to the treatment, the analysis is still structured and driven by the statements of the analysand, as it is in these statements that something of the position of enunciation can be read. But from Seminar XX, Lacan seeks to find other ways of intervening in subjective organization than those associated with classic psychoanalytic interpretation. Classic methods of interpretation, by introducing more signifying material in the treatment, in fact encourage meaning-making by bringing yet more water to the mill of the unconscious. By contrast, the cut isolates jouissance in speech and prevents the proliferation of meaning that makes analysis interminable.

The status of the real is the strongest marker of the break that distinguishes the later Lacan. In the first period, the real is more or less akin to reality, a backdrop to the symbolic-imaginary dialectic. From Seminar VII, *The Ethics of Psychoanalysis,* the real begins to occupy a central position: passing from the background to the beyond of the symbolic, it comes to the fore for the first time in Lacan's teaching. The real, in its most radical, ungraspable, unthinkable dimension becomes *das Ding,* the most intimate, yet excluded, partner of the speaking being, referred to by Lacan for the first time in Seminar VII as the extimate. In the later teaching, starting with Seminar XX, the real becomes the real of the body, indexed on the absence of sexual relation. And in the course of the analytic treatment the subject approaches—insofar as it is possible—this real in speech.

Clearly, this last shift, which plays down the function of meaning in the analytic treatment, entails a thorough rearticulation of the key concepts of psychoanalysis, as well as a new clinical orientation. In fact, the originality of the later Lacan is such that the texts of the final decade are still being worked through today in the Lacanian Schools, providing the foundations for current developments in psychoanalytic theory and practice, and producing effects of transmission that this volume begins to map.

The present collection aims to guide English-speaking readers through the developments of analytic theory and practice generated by Lacan in his later teaching. The body of work referred to here as the later Lacan is problematic in at least one initial respect for an English-speaking audience: of the later seminars, only Seminar XX exists in official translation. A further obstacle presented by Lacan's later teaching resides in the inherent complexity of his thought, a difficulty that some find compounded by the idiosyncrasy of his style. Although these difficulties are familiar to readers of Lacan, in the later work, Lacan—influenced by his work on Joyce and driven by his interest in *lalangue,* or language as jouissance—gave himself a free linguistic rein. The result is that some of the later texts and seminars (a case in point being "L'Étourdit," *Autres Écrits,* Paris: Seuil, 2001) are real word-fests that are near-ungraspable without the context provided by a community working in a rigorous orientation. Finally, whereas in previous seminars, readers could refer to the classic texts of psychoanalysis considered by Lacan to direct their understanding, the later teaching is very much Lacan's singular elaboration. Mathematics freely mingles with literature and topology; wordplays, neologisms, and knots bounce off one another, to the point that, arguably, without the dedicated work of exegesis and transmission centered around Miller's own seminar,[9] some of Lacan's texts would probably remain too obscure for most, despite the beautiful logic and simplicity often harbored by Lacan's baroquely crafted languages.

For these three reasons—the unavailability of Lacan's own later seminars in English and the shortage of commentaries on this period, the inherent difficulty of the concepts being developed and of the texts themselves, and the move away from classic psychoanalytic references and terminology—we decided to reproduce in a single volume, and with revised translations, a selection of texts initially published over a period of seven years in the *Psychoanalytical Notebooks of the London Society of the New Lacanian School.* Throughout, we have sought to balance theoretical elaborations with clinical material, whether this material is derived from an author's own clinical experience or from classic cases within the psychoanalytic literature. The result is a collection of absolutely fundamental texts written by a mixture of established and new Lacanian practitioners, all of whom belong either to the last school founded by Lacan before his death, the *Ecole de la cause freudienne* in Paris, or to other schools of the *World Association of Psychoanalysis,* founded by Jacques-Alain Miller in 1992.

Contributors to this volume include a number of Parisian analysts who are also involved in transmission and clinical formation at the Department of Psychoanalysis of Paris VIII University and its Clinical Section. The Director of this Department is Jacques-Alain Miller, and Marie-Hélène Brousse, Jean-Louis Gault, Pierre-Gilles Guéguen, Eric Laurent, Esthela Solano-Suárez, and Herbert Wachsberger all take part—and have done so for many years—in the formation of clinical practitioners in France, and also abroad through seminars and conferences. Alexandre Stevens is the founder of the Courtil Clinic in Belgium and coordinator of the Brussels Clinical Section. And the remaining four contributors, Richard Klein, Gabriela van den Hoven, and ourselves, are active members of the London group.

These texts are organized according to the key themes of Lacan's later work, starting with the concept of the letter—or what in language is real, for it always returns to the same place—and the limits this concept introduces for a classic understanding of interpretation (Part I). We then chose to include a number of texts mapping Lacan's shift from the Freudian symptom, as a message to be deciphered, to the sinthome—or the subject's elective and singular mode of inscription in language (Part II). These two concepts, the letter and the sinthome, punctuate Lacan's gradual reformulation of the psychoanalytic clinic of psychosis (Part III). Further, the Lacanian concepts devoted to circumscribing the manifestations of the drive in language have also been affected by this new version of the unconscious, and so we have dedicated a section to jouissance, the object, and anxiety (Part IV). Lastly, the consequences of these elaborations are drawn out, in a return to the fundamental questions of psychoanalysis, in relation to sexuation: love, sexuality—reinstated as traumatic for all—and the question of sexual and gendered identity (Part V).

The reception of Lacan's work in the English-speaking world often takes place outside the clinical environment that informed his thought. We hope that this volume will attest to the pertinence of Lacan's later teaching for the treatment of contemporary symptoms. These symptoms have 'scientific' names such as post-traumatic stress disorder, eating disorder, obsessive-compulsive disorder, and so on. This proliferation of 'disorders' provides convenient name-tags under which the contemporary subject lodges his singular discontent, but they come at a price: the 'closing' of the very unconscious psychoanalysis seeks to keep open.

Lacan's work in the last period of his teaching is extremely important clinically. The foremost consequence of the later Lacan, in terms of analytic practice, is that it casts a new light on the differential clinic, in particular the neurosis/psychosis diagnosis. It is with the last phase of Lacan's teaching that the differential clinic, indexed on the Name-of-the-Father (repressed in neurosis, foreclosed in psychosis) begins to orient itself on the ground common to both structures. With a clinic indexed on jouissance rather than on the signifier, different structures become different ways of treating jouissance, and of enjoying language. The analytic treatment must therefore take its bearings from the subject's position of jouissance rather than on repressed meaning.

A clinical orientation on jouissance as it is ciphered in the subject's discourse foregrounds singularity and so dignity. Subjects are not to be cured; they are neither deficient nor helpless victims of their family circumstances. We recall that Freud saw sexuality as the root cause of neurosis; but for Lacan it is the absence of sexual relation that differentiates the human subject from animals. Humans cannot behave instinctively; they need a symptom, or a construct, an invention of their own, to be inscribed in the social bond. Unlike cognitive-behavioral therapies, for the later Lacan the symptom is thus neither to be removed nor to be cured, for the symptom is a real invention of the subject that anchors him or her in language.

Psychoanalysis may not seek to remove the symptom, and so not be a 'therapy' in the usual sense, yet it has profoundly therapeutic effects. So in what way does psychoanalysis improve the life of a given subject? Following the later Lacan, the analyst takes his or her bearings from the fantasy rather than the meaning of the symptoms complained about by the analysand, and the therapeutic benefits proceed from a radical decrease in suffering, obtained not through an eradication of the symptom but through a reduction of the symptom to the sinthome. This reduction entails an isolation of—and separation from—the fantasy. This analytic strategy, driven by what Lacan was the first to recognize as the 'desire of the analyst', denotes an uncompromising belief in the possibility that the dignity of the subject can return in the separation from the fantasy. It is the fantasy that gives consistency to the Other, and a consistent Other commands alienation. Dignity, then, for the neurotic subject, is asserted in a process of separation from one's own investment in one's position of alienation.

Lacan's later teaching also foregrounds the dignity of the psychotic subject. For where an oedipal clinic as good as excluded psychosis from the realm of psychoanalysis (Freud thought that analysis was not suitable for psychotic subjects), Lacan's work in the last period of his teaching shows that, on the contrary, psychotic subjects have much to expect from the analytic treatment once it is understood that psychosis is not an irredeemable deficiency but rather another form of subjective organization. Of course the analytic process is different according to the structure of the patient. First, transference to a subject supposed to know does not exist in psychosis, where the Other does not exist as such and the subject is stuck in the position of object. There can be transference in psychosis, but it will take the form of an imaginary identification, erotomania, persecution, and so on, and these transferential modalities require cautious handling. Second, interpretation cannot be used in the same way as with a neurotic subject. The analyst may seem too 'knowing' and produce a paranoid effect: "the analyst knows everything about me." Third, while the neurotic subject needs to be disalienated *from* the signifier, the psychotic subject must find ways to treat his jouissance *with* the signifier. In short, the differential direction of the treatment is as follows: from the symbolic to the real of the symptom in neurosis, and from the real to the symbolic in psychosis. The later Lacan therefore provides an orientation for the analytic *treatment* of psychosis by means of the signifier, and with the support of the analyst.

Another fundamental advance of the later Lacan concerns the feminine clinic, which Lacan takes beyond the phallus and the *Penisneid* identified by Freud as a stumbling block in the clinic of women. In Seminar XXIII, Lacan proposes the concept of *ravage* as a counterpoint to that of sinthome: "if a woman is a sinthome for any man, it is absolutely clear that there is a need to find another name for what a man is for a woman, since the sinthome is precisely characterised by non-equivalence. We can say that a man is for a woman anything you like, namely an affliction worse than a sinthome . . . it is ravage itself."[10] The concepts of ravage and feminine jouissance pave the way for the elaboration of a true clinic of femininity, and the work of Marie-Hélène Brousse, here and elsewhere, is groundbreaking in this respect.

So the later Lacan provides us with the necessary tools to approach the contemporary psychoanalytic clinics of psychosis and ravage. But what of his teaching is applied most innovatively to cases of psychosis and the feminine clinic can also be of use for *every* subject in analysis: for if Lacan's orientation on jouissance makes analysis impossible, it is also what makes it terminable.

This volume seeks to broaden the knowledge of the later Lacan in the English-speaking world, where the later teaching is often assimilated with, and reduced to, Lacan's work on James Joyce and the sinthome. The texts collected in this volume make it clear that Lacan's work on Joyce is inscribed in a much broader reformulation of analytic theory and practice, and that contemporary psychoanalysis as a whole bears the mark of Lacan's later teaching.

The wealth of this orientation is apparent in clinical developments in 'Lacanian countries' (France, Spain, Italy, Argentina, etc.) where, beyond very interesting developments on the treatment of psychosis and the feminine clinic, there is also groundbreaking work on the "rapid therapeutic effects in psychoanalysis."[11] These rapid therapeutic effects are achieved using the psychoanalytic tools of transference and interpretation (in its redefined modalities); they do not assimilate psychoanalysis to the short therapies practiced under other auspices. On the contrary, short treatments in the Lacanian orientation bring to bear the insights derived from analytic technique and from long analyses on the treatment of subjects requiring punctual support. Structures in the Lacanian orientation are now in place—and more are being created—to receive people who have encountered a sudden trauma (as in the case of the Madrid clinic opened for the victims of the bombings of 11 March 2003) or who are facing a particularly tricky conjuncture requiring that they be accompanied for a 'cycle' of their life [as in the case of the *Centre psychanalytique de consultations et traitement* (CPCT) in Paris, which receives people for free for a duration of four months, renewable once].

Concurrently with these innovations, which incarnate analytic responses to today's symptoms, the psychoanalytic community is also busy defusing a number of threats to its continued existence. Indeed, contemporary modes of governmentality, fixated on the management of risk, fueled by the exigencies of managerialism, and operating within the sometimes surreal parameters of the evaluation-culture, foster the 'closing of the unconscious' through ready-made, pseudoscientific signifiers to name the discontents that are rife in our civilization.

Psychoanalysis, obviously at odds with the aims of governmentality, has recently been under attack in a number of countries. In France, for instance, the proponents of cognitive-behavioral therapies, newcomers in the field of mental health in that country, are actively seeking to marginalize psychoanalysis, which they argue is not 'evaluable' and so not scientific. In the afterword to this volume, Jacques-Alain Miller points to the violence of cognitive-behavioral therapy (CBT), contrasting it with the respect with which psychoanalysis approaches the subject. Psychoanalysis refutes the universalization of the discourse of science exactly because the latter forecloses singularity, and thus the dignity of the subject. It stands against the dehumanization proposed by CBT, whose pernicious appeal lies in that it feeds fantasies of normalization.

These developments attest to the indissociability of the clinical and the political in psychoanalysis. But they also of course attest to the interpretative power of the psychoanalytic—and particularly the later Lacanian—framework, both in clinical practice and beyond it.

Notes

1. These concepts were introduced in the conference considered to have marked the beginning of Lacan's public teaching, "Le symbolique, l'imaginaire et le réel" (1953), in J. Lacan, *Des noms-du-père* (Paris: Seuil, 2005).

2. See *Reading Seminar I & II: Lacan's Return to Freud,* ed. R. Feldstein, B. Fink, and M. Jaanus (Albany: SUNY Press, 1996).

3. J. Lacan, *Le Séminaire livre X: L'angoisse* (Paris: Seuil 2004).

4. See *Reading Seminar XI: Lacan's Four Fundamental Concepts of Psychoanalysis,* ed. R. Feldstein, B. Fink, and M. Jaanus (Albany: SUNY Press, 1995).

5. J. Lacan, Seminar XX, *Encore: On Feminine Sexuality 1972–1973,* trans. B. Fink (New York & London: Norton, 1998), p. 9.

6. See "Preface to the English-language edition" in *Seminar XI* (London and New York: Penguin, 1977), written in 1976 and in which Lacan refers to the unconscious as real: "the unconscious, I would say, is real," p. vii.

7. Seminar XX, op. cit., p. 55.

8. Ibid., pp. 118–119.

9. *L'orientation lacanienne* is J.-A. Miller's weekly seminar in Paris and is open to the public.

10. J. Lacan, *Le Séminaire XXIII: Le Sinthome* (Paris: Seuil 2005), p. 101.

11. *Effets thérapeutiques rapides en psychanalyse: La conversation de Barcelone* (Paris: Navarin, 2005).

Acknowledgments

The editors would like to thank Jacques-Alain Miller for supporting this project and Pierre-Gilles Guéguen for his invaluable editorial input. We would also like to express our gratitude to Judith Miller for graciously allowing us to reproduce images of her father from her beautiful book, *Album Jacques Lacan* (Paris: Seuil, 1991), as well as the photographer, Fritz Senn (of the Zürich James Joyce Foundation) for kindly granting us the right to use his photos. And we are very grateful to our contributors for allowing us to collect their work in this volume. Finally, we would like to thank Colin Perrin for suggesting this edited collection.

Translations of texts by Marie-Hélène Brousse, Jean-Louis Gault, Pierre-Gilles Guéguen, Eric Laurent, Jacques-Alain Miller, Esthela Solano-Suárez, Alexandre Stevens and Herbert Wachsberger were carried out by Heather Chamberlain, Vincent Dachy, Philip Dravers, Richard Klein, Bridget Macdonald, Adrian Price, Marc Thomas, Véronique Voruz, Victoria Woollard, and Bogdan Wolf for the *Psychoanalytical Notebooks,* edited by Bogdan Wolf since its creation in 1998. Many heartfelt thanks to them.

PART I

The Letter and the Limits
of Interpretation

Interpretation in Reverse

Jacques-Alain Miller

You're not saying anything?

Oh, I am, I am saying something. I am saying
that the age of interpretation is behind us.

This is what everyone is saying, though they don't know it yet. And this
is why these *Journées* on interpretation needed an interpretation.

The age of interpretation is behind us. Lacan knew it, but he did not
say it: he hinted at it [*il le faisait entendre*], and we are just beginning to
read it. We talk about "interpretation," we use the word all the time; it
ensures that the 'history' of psychoanalysis lives through us. But we say
interpretation in the same way that we say the unconscious, no longer
thinking of consciousness and of refuting it. The "unconscious," "interpretation," these are the words of the tribe under the cover of which the
new sense, advancing in disguise, creeps in.

What is the unconscious? How are we to interpret this concept now
that we no longer relate it to consciousness, but rather to the function of
speech in the field of language? Do we not all know that the unconscious
is wholly situated in the space [*décalage*] that is repeatedly produced
between what I want to say and what I do say—*as if* the signifier deflected
the programmed trajectory of the signified, which provides the material of
interpretation—*as if* the signifier had a way of interpreting what I want to
say. This is the space in which Freud situated what he named the unconscious—*as if* another wanting-to-say [*vouloir-dire*], that of the signifier itself and which Lacan designated as 'the desire of the Other', substituted
itself for my wanting-to-say, which is my 'intention of signification'.

This is so simple! So well known! So why did it take so long for the
conclusion inscribed by these statements [*ces dits*] to come to light—

namely, the conclusion that interpretation is nothing other than the unconscious, that interpretation is the unconscious itself? If Lacan does not include interpretation among the fundamental concepts of psychoanalysis, is it not because interpretation is included in the very concept of the unconscious? Does the equivalence between the unconscious and interpretation not emerge at the end of the Seminar *Desire and Its Interpretation,* with the paradox that unconscious desire *is* its interpretation? Is the equivalence unconscious/interpretation not what is restated in the form of the concept of the subject supposed to know? And because I say it once more today, will it be taken on board at last?

It is a lure, and even an impasse, to unilateralize interpretation on the side of the analyst, as his intervention, his action, his act, his statement [*son dit*], his saying [*son dire*]. People have probably been too fixated on the *speech act* of the analyst to notice the equivalence I mentioned between the unconscious and interpretation—here the time for comprehending has unduly prolonged itself.

Analytic theories of interpretation merely attest to the narcissism of analysts. It is time to conclude. Interpretation is primarily the interpretation of the unconscious, in the subjective sense of the genitive—it is the unconscious that interprets. Analytical interpretation comes second. It takes its bearings on the interpretation of the unconscious, and this accounts for the erroneous belief that it is the unconscious of the analyst that interprets.

When people fail to start from the premise that the unconscious interprets, they always end up by making an object-language of the unconscious and a metalanguage of interpretation. Yet interpretation is not stratified in relation to the unconscious; interpretation is not of another order—it is inscribed in the same register and is constitutive of this register. When the analyst takes over [the task of interpretation], he does not do anything else than the unconscious. He takes over from the unconscious. Except that he takes interpretation from the *wild* state it proves to be in in the unconscious to the *reasoned* state where he strives to bring it.

Introducing resonances [*faire résonner*], alluding, implying, being silent, being the oracle, quoting, being enigmatic, half-saying things, revealing—but who does this? Who does these things better than you do? Who handles this rhetoric as if by birth, while you exert yourselves to learn its rudiments? Who, but the unconscious itself! The whole theory of interpretation has only ever had one goal—to teach you to speak like the unconscious.

What is the minimal interpretation, the "I could not have put it better myself" [*je ne te le fais pas dire*]? It simply amounts to putting what is said [*le dit*] in quotation marks, to decontextualizing it in order to make a new sense emerge. But is this not what the unconscious of the dream does, as Freud discovered with what he named "the day's residues"?

The unconscious interprets. And the analyst, if he interprets, interprets in its wake. In the end, there is no other avenue than identifying with the unconscious itself. It is the principle of a new narcissism, which is no longer that of a strong ego. "You're not saying anything?" Quite. To be silent here is a lesser evil. Because all the unconscious ever did is interpreting, and as a rule it does it better than the analyst. If the analyst is silent, it is because the unconscious interprets. And yet the unconscious also wants to be interpreted. It offers itself for interpretation. If the unconscious did not want to be interpreted, if the unconscious desire of the dream was not, in its deepest phase, a desire to be interpreted—Lacan says so—a desire to make sense, there would be no analyst.

Let us go along with the paradox. The unconscious interprets, and it wants to be interpreted. The contradiction only exists for a rudimentary concept of interpretation: interpretation always calls for interpretation. To say it otherwise: to interpret is to decipher. But to decipher is to cipher again. The movement only stops on a satisfaction. This is exactly what Freud says when he inscribes the dream as discourse in the register of the primary process, as a wish fulfillment. And Lacan deciphers it for us by saying that jouissance lies in ciphering. But then—how does jouissance lie in ciphering? What is its being in ciphering? And where does it dwell in ciphering?

Let's say it abruptly, as befits these brief communications that bring style and spice to these *Journées*—there is nothing in the structure of language that enables us to respond accurately to this question, unless we adjust this structure.

Last year I fatigued the audience of my course by taking them along the meandering path Lacan took when he tried to integrate the Freudian libido within the structure of language—more precisely, [he tried to integrate it] in the locus of the signified, giving jouissance, if I may say so, the very being of sense.

Jouissance, *sens joui* [enjoyed sense]—the homophony Lacan surprises us with in his [text] *Television* is the very principle of the program inaugurated, if not by "Function and Field of Speech and Language," at least by his deciphering in "The Agency of the Letter." This program is to reduce libido to the being of sense.

I have [already] punctuated the main moments of this elaboration; there are five. The final moment is the very disqualification of object *a*. What Lacan christened *objet petit a* is the ultimate waste of a grandiose attempt, the attempt to integrate jouissance in the structure of language—even if it meant extending this structure to the structure of discourse.

Beyond this, another dimension opens up where the structure of language itself is relativized and merely appears as an elaboration of knowledge [*savoir*] on *lalangue*. The term "signifier" fails to grasp what is at stake since it is designed to grasp the effect of the signified, and it struggles to account for the jouissance produced. From then on, interpretation will never again be what it used to be. The age of interpretation, the age in which Freud turned the universal discourse upside down by means of interpretation, is over.

Freud started with the dream, which has always lent itself to interpretation. He moved on to the symptom, conceived on the model of the dream, as a message to decipher. On his way he had already encountered the negative therapeutic reaction, masochism, and the fantasy.

What Lacan continues to call "interpretation" is no longer the same, if only because it is not indexed on the symptom but on the fantasy. And we keep saying that the fantasy is not to be interpreted but to be constructed, don't we? The fantasy is a phrase that is enjoyed [*qui se jouit*], a ciphered message that harbors jouissance. The symptom itself is to be thought from the fantasy, and this is what Lacan calls the sinthome.

A practice that targets the sinthome in the subject does not interpret like the unconscious. To interpret like the unconscious is to remain in the service of the pleasure principle. To place oneself in the service of the reality principle does not change anything, since the reality principle itself is in the service of the pleasure principle. To interpret in the service of the pleasure principle—you needn't look anywhere else for the principle of interminable analysis. This is not what Lacan calls "the way to a true awakening for the subject."

It remains for us to say what interpreting beyond the pleasure principle could be—interpreting against the grain of the unconscious. There, the word "interpretation" is only valid as a place-holder for another, which cannot be silence. Just as we must abandon the symptom as reference and use the fantasy instead, to think the symptom from the fantasy, so we must abandon neurosis and use psychosis as reference, to think neurosis from psychosis.

The signifier as such, that is, as cipher [*chiffre*], as separated from the effects of signification, calls for interpretation as such. The signifier on its own is always an enigma and this is why it craves interpretation. This interpretation requires the implication of another signifier, from which a new sense emerges. This is the structure I highlighted at the Clinical Section of Buenos Aires, in a colloquium on delusion and the elementary phenomenon.

The elementary phenomenon is a particularly pure demonstration of the presence of the signifier all alone, in sufferance—waiting for the other signifier that would give it a meaning—and as a rule the binary signifier of knowledge appears there, which in the event does not conceal its delusional nature. It has a perfectly good name: the delusion of interpretation. This is the way of all interpretation: interpretation has the structure of delusion, and this is why Freud does not hesitate to put the delusion of Schreber and the theory of the libido on the same plane, without any stratification. If the interpretation that the analyst has to offer the patient is of the order of delusion, then indeed it is probably better to remain silent. This is a cautionary maxim.

There is another way, which is neither that of delusion nor of the silence of prudence. We will continue to call this way "interpretation," although it no longer has anything to do with the system of interpretation, save for being its reverse side. To say it with the concision required by these *Journées,* the other way consists in withholding S_2, in not bringing it in—so as to circumscribe S_1. It amounts to bringing the subject back to his truly elementary signifiers, on which he has, in his neurosis, had a delusion.

The unary signifier, which as such is nonsensical, means that the elementary phenomenon is primordial. The reverse of interpretation consists in circumscribing the signifier as the elementary phenomenon of the subject, and as it was before it was articulated in the formation of the unconscious that gives it the sense of a delusion.

When interpretation emulates the unconscious, when it mobilizes the subtlest resources of rhetoric, when it molds itself onto the structure of the formations of the unconscious, it feeds the delusion that it should be starving. If there is deciphering here, it is a deciphering that does not produce sense.

Psychosis, here as elsewhere, strips the structure bare. Just as mental automatism exposes the fundamental xenopathy of speech, so the elementary phenomenon is there to manifest the original state of the subject's relation to *lalangue.* The subject knows that what is said [*le dit*] concerns him, that there is some signification, although he does not know which one.

This is why, at this point precisely, as he advances in the other dimension of interpretation, Lacan resorts to *Finnegans Wake,* namely, to a text that unceasingly plays on the relations between speech and writing, sound and sense, a text full of condensations, equivocations, homophonies, but nevertheless has nothing to do with the old unconscious. In *Finnegans Wake,* every quilting point is made obsolete. This is why, despite heroic efforts, this text can neither be interpreted nor translated. That's because it is not itself an interpretation, and it wonderfully brings the subject of reading back to perplexity as the elementary phenomenon of the subject in *lalangue.*

Let's say that in the text, S_1 always absorbs S_2. The words which would translate its sense into another language are as if devoured in advance by this very text, as if it was translating itself. Consequently, the relation between signifier and signified does not take the form of the unconscious. You will never be able to separate what Joyce wanted to say from what he said—this is integral transmission, but in a mode that is the reverse of the matheme.

The *zero effect* of the elementary phenomenon is obtained here through an *aleph effect,* which opens onto the infinity of the semantic, or, better, onto the flight of sense.

What we still call "interpretation," although analytic practice is evermore post-interpretative, is revealing no doubt, but of what if not of an irreducible opacity in the relation of the subject to *lalangue.* And this is why interpretation—this post-interpretation—is no longer, if we are to be precise, a punctuation.

Punctuation belongs to the system of signification; it is still semantic; it still produces a quilting point. This is why the post-interpretative practice, which takes over from interpretation on a daily basis, takes its bearings on the cut rather than on punctuation.

For now, let us imagine this cut as a separation between S$_1$ and S$_2$, the very one that is inscribed on the bottom line of the matheme of the 'analytic discourse': S$_2$ // S$_1$. The consequences are fundamental for the very construction of what we call the analytic session. The question is not to know whether the session is long or short, silent or wordy. Either the session is a semantic unity, in which S$_2$ comes to punctuate the elaboration—delusion in the service of the Name-of-the-Father (as many sessions are)—or the analytic session is an asemantic unit returning the subject to the opacity of his jouissance. This implies that it be cut before it can loop back upon itself. So here I am opposing the path of perplexity to the path of elaboration. Don't worry about elaboration; there will always be too much of it.

I propose that these *Journées* reflect on the following: properly analytic interpretation—let's keep the word—functions against the grain of the unconscious.

This is a summary of one of Jacques-Alain Miller's responses to questions from the audience: We begin from Serge Cottet's spot-on diagnosis—"the decline of interpretation"—that I picked up on last year in his presentation at the Clinical Section. He signaled some difficulties that he situated in the order of a certain symptom. I tried to bring out the good side of this 'decline', for the term echoes darkly with 'grandeur and decadence'. I placed what at first sight appears as a decline of interpretation in a positive light. I sublimated this decline into a post-interpretative practice. When did this practice start? With Freud himself, it is impossible not to see that.

Author's note: I had initially announced this text in the program for the Journées *under the title* "The Other Side of Interpretation." *I presented it in three sentences:* "Interpretation is dead. It will not be resuscitated. If a practice is truly contemporary, it is ineluctably post-interpretative although it does not really know it yet." *This oral communication was designed to unsettle the average opinion, to produce surprise. It did do that, and more. Did this amount to success? Perhaps not. Some, turning around, drowned the essence of this communication (on this point, see my first thoughts:* "L'oubli de l'interprétation" *in* La lettre mensuelle No. 144, December 1995, pp. 1–2). *This text was transcribed by C. Bonningue. I read it and made few corrections.*

Discretion of the Analyst in the Post-interpretative Era

Pierre-Gilles Guéguen

I borrow the term "post-interpretative era" from Jacques-Alain Miller, who used it to describe the situation of psychoanalysis today. He proposed a thesis, "the unconscious interprets," and this thesis corresponds to what psychoanalysis—as deduced from the work of Lacan—is.[1] I propose to develop some of the consequences of this thesis for psychoanalytical practice, at least those that I can perceive at present. Others will no doubt appear, as we need the time for comprehending.

If, today, a practice that takes account of the thesis "the unconscious interprets" can be said to be discretionary for various reasons, it is not for all that any less determined. Lacan is no more, nor is the time when his stature, so dominant in the intellectual world and in the world of psychoanalysis, constituted for many either a scandal or a cause for hypnotic admiration, especially when the question of short sessions provoked condemnation. The contemporary figure of the analyst is different, although his practice is still often congested with a hardly discrete mimetism of the dead master rather than with a fidelity to his work and his concepts.

But if I speak of discretion, it is rather to evoke three consequences entailed by the thesis "the unconscious interprets" for analytical practice.

- The analyst is discrete because he is effaced in his interpretative action behind the one of the unconscious. He leaves it up to the unconscious, only to take over in "the interloan" [*l'entreprêt*].[2] This does not mean that he should abstain from all intervention or find refuge in the convenience of textbook neutrality—quite the contrary.

- The analyst acts with discretion: his discernment (the sense given by the *Littré* dictionary to *discrétion*) is required in his action, his judgment is called for, and this just as much if he leaves its place to the work of the unconscious.
- Lastly, analytical practice is a practice of the discrete, of the discontinued. If analytical practice is based on the interpretation of the unconscious, then it has to be homogeneous with its pulsating structure, its structure of opening and closing. This statement entails precise consequences, especially for grasping what distinguishes psychoanalysis in the Lacanian orientation from other 'postmodern' practices and other conceptions of the unconscious. In any case, it is a necessary condition to situate psychoanalysis, as Freud and Lacan did, in its articulation with science and not against it as it too often seems to be the case today.[3]

The Discrete Analyst: Leaving It Up to the Unconscious

The action of the analyst has to be subordinated to the interpretation emanating from the unconscious. This is not how Freud initially practiced. In the beginning, he often translated an object-language, that of the dream among others, into a metalanguage of symbols. The *Traumdeutung,* which testifies to this in a number of places, was nevertheless corrected by the theory of double inscription that was to prove so pleasing to Lacan's students that it ended up annoying him.[4]

The break with Jung allowed a radical recentering, that of the *Metapsychology,* on this point. The theory of the unconscious then developed by the inventor of psychoanalysis shows that the decisive step was not so much the distinction between the manifest and latent contents of the dream, but rather his uncovering of free association.

The move to put the associations of the dreamer and the contents of the dream on the same plane (an apparently innocent move but one that is in fact profoundly iconoclastic) gave psychoanalytical practice a basis that Lacan, in turn, will articulate in a number of famous formulas, which today have become aphorisms: "There is no metalanguage" or "There is no Other of the Other." On the side of the analyst, the method of "floating attention" corresponds to the free association of the analysand; they are inextricably linked. They denote the little interest

Freud has for the signification of the patient's statements for the patient's intentionality. Freud does not subscribe to the tradition of Dilthey.[5] What interests Freud, and it is there that his method is homogeneous with his theory of the unconscious, is the deciphering of the unconscious enunciation in the statements, the means of seizing the inscription of the repressed movements of the drive budding in the statements [*les dits*] (what is read from the repressed drive in what is said). The elaboration of the significations of the dream, of its relation to the reality or history of the patient, is only a means to this end. The Freudian texts of the 1920s on the dream are in this respect quite revealing of his position:[6] the dream is presented there as an activity in the service of jouissance ("a piece of phantasy working on behalf of the maintenance of sleep"), and the deciphering of its rebus is far from being an obligatory task for Freud; it is to be done if the analyst deems it necessary but is not an absolute requirement.

In 1912, and in the same sense, Freud had already posed that the text of the dream is as such inexhaustible, and had recommended that the analyst should only communicate his point of view with reserve.[7] And he does not consider it necessary to come back from one session to the next to the analysis of the same dream. It is clear that a break in the pursuit of the conscious discourse is not detrimental; it is even advisable for the effectuation of the analytical task. The analyst has three objectives: to situate the fulfillment of desire in the dream, to evaluate the "pressure of resistance" (which conditions the possibility of an intervention), and, above all, to search for the "cause of the distortion," and for Freud this is the key point.

Lacan took a long time to refind this Freudian liberty. (He will evoke in this respect his "ten years of bed-sharing with Jaspers"). Lacan refinds it with brilliance by bringing forth the function of speech and the field of language in his Rome Report. Nevertheless, psychoanalysis's breakaway out of the rut into which it had fallen will also entail its own unpredictable consequences. The passion for the formations of the unconscious and the identification of the concept of the unconscious to the laws of language (metaphor and metonymy) led some of Lacan's students to an erratic use of homophony, transforming in the worst cases the psychoanalytical treatment into an exchange of formations of the unconscious, those of the analyst coming into rivalry with those of the analysand. In *L'Étourdit,* in a paragraph that sounds like he is setting the record straight for the benefit of his students, Lacan specifies that homophony is indeed one of the chosen modes of interpretation (in the sense of the analyst's intervention) on the condition "that the analyst makes use of it where suitable."[8] He reminds us that the point is to get hold of it to produce the *Spaltung* of the subject. We can understand this as a means of provoking the split in the analysand, the division that is the mark and the consequence of interpretation by the unconscious.

But the thesis "the unconscious interprets" also aims to make the analyst revert to a certain discretion as regards the appreciation of the efficacy of his action. Freud laid down foundations that have perhaps been slightly forgotten today. If the unconscious interprets (interweaving jouissance and sense in its formations), it also decides the outcome of any intervention of the analyst. It is the unconscious that indicates whether or not the analyst was able to touch the cause of desire. Freud noted this in particular in relation to dreams: it matters little whether they lie or tell the truth, whether the analysand lies, whether he accepts or refuses the analyst's intervention. The result of an interpretation can only be assessed by the production of new material: another formation of the unconscious, the production of a symptom (even a negative therapeutic reaction)[9] or a simple negation ("I hadn't thought about it"). The question is not to know which of the two, the analyst or the analysand, is right, as "there is no confrontation at this level. When there is a confrontation, it is because we are on the imaginary axis."[10] So what crowns the success of an intervention is a new manifestation of the drive that calls for a new lifting of repression.

For Lacan, for a long time the true interpretation was the one that revived desire, that carried the mark of desire as a lack-of-being. To renew the division of the subject, to bring out S_1 —"the signifier—to what irreducible, traumatic, non-meaning he is, as a subject, subjected"[11] is doubtlessly a facet of the unconscious. However S_1, as a rule, calls for an S_2, and the effect of producing lack-of-being is never equivalent to pure desire. The concept of desire has two values. If desire revives signification through the produced void, it also goes in circles. We like to praise the celestial bird, but there is also the ungraspable ferret that rages endlessly in its cage of dissatisfaction, of impossibility or avoidance.[12] And what remains unperceived in the exaltation of desire is that it is also, just like sense, a carrier of jouissance. "The true consent, the consent of being which is the one the analytical work seeks to produce, is a consent to the unconscious as repressed, that is to say as carrier of jouissance."[13] Contemporary interpretation, the one that leads to the pass, should therefore lead in this direction, and bear at the same time on $-\varphi$ and a, the phallus of castration and the remainder of jouissance: this is where the thesis "interpretation in reverse" complements the thesis "the unconscious interprets."

The Discretion of the Analyst: His Discernment, His Judgment

The use of the term *interpretation* has spread and it now designates all aspects of the analyst's action in a generic fashion. It has numerous denotations in language (translation, falsification, performance, acting, declaring the will of higher forces, give meaning, etc.).

The "death of interpretation"[14] does not mean that the analyst no longer intervenes in the treatment. What is targeted is the interpretation in which the analyst injects sense whimsically, without orienting himself on the unconscious of the patient: interpretation in the weak sense of the word. By contrast, the "duty to interpret,"[15] which Lacan underlined in his time, acquires all the more depth. The analyst is bound to this duty, he "pays with words . . . , with his person . . . and with that which is essential in his most intimate judgment."[16] How he exercises this duty nevertheless remains within his discretion, and he uses it when he deems it necessary, against the backdrop of silence, with parsimony and with good reason. He is the sole judge of his *timing,* of his tactfulness. Lacan reminded us of this with solemnity: "as alone as I have always been in my relation to the psychoanalytic cause."[17]

If the thesis "the unconscious interprets" in no way exonerates the analyst from having to intervene—since, just as well, as Lacan indicated it, he "is part of the concept of the unconscious as he constitutes its address"[18]—it nevertheless forces us to question anew what the analyst does. His task is distributed between different dimensions: to interpret (in the narrow sense), to construct, to communicate, to support the transference.

To Interpret

What does the thesis that "the unconscious interprets" bring on this point? Let us note, to begin with, that it is a new formulation. Neither Lacan nor Freud had posed it before.[19] The formulation does, however, evoke the famous formula "desire is its interpretation." And yet, the two formulas are not equivalent. "The unconscious interprets" adds that interpretation, understood in the broad sense of the analyst's intervention in the treatment, can certainly provoke desire, the lack-of-being, but frequently also the jouissance that is incarcerated in *lalangue*. And indeed, one can enjoy [*jouir*] one's unconscious or, more precisely, the formations of one's unconscious or the interpretations of one's analyst. But one can no longer enjoy the interpretation by the unconscious in the strict sense used by J.-A. Miller. That is why the thesis that "the unconscious interprets" calls for the complementary thesis of "interpretation in reverse."

What does the Freudian interpretation do? It certainly goes against signification, against the discourse of the subject's ego, but it targets a sexual sense. The drive remains subjected to the oedipal myth, to the function of the imaginary father. In this framework, consequently, the end of analysis stumbles against the rock of castration: impossible for women to be detached from the father, impossible for a man to accept being 'cured' by another man.

The interpretation according to Lacan aims elsewhere: it targets the enunciation and not the statement. It goes against signification, no doubt, but also against sexual sense, it targets the cause of desire, this cause of distortion that Freud was able to isolate. This also means that interpretation seeks to direct its effect beyond the Oedipus or the family romance, beyond the Freudian primal scene in which the woman always remains contaminated by the mother. In the final analysis, for Lacan the idea is to expose, by means of interpretation, the last signifier, the signifier of the primarily repressed. It is the attempt of the metaphorical interpretation, which favors highlighting the phallus as signifier of desire. We are however hindered by the fact that desire itself is enclosed within the limits of fantasy.[20] In his later work, with the elaboration of object *a* and, above all, the tables of sexuation, Lacan proposes the place of the drives as the target of interpretation, that of the absence of the sexual relation. It is a place "inhabited by silence,"[21] for it corresponds to what cannot be said (no more than desire could be said directly), and also to what is enjoyed [*se jouit*] beyond what is said (surplus enjoyment [*plus-de-jouir*]). So we must resort to metonymical interpretation. It brings the subject back to his or her division, finding its formula in the interpretative scansion that does not decide meaning for the subject but forces the latter to decide upon it. The 'little extra' [*plus*] added by the analyst to the formation of the unconscious, or to the patient's own analysis, is an almost-nothing, perhaps even a simple temporal break. It signifies in any case: "I agree with you but you are the one who said it!" [*je ne te l'ai pas fait dire*].

Let us now move on to what J.-A. Miller proposes with his "interpretation in reverse." I will stress two aspects of his proposition. This thesis takes account of the fact that interpretation has to be homogeneous with the analyzing task, and so ultimately targets the drive. This means that interpretation must bring about a convergence of the analysand's statements [*dits*] (Lacan's interest in this convergence is apparent in his work on the Fibonacci series and his reference to the golden number). It would be inaccurate to think that Freud had already grasped this, but we can nevertheless take the view that he had a certain intuition of this [convergence].22 Nevertheless, the thesis "interpretation in reverse" proposes something else. What matters is to obtain a crossing of the limit, not only the convergence toward the silent saying [*dire*] but also the subversion of this silence. J.-A. Miller described this subversion as what does not enter the semantic flow, whereas he notes that the scansion, since it punctuates, brings one back to it. That is why he opposes this interpretation to scansion and calls it the cut, thereby giving back its precision and weight to Lacan's term. The step made here consists in isolating a new modality of interpretation. "It does not interpret in the service of the pleasure principle,"23 that is, for jouissance. It brings us back, not to the division of the subject, but to what he calls, by reference to psychosis, "perplexity." It is the beyond of the defense of the subject that is then targeted, not desire that itself "is of defense." The practice of the cut, compared to the practice of punctuation, is asemantic, and it touches directly what is enjoyed in saying [*le joui dans le dire*]. It corresponds to the moment of concluding in the pass.

To Construct

On this point, Freud and Lacan take a similar view of the task of the analyst: there is no doubt that it is up to him to construct. In this respect, [Freud's] "Constructions in Analysis" (SE XXIII) remains exemplary. Construction, unlike interpretation, draws scattered and heterogeneous elements together in a linear causality, and is a discretionary practice of sense (but not of signification). It aims for the internal coherence of the analytic experience. Freud reserved the task of construction for himself and left that of remembering to the analysand; for him, to construct meant to assure oneself of the truth of the analysis.

This operation targets at least one aspect of truth, that of internal coherence. To construct is to assure oneself of consistency, of rules of deduction. This is why, in analysis, the construction and elaboration of the axiom of the fundamental fantasy are homogeneous with one another. Together they contribute to situating the place of object *a*, which, in psychoanalysis, has the status of logical consistency. This operation is necessary due to the fact that, on the side of the unconscious (as emphasized by Freud through the interpretation of dreams and as noted by Lacan in the "Introduction to the German edition of *Écrits*"), meaning escapes. But while Freud did not really distinguish construction from interpretation, Lacan separates them very clearly. Construction aims at the internal consistency of the analytical work, namely, a truth of *fixion*, while interpretation finds its efficiency in the allusive virtues of language in order to create a point of emptiness in the response of the Other and thus produce a half-saying [*mi-dire*] of truth. In a commentary of "Constructions in Analysis," Jacques-Alain Miller affirms that "the Lacanian analyst must construct, that goes without saying,"[24] and he adds that if Lacan is not interested in construction as such, it is because in his work it is called structure (in the sense of clinical structure). Thus, interpretation in reverse takes its bearings solely on construction.

To Communicate

It is in this respect that the judgment of the analyst is mostly solicited. When should we produce an interpretation, when should we communicate a construction, but also in what form, and with what content?

Freud never shied away from stating his opinion. He never worried about a potential effect of suggestion and measured the value of his intervention with the indirect confirmation of the unconscious. The problem is situated otherwise for Lacan. As for Freud in the case of the Wolf Man, the point is still to obtain certainty in the patient, but in a way that is regulated by the crossing of the fantasy and subjective destitution, both being limit-operations. And yet the end must win the conviction of the patient—it is even required. Here again, and perhaps one should say particularly here, confirmation is to be sought more in the indirect ratification by the unconscious than in the assent of the patient.[25]

As to knowing whether the analyst must be silent or communicate, there is a lot of suspicion on that point: the suspicion that silence, recommended by Lacan as the background against which interpretation could unfold and then also as minimal principle of interpretation-scansion, the one that avoids suggestion, may often translate as faint-heartedness on the analyst's part—a silence of convenience, a lesser evil in a way. It is true in many cases, but it is important to give its right place to this silence, and to the scansion that leaves it up to the analysand to receive from the Other his own message in an inverted form. Nevertheless, it is Lacan himself who was able to measure how much the systematic practice of silence, punctuation without a way out of the semantic system, contributed to turn analysis into an infinite task, as infinite as the productions of the unconscious. This is why, in the later years of his teaching, he incites analysts to speak up, in his own terms "to open their mouths" [*l'ouvrir*], but also not to feed the symptom with sense.[26] These indications may seem contradictory.

And, in fact, the interventions of analysts can be shared out between two polarities, those that make the $-\varphi$ appear on the one hand, and *a* on the other. The idea is to stimulate the stream of desire, when it is threatened by the premature attack of the signifying chain, through interpretation: by evoking the unconscious knowledge yet to be explored (metaphoric interpretation). On the other hand, we must also deflate the signifying efflorescence; jam the jouissance of empty speech. This we do rather by interpreting with the structure (metonymic mode of interpretation). Most frequently, the scansion punctuates the session by signaling a partial point of possible conclusion.

But the interpretation of the unconscious, correlated to the interpretation in reverse of the analyst, namely, interpretation in a restricted sense, that which indicates a true act of the analyst, has another mission: it must radically separate jouissance from the signifying chain that carries it. It is not only the formula "the word is the murder of the thing" that applies here—a formula that, when read in its weaker sense, has allowed some to think that all the virtues of psychoanalysis could be reduced to a practice of expression, of "verbalization." The reference is taken from the later Lacan, who equivocates between jouissance and enjoyed-sense [*sens-joui*]. Thus, one should reserve the term "analytic act" (which produces a new subject) for this type of interpretation, which makes an S_1 emerge all alone by plucking it, in a way, out of the signifying chain and its implacable recommencement. We immediately see that such an interpretation must precipitate the moment of concluding for the analysand by calling forth certitude and consent.

To Support the Transference

According to Lacan's formula, the analyst supports the transference. He localizes the semblants. This does not depend on his judgment but on what he offers through the position that he occupies. So he does not cause transference, which anybody can do, as much as he causes the work of the analysand's unconscious through transference. There, on the other hand, his judgment is required.

Lacan defined transference as a pure dialectic, in opposition both to the conception of transference as a phenomenal repetition and to the pedagogical role of the analyst (deviations that the practice in the IPA had permitted). That is, that he refutes any psychologization of the treatment in order to emphasize radically that "the conception of the case-history is *identical* to the progress of the subject, that is, to the reality of the treatment."[27]

Nevertheless, he will later on be led to correct what in this definition could be excessively nominalistic (albeit a realist nominalism) in order to take account of jouissance. Transference is then presented as the permanent mode of constituting objects, and from Seminar XI onward, transference and interpretation are inextricably bound up.

Transference, insofar as it is mobilized by analysis, is not the pure repetition of past loves [*énamorations*]; it is linked to the moments of opening and closing of the unconscious. Once we accept that the unconscious is interpretation, transference presents itself as the supposition of knowledge in the unconscious (cf. the algorithm of transference [in Lacan's "Proposition"]).

In specifying the kind of interpretation that goes with the thesis that "the unconscious interprets," that is, the cut that dries up the Zuyderzee of the unconscious and isolates the S_1 without S_2, J.-A. Miller clarifies the question of the fall of the subject supposed to know at the end of an analysis and its corollary: the canceling of one's subscription to the unconscious. This echoes with a proposition that J.-A. Miller had already put forward concerning the couple transference and interpretation: to ground transference on the subject supposed to know, as Lacan did before anybody else, means that transference is first of all *interpretandum,* to be interpreted. Not to interpret by targeting the repetition of infantile experiences, but by interpreting the cause of desire; in other words by bringing interpretation to bear on the signifying interval (and so with the half-saying [*mi-dire*], with equivocation).

"The desire of the analyst, implicated in his interpretation, goes against identification, which is to say that it goes towards being. And we could not recognize as Lacanian the analyst who only makes meta-phoric interpretations, that is to say who delivers, already worked out, the master signifier into the hands of his analysand."[28] The interpreta-tion as cut aims to isolate indirectly the repressed master signifier and, in that, it opposes the proliferation of added meanings, particularly those that could stem from the intervention of the analyst. Equivoca-tion, yes, if it is metonymic, between enigma and citation; metaphor, no.

Discretion in the Analytic Act

Incontestably, the thesis that "the unconscious interprets" emphasizes discretion, discontinuity in the mathematical sense (quantities that only vary as whole values). It brings to light the fact that the uncon-scious is only inscribed through ruptures, ruptures in sense and rup-tures in the enjoyed [*joui*]. 'In-nate' [*in-né*] unconscious, unconscious of revelation, apophantic. This is how the unconscious has manifested itself since Freud, but it took Lacan to remind us: through surprise. And, let's face it, mostly unpleasant surprise, as a rupture in meaning and signification, as an unknown jouissance, repressed and quite frankly bad. So the unconscious is not the unknown that all psycholo-gies happily accommodate; it is primarily of the order of encounter and revelation;[29] it is not the expression of feelings. Thoughts carry it, but it is primarily explosion, perplexity.[30] This is even why it has an ethical status. Freud showed it clearly, for example, in 1925: "Obviously, one must hold oneself responsible for the evil impulses of one's dreams. What else is one to do with them? Unless the content of the dream (rightly understood) is inspired by alien spirits, it is a part of my own being."[31] This represents a rupture in both ideals and in the thread of conscious thought: the ego is manhandled. Lacan assigns the subject $\mathoh{S}$ to this place, the place where the *id* was and where the *I* must come into being. The unconscious is the rupture that makes this gap appear, but for it to inscribe itself an act is necessary, as such "firmly distinguished from [the status of] the doing":[32] an act of speech from the analyst.

To speak of interpretation as being deployed on the other side of sense and of interpretation, as Jacques-Alain Miller does, is to emphasize that, when interpretation amounts to an act of the analyst, it must not only come second to the action of the unconscious but also act like the unconscious. In other words, it must produce through subtraction of sense what Lacan calls nonsense [*insensé*] in Seminar XI, and which cannot be attained any old way, since it targets the cause of desire.

Yet the unconscious is not there a priori in analysis; what is there from the beginning is the symptom and its trail of complaints; what is there as given is malaise, suffering, unhappy consciousness that seeks to pour out in the other, at the same time as it produces the other as the source of its troubles. These are the paradoxes of reflexive consciousness linked to retaliatory aggressivity, the commonplaces of psychology and psychotherapies.

For an analysis to begin, there must be a rupture in this register: we need interpretation in the strong sense. No doubt, this interpretation is not the one of the end, but it is the one that opens the unconscious. This is to say that it brings to light a principle of rupture. Lacan says as much in "Science and Truth":[33] the subject of psychoanalysis, that of the *Spaltung,* cannot be approached through the empirical fact, the practice of analysis supposes an *epoché,* a reduction. This reduction always rests on the absence of a relation, absence of a relation between jouissance and the formalism of science, absence of a relation between the symbolic and the real in psychoanalysis. In 1965, Lacan thinks that truth as cause allows in psychoanalysis to drill the place of the subject, the place that restitutes the subject foreclosed by science.

The thesis "the unconscious interprets" emphasizes once more the rupture between the enjoyed [*joui*] in the real and the symbolized. But it adds to the Lacan of that time, whose peak in formalization is to be found in "Position of the Unconscious," the Lacan of the *Other Side of Psychoanalysis,* and for whom truth is the sister of jouissance.

The interpretation in reverse aims at the cause in the real and at the cut that produces the subject having cancelled his subscription to the unconscious,[34] not the truth of the subject but a *véri-fixé* subject[35]—that is, to say with a certainty as to his jouissance, his mode of enjoyment [*mode de jouir*].

Note: This text was presented at the Colloque de Bretagne *(1996) and at J.-A. Miller's Seminar (19 June 1996).*

Notes

1. See J.-A. Miller, "Interpretation in Reverse" (in this volume).
2. J. Lacan, *Television* (London & New York: Norton 1990), p. 46.
3. See the conversation between J.-A. Miller and François Ewald in the issue of the *Magazine littéraire* on Freud.
4. J. Lacan, *Le Séminaire XVIII, D'un discours qui ne serait pas du semblant* (1970/71), unpublished.
5. W. Dilthey, *Selected Writings* (Cambridge: CUP, 1976) edited, translated, and introduced by H. P. Rickman.
6. S. Freud, "Remarks on the Theory and Practice of Dream-Interpretation" (1923) SE XIX; "Josef Popper-Lynkeus and the Theory of Dreams" (1923) SE XIX; "Some Additional Notes upon Dream-Interpretation as a Whole" (1925) SE XIX. Especially the last text that begins with the paragraph entitled "The limits to the possibility of interpretation," p. 127 for the quote.
7. S. Freud, "Recommendations to Physicians Practising Psychoanalysis," SE XII.
8. J. Lacan, *L'Étourdit* (1972), *Scilicet No. 4* (Paris: Seuil, 1973), p. 48 (also in *Autres Écrits,* Paris: Seuil, 2001), p. 491.
9. J.-A. Miller insists on this point in "Marginalia de Constructions dans l'analyse," *Cahier No 3.*
10. J.-A. Miller, ibid., p. 24.
11. J. Lacan, *The Four Fundamental Concepts* (London: Penguin, 1977), p. 251.
12. See on this point J.-A. Miller's Seminar *Donc* (seminar 12 January 1994).
13. J.-A. Miller, "Marginalia de Constructions en analyse," op. cit., p. 27.
14. J.-A. Miller's formula from "Interpretation in Reverse."
15. J. Lacan, *Le Séminaire XI, Les quatre concepts fondamentaux de la psychanalyse* (Paris: Seuil, 1973) "Postface," p. 252, also in *Autres écrits,* op. cit., p. 504.
16. J. Lacan, "The Direction of the Treatment and the Principles of Its Power" in *Écrits* (London: Routledge, 1977), p. 227.
17. J. Lacan, "Founding Act" in *Television,* op. cit., p. 97.
18. J. Lacan, *Seminar XI,* op. cit.
19. In *Seminar XI,* Lacan gives a similar indication: "The analyst's interpretation merely reflects the fact that the unconscious, if it is what I say it is, namely, a play of the signifier, has already in its formations—dreams, slips of the tongue or pen, witticisms or symptoms—proceeded by interpretation" (*Seminar XI,* p. 130).

However, "the unconscious interprets" radicalizes the import of this thesis; what is at stake is both to remind the contemporary analyst of it, and to combine it with the thesis of interpretation that removes sense. Seminar XI is to be read alongside *Seminar XX* and *L'Étourdit*.

20. J.-A. Miller insisted on this point in his seminar *Donc,* where he developed it on the basis of Lacan's indications (e.g., in *Seminar XI*).

21. C. Soler, "Silences" in *La Cause freudienne,* No. 32, p. 30. Colette Soler coined this beautiful expression.

22. For example, in 1925, he states that when the subject's resistance does not preclude the work of the unconscious, the associations on dreams initially diverge but then rapidly converge toward a conclusion in the direction of the fantasy of desire.

23. J.-A. Miller, "Interpretation in Reverse," op. cit.

24. J.-A. Miller, "Marginalia de Constructions en analyse," op. cit.

25. J.-A. Miller, "To Interpret the Cause from Freud to Lacan" in *Newsletter of the Freudian Field No. 3,* Spring/Fall, 1989, pp. 30–50. In this article in particular, the link between the cause in psychoanalysis and the principle of the discrete is developed.

26. J. Lacan, "Geneva Lecture on the Symptom" in *Analysis* No. 1, trans. R. Grigg (Melbourne: Centre for Psychoanalytic Research, 1989). In this paper, Lacan defines a symptom as a voracious fish that should not be fed with sense.

27. J. Lacan, "Intervention on Transference" in *Feminine Sexuality,* ed. Jacqueline Rose and Juliet Mitchell (London & New York: Norton, 1982), p. 64.

28. J.-A. Miller, "Interprétation et transfert" in *Actes des Journées de l'ECF No. 6.*

29. In Seminar XI, Lacan uses the terms "not-born," "not-realized."

30. It is purposefully that Jacques-Alain Miller uses this term, traditionally employed in the field of psychosis, with reference to his thesis of "generalized foreclosure."

31. S. Freud, *Some Additional Notes upon Dream-Interpretation,* op. cit., p. 133.

32. J. Lacan, "De la psychanalyse dans ses rapports avec la réalité" (1967) in *Scilicet No. 1* (Paris: Seuil, 1968), p. 56.

33. As well as in Seminar XI.

34. The theorization "the unconscious interprets" is essential to operate the right cut between the operation of psychoanalysis and, on the one hand, a logical formalism that will never be able to deal with jouissance, and, on the other, a nauseating hermeneutics that, for example, allows Paul Ricoeur to say: "One does not sufficiently underline the role of conscience-as-witness, that of the analyst, in the constitution of the unconscious as reality" (Paul Ricoeur, *Le conflit des interprétations,* Paris: Seuil, 1969), p. 107.

35. In this perspective, the reduction carried out by psychoanalysis does not amount to identifying cause and truth of the subject. It is not the same thing to say, as J.-A.

Miller does, that the subject reelects the unconscious and responds from this place with a consent. Lacan's famous formula "burned circle in the jungle of the drives" (*Écrits,* Paris: Seuil, 1966, p. 666) seems adequate to evoke at the same time one's canceling of one's subscription to the unconscious, subjective destitution, consent to primarily repressed jouissance, and the effect of being that it implies. It is possible to serialize proximate terms that concern the end of analysis. It is no longer a subjective division referring to lack-of-being that is at stake here, but the constitutive division of the speaking being [*parlêtre*] that reelects the defect in the Other correlative to the subject, defect from which the Oedipal delusion has constructed itself for the neurotic.

The Purloined Letter and the Tao of the Psychoanalyst

Eric Laurent

Last time I found myself here, at the end of the course *L'Autre qui n'existe pas et ses comités d'éthique,* Jacques-Alain Miller spoke of the possibility of continuing the work of the seminar that had begun that year. This is really what is coming to be realized today, since I envisage this session and the offer that he has given me to speak at his course as an occasion to communicate certain results of my teaching this year, halfway through the university year. I proposed, in effect, to study the function of the plus-One for Lacan, at least certain aspects of this function, in taking into account at once the aspect of the hole and the aspect of the plus-One, that underlies the utilization or the reference to the function of the plus-One.

We had the occasion, last year, to approach the link of this function of the plus-One with the place of the father and the Name-of-the-Father. This place of the plus-One is to be gone into in depth for the psychoanalyst, especially from the perspective of Lacan's *Séminaire V, Les formations de l'inconscient* in the current presentation that Jacques-Alain Miller has made of it. This seminar puts the accent on a place that is extimate to the system of language [*la langue*], distinguished insofar as it is outside the system and yet inside. This place authorizes new meanings that are produced each time that the effect of a *Witz* inscribes a totally new usage or a new way of speaking in language and it allows them to be admitted.

In the perspective constructed from this role of admission that the function of the plus-One fulfills, I wondered how to articulate the latter with the function of the psychoanalyst, which consists in editing the text, in punctuating it.

Thus, how to articulate the one who admits new meanings, the effect of sense, with the one whose practice is indexed less on the effect of sense than on scansion; without of course neglecting the fact that the scansion implied by the editing of the text distributes signification and produces effects of sense.

This is not, however, the whole of the definition of this place, which is centered more on punctuation than on sense. It is from this perspective that I have taken up the reading of "Lituraterre" again, an eminent text, in the series of texts by Lacan dating from the beginning of the seventies, to broach the question of the place of the letter, of its relation to semblants and to the effect of sense.

I took up "Lituraterre" again, with all the more keenness that it appeared to me that Jacques-Alain Miller, at the beginning of his course this year, had supplied the matheme that was missing for a clear reading of this text, which is not considered, in general, to be a text that is easy to access.

The Double Function of the Letter

The entire text of "Lituraterre" is centered on two aspects of the function of the letter: the letter insofar as it makes a hole and the letter insofar as it makes an object (*a*).

This text is articulated, in fact, around a reflection on the history of writing, much more than on a history of literature, on a history of writing, to which correspond two approaches, two apologues, two modes of consideration.

The two approaches to writing correspond to two traditions, Western and Oriental, that Lacan examines one after the other. To each of the two modes of writing, alphabetic or ideographic, corresponds an apologue. For the first, it is "The Purloined Letter," for the second, I will say that it is a story of water: from high in his plane, crossing the Siberian desert, Lacan sees rivers. It seemed to me that it was a question of the same apologue, and, in any case, it really is a question of grasping in what way the one and the other designate, deliver a message on the letter that indicates the same point.

"Lituraterre" is clearly the rewriting, in the seventies, of "The Agency of the Letter in the Unconscious," a text in which Lacan was also particularly interested in two modes of writing, Greek and Chinese, but in another way. Thus, on page 504 of the *Écrits,* the opposition between them is evoked: " . . .is it your figure that traces our destiny for us in the tortoise-shell cracked by the fire, or your lightning that causes the slow shift in the axis of being to surge up from an unnameable night into the Ἐν πάντα of language".

This sentence refers to Chinese writing, which everybody grants derives from a divinatory practice that consists in placing tortoiseshells in a fire and, in the cracks that appear upon them, to foresee destiny, the message of the gods, the writing.

The paths of writing in China are thus based on divinatory practices with which you know to what extent China remains encumbered. Hence, the Bank of China in Hong Kong was only built after some divinatory practices were performed in order to be assured of the circulation of different fluids, and so on.

Thus, we have, on the one hand, divination by tortoiseshells placed in the fire and, on the other hand, lightning, the Heraclitian lightning that makes the slow mutation of Being surge forth from the night, and the way in which the One, being condensed in one phrase, comes to name the innumerability of things.

This passage of "The Agency of the Letter," in which Lacan shares with us his meditation on the different modes according to which Being comes to language, leads us to the diagrams of metaphor and metonymy that appear to him, he says, to operate in Chinese poetry as well as in Western poetry. It is the bar [*barre*] that appears to him as the veritable axis [*arbre*] that organizes the division between them.

Here, in "Lituraterre," Lacan rereads and reinterprets this place of the bar, whereas, before, he situated it as the reason for the unconscious, as repetition: either it repeated itself below the bar and it was metonymy,

The bar ————

⟶

Metonymy

or it crossed the bar, and it was metaphor that punctuated the incessant sliding of the signifier over the signified.

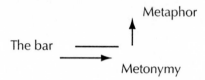

Metaphor

The bar ————

Metonymy

Lacan reconsiders his approach in an amusing way: "[I situated the letter as] reason for the unconscious. Does this not suffice to designate what in the letter, because it needs to insist, is not there rightfully, however much it may pretend to be?" ("Lituraterre," 13)

Thus, he takes up once more the Saussurian algorithm, with this 'rightfully,'

$$\frac{S}{s}$$

Once the question has been displaced and his teaching has reached the point at which metaphor and metonymy are linked, he wants to take a step further.

We have here a first misunderstanding. The misunderstanding, he says, is that in 1970 he is speaking in the context of the promotion of the written. The context is the implication, differently accentuated at the time by a certain number of authors (Derrida is the most eminent among them; one can also cite Barthes, since Lacan makes reference to him in his text, and, to a lesser or other extent, Michel Foucault), of Lévi-Straussian structuralism, which is too centered, according to them, on structural phonology and on the privileging, they say, of the voice, of speech.

Indeed, the philosophical chorus, which had been dumbfounded for ten years by the approach of Lévi-Strauss, started a comeback, in which Derrida's lecture on Freud in 1966 at the Institut de psychanalyse was to mark an important scansion. Lacan replies here, dryly, clearly, and vigorously to Derrida, fairly vigorously to Barthes, and leaves other authors to one side.

From the start, one can reduce the misunderstanding. Lacan does not want to get involved in the promotion of the written. He says, rather, that he delights in the fact that it is our epoch that has truly taken up the reading of Rabelais. Thus, he insists not on the promotion of the written, but on reading: to read Rabelais. What does it mean for this epoch to read Rabelais? He is a monument that has already been visited; what's more, Michelet has made him into the great man of the Renaissance. However, it is our epoch that has focused the reading of Rabelais on his laughter. It is the works of the Russian formalist Michael Bakhtin that have attracted the attention of critics to Rabelais's laughter. Altogether, Rabelais as *homme d'esprit* is known from the diffusion of these works, produced in Russia toward the end of the twenties and subsequently diffused throughout Europe. There is, on the one hand, this Russian school, which makes of Rabelais the laughter of the people of the Renaissance, replying to the collapse of scholastic semblants, and then you have other readings, notably that of the English with Michael Screech who, instead of considering Rabelais's laughter as a popular laughter, shows that it is the laughter of the humanists and that Rabelais's most smutty jokes are derived in general, with very precise references, from a piece of writing by Erasmus.

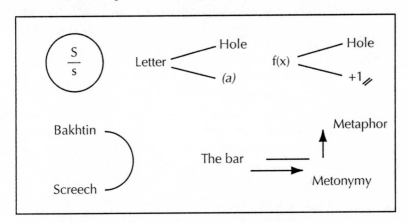

Let us leave these battles and simply highlight what our epoch brings to the fore; it is the effect of assuagement produced by these writings of Rabelais that is very important. The first texts of Kant were received with floods of tears; as a moral effect it was so beautiful that it made generations of students cry; with Rabelais it was, and still is, laughter. And this is what is beautiful in their achievement: such writings provoke passions, like Lacan's *Écrits* in 1966, that made people laugh and cry at the same time.

So, it is necessary to emphasize this all the more given that Lacan borrowed the writing of the sinthome from Rabelais, and he ended up by making it his banner. To declare in this way that the letter, in literature, must be grasped in the effect that it has and not in its signification, clarifies the place that the two apologues developed by Lacan will occupy: "The Purloined Letter" and the apologue that I will entitle *Flight over the Letter*.

I will recall that *Flight over the Letter* [*Vol sur la lettre*], the aerial flight over the letter, is written on the ground. Evidently, "The Purloined Letter" [*La lettre volée*] is not here for nothing, given the fact that it is from a story of flight [*vol*] that Lacan constructed the second apologue.

What the Letter Is Not

It is a matter of considering, first, what the letter is not. The letter is not an imprint, and Lacan is precise about this. Contrary to what Freud says in "The Mystic Writing Pad" where, departing from the inscription or from the instance of the letter in the unconscious, he speaks about it as printing with these little tools, slates said to be magic that children are no longer familiar with today—they have computer screens. There were two sheets on which one pressed and made an imprint; you lifted the two sheets and suddenly there was nothing there. Nowadays, you simply turn off the computer screen. This metaphor of writing appears incorrect to Lacan; it does not seem to him that writing is printing. Here, he attacks what Derrida had advanced in his lecture of 1966, where it was a question of the first fundamental trace, a primary imprint, outside sense, which sense would then try to catch up with, never managing to reabsorb the primary outside-sense that makes a trace.

Hence, it is not an imprint, and, second, it is not an instrument. Indeed, he says "That it [the letter] is an instrument specific to the writing of discourse [that one can write discourse with the letter] does not render it improper to designate a word taken for another [this is a metaphor since with writing you can write discourse, you can always write a word that comes in the place of another],

$$\frac{\cancel{S}}{S}$$

or even a word taken up by another [and this is metonymy,

$$S \xrightarrow{\cancel{S}} S$$

hence, in "The Agency of the Letter," Lacan gave as an example the way in which the word *tête* is taken up in *tempête*], in the sentence, and so to symbolize certain signifying effects, but it does not require that it be primary in these effects."

$$T[emp]ête \qquad S \xrightarrow{\cancel{S}} S$$

It is here that Lacan himself puts into question the 'primary' place of the bar, and struggles against the thesis of a primary imprint or the character of a primary instrument that the letter would have. In this way, he challenges the primary place of the bar that divides metaphor and metonymy. He says that this can serve for that, but it is not sufficient.

Thus, he criticizes himself, as he often does: if it is not an instrument, if it is neither trace nor imprint, what consequence can be drawn?

It seems to me that Lacan relates the ensemble of what has been considered as the genesis of writing, or as the history of writing in the West, back to a nonpertinent knowledge [*savoir*]. In one paragraph, quite an admirable one as a matter of fact, he says, "The question is to know whether what the textbooks seem to make a display of, namely that literature is the using up of leftovers, is an affair of collocation in the written of what would firstly be song, spoken myth, or dramatic procession."

Indeed, it is written everywhere, at least in the serious textbooks on the history of writing, that at a certain moment the Greeks judged it timely to reunite the hymns with the gods, the songs, the myths that they recounted to each other or the dramatic processions, that is, the tragedies, and to put them down on paper. In fact, we still have the written record of the order that Pericles gave one day to establish the best possible version of Homer's texts, this version that was the glory of Athens, until the Hellenic sovereign, one of the Ptolemaists, in fact, laid his hands on it and took it to the library at Alexandria.

Thus, there are these "collocations," as Lacan says, "in the written, of what would be, firstly, song, spoken myth, dramatic procession." Here we have what writing would be: a means of allowing this, and thus transforming all these texts into a useful instrument.

Now, what all these textbooks well and truly avoid is the effect of jouissance thus produced. What was it, for Pericles, to gather together Homer's texts? What did it inscribe, other than his nostalgia for not having been one of Homer's heroes? Would he have suffered a slight effect of passivation from it, this first tyrant, unless he was not, already, the second, and hence, already nostalgic for the time when there were real men? So here we have what brings us back to "The Purloined Letter." There's a letter, a love letter addressed to the queen by her lover, which undergoes a detour, with the paradox that those who come to be in possession of the letter start, shall we say, to busy themselves with their appearance. The unscrupulous minister, the plain-speaking man, the chap who is "up-for-anything," for any kind of treason, who is a bit like Alcibiades, takes the letter in order to do what appears to him to be opportune and thereby becomes a dandy of the nineteenth century. He becomes Lord Byron, he busies himself with his tie, with his posture; he is on his sofa and he poses, while the police bustle about him, seeming to say to them: "Well done, if you find it." Finally, he ends up back there in the position of the dandy, mocking the men of action. Dupin who, being more cunning, armed with his green glasses, is going to snatch the letter from the minister, and in so doing will find himself likewise encumbered, in a different way but with the same traits of dandyism. He ends up in the style of Edgar Allan Poe, of Baudelaire. He also becomes a man of the nineteenth century.

Lacan summarizes this in the following way: "The letter produces an effect of feminization." This term has an initial sense that is Freudian, since for Freud the feminine position consists of actively searching for passive aims; it is the 'feminine masquerade'. We have an initial sense of the position of passivation of these men of action. In a second and more profound sense, among all these people who bustle around and who, in fact, are all men, the grand enigma is the position of the queen. As for her, amid all this, what does she want—what does the woman want?

This second level allows us to note that the feminization induced by the letter, that is, the very sense or senses of the tale, the effects of signification, the story itself, all that is told in the tale, do not account for the position of jouissance, for the enigma of her position. It suffices that this enigmatic place be a place in reserve. In this respect, the place of jouissance surges up as, at once enigma, a hole in sense, and, at the same time, the place of this jouissance. To read "The Purloined Letter" against the grain of signification, one must distinguish the share of jouissance *(a)* and the effect of sense or the effect of signification introduced by the path taken by the signifier.

Thus, Lacan is opposed to the philosophical position that simply organizes itself according to the perspective of the opposition of sense and outside-sense, and does so in relation to Being.

Sense / outside-sense

Being, as that which has some sense, is the status from which the philosopher interrogates contemporary non-sense. To put this in Heideggarian terms, which Derrida cites, it is 'Being crossed out [*barré en croix*]'; crossed out or barred being the status of modern non-sense in which the subject, given over to nothingness, moves. It is the status of modern subjectivity: Being and nothingness.

$$\frac{Being}{\cancel{Being}} = Sense / outside\text{-}sense$$

Lacan, on the contrary, shows that it is not from this perspective that the question of sense and of outside-sense must be understood, but from that of the opposition between the effect of signification and the place of jouissance. Writing allows this place of jouissance to be registered; it inscribes what Pericles did in gathering the hymns and what Edgar Allan Poe did in naming the jouissance of his time, the place of the dandy reflecting a contempt for a man of action. In other words, a certain mode of the man of action (par excellence, that of the entrepreneur) is going to be inspired by the dandy's withdrawal from the world.

Thus, each time, we have an inscription and a trace of something that is primary and exceeds all the significations in play, and each time it is this harboring, this very reception, of the jouissance in the letter, in writing, that comes to inscribe itself.

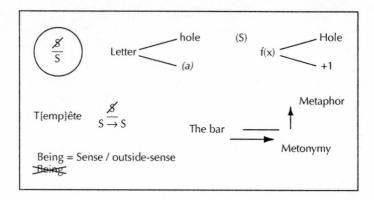

What are the relations—and it is really these that Lacan will interrogate in this text—between the effect of signification and jouissance? He can no longer content himself with what he had introduced with metonymy, where the effect of sense, the metonymic flight [*fuite*]¹ of sense, was equivalent to the metonymic object. It is here that we must have recourse to what Jacques-Alain Miller raised in his *Course* of 1987–1988, *Ce qui fait insigne*. At that time, he broached Lacan's texts from the seventies (*L'Étourdit, Joyce-le-Sinthome,* and *R.S.I*) around a problematic articulating the real and sense.

Real / Sense

It is a problematic that has been established explicitly in the teaching of Jacques-Alain Miller since 1987, and that he pursued throughout that year in order to make us perceive the consequences to be drawn from this approach, in what way it touches the heart of our practice.

Three Reals

In 1987, toward the month of June, when he was bringing his *Course* to a close, J.-A. Miller was speaking of the function and noting that, in approaching the real, it is necessary to distinguish the real in science, the real in the symptom, and the real in the analytic operation. He proposed, after a series of simplifications, to inscribe in the place of the hole, in the hole that any function supposes, the categories of the real, symbolic, and imaginary.

The real that science knows is mathematisable, it presents itself under a symbolic form:

$$f(R) = S$$

In the symptom, the symbolic becomes real in the psychoanalytic sense:

$$f(S) = R$$

Lacan's idea is that it would be wonderful for psychoanalysis to propose that a certain function of the signified, not of the signifier, gives us a real—that is, in operating on the effects of sense, we might have a function where the effect of sense touches the real.

$$f(s) = R$$

Within the manifold problematic of the seventies, "Lituraterre," in trying to catch the links of sense and of the real, is eminently situated from this perspective.

> Real / sense
> $f(R) = S$
> $f(S) = R$
> $f(s) = R$

How can we account for the fact that some real is produced by means of the effect of sense? It is necessary to distinguish the register of alienation—by means of which a subject inscribes himself in the Other, where the effects of sense are produced by the primary identification—from that of separation—where the place of jouissance is inscribed, marking the place of the lost object through the effects of sense (e.g., Pericles's nostalgia circulating between the lines of Homer's poem).

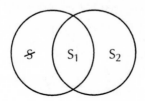

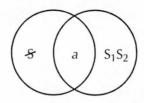

It is with the apparatus of these schemas, which Jacques-Alain Miller established while transcribing Seminar XI for us, that we are going to approach the second apologue.

"I'm coming back from a journey in Japan," says Lacan. The anecdote is that of a flight over a desert, Siberia, a route that, he says, he is taking for the first time—this is a real thumbing of the nose at the imprecise routes of Derrida—he travels thus for the first time by a polar route that has just opened (the Russians accepted this route, which allowed, in fact, a reduction of four or five hours by plane on the journey back from Tokyo to the West, but it is a desert route, for the Soviets wanted to be sure that no spy plane would photograph their installations. Besides, it is fairly reasonable seeing as, since then, we have learned that all the commercial planes were at the very least equipped with small spying devices).

Here we have an impossible route in the complete desert, the Siberian plain, truly more deserted than any other and, what is more, a plain that is totally plain: no mountains, but only water, rivers.

So, OK, we can see the montage between "The Purloined Letter" and the flight. Then in the montage, he says, it is wonderful; he sees the rivers as a kind of trace from where the imaginary is abolished and he says it in the style of Mallarmé: "Such as it invincibly came to me . . . from between the clouds, the streaming, the sole trace to appear, that forges, more than it brings out, the relief at this latitude, in what constitutes the plain of Siberia, a plain desolate of any vegetation but for reflections, reflections which push into the shadow all that does not shimmer."

Indeed, it is written in Mallarmé's style; this is a French on which you really have to rack your brain to understand the exact construction— where are the relatives, is the subject in apposition, where? how? It is language at work.

We can see, thus, this abolition of the imaginary: "reflections push into the shadow all that does not shimmer." It is not the sign, for the sign indicates something, but we have this trace that does not even come to underscore a preexisting aspect of the world. It is not even the opposition of the river and the mountain; there is no deception—no opening out of a path—it is a pure trace that operates.

He tells us he is coming back from Japan, but, as he says, he is coming back, above all, from a certain relation to writing. He draws his inspiration mainly from China. During those years, he reflected deeply on Chinese. We know from François Cheng, and from the interview published in the Freudian magazine *L'Âne* No 48, that between 1969 and 1973 he had very thorough conversations with Lacan once a week on the Chinese classics and on three of them in particular: Lao Tzu, Mencius, and Shih-t'ao. Cheng had published the latter's treatise on painting as an addendum to his essay on Chinese painting *Le vide et le plein* published by Seuil in 1977. Furthermore, the combination of the characters "mountain" and "water" in Chinese means the landscape in general. Obviously, it is not without this reference to Chinese painting that Lacan reads Siberia as calligraphy, as a pure trace that operates without indicating, without signifying what is there: nothing human, not a single human product on the horizon, that is, no dustbins (the human par excellence—here it is the dustbin, rubbish); this is what industrial China is going to produce by way of radioactive rubbish and which always leaves a trace. Here the beginning of Beckett's *Endgame* is evoked: "no trace of living life, hurry up, sprinkle on some powder." This is the pure operation of the letter taking place. "And there," he says, is established "the dimension, the demansion . . . of the *nomorthunwonn* [*papeludun*],[2] that which is evoked by the part of the subject, the part I set up in the *Wonn-mor* [*Hun-en-peluce*],[3] as such it fills the anguish of the *l'Achose*."

The One more [*Un en plus*], one could say, the One more with which the anguish of *l'Achose* is filled, is the object *(a)*, and in what form if not that of the teddy bear [*l'ours en peluche*]?

(a)

It is the teddy bear as a reservoir of fundamental libido that one adds to the Other, that each of us adds to the Other, which, when the Other has gone and leaves you all alone, left to your own anguish, your anguish deserted of *l'Achose,* you cling to once more. You hang on like a wretch, to your bobbin, to your teddy bear, and then, when you grow up, you cling to other objects that attempt to replace this, but evidently do so in vain.

So you approach, as you can, what allows you to hold on, and here where there once was the hole, where the hole of *l'Achose* appeared, the void, hey presto!, the *One more* [*Un en peluce*], of which it is very important that there's no more than one, is lodged.

$$\frac{\text{Hole}}{(a)}$$

You know, if you have a mother who spends her time taking away your teddy bear and washing it, so it is clean, because it is dribbled, my dear, well, that is no good. In the seventies, this gave rise to the cult of the teddy bear; it gave rise to some stinking, appalling things, that were not to be washed. Neither must one fall into excess, but, finally, it is like everything—good maternal care is a question of tact; you have to make do, without extremes, not being dogmatic or too fanatical about a thing because, in the advice given to mothers when they become fanatical about a solution, Doctor Spock said: above all, you must not physically abuse a child; that turns out bad. In any case, when it is necessary to discipline a child, it gives rise to a great deal of ravage due to a dogmatism of nonviolence, it topples over in the other direction, so there is no method but for a sufficiently bad one.

Littoral

All this, ultimately, is to say how the subject is established. The subject, when he cannot be represented, when he is no longer represented in the Other, when the Other is no longer the place where he is alienated, or where he inscribes himself, but becomes the desert of *l'Achose,* then, instead, the subject clings to what is its fastening point, the object *(a)*. And the letter, Lacan tells us, becomes littoral: "between knowledge [*savoir*] and jouissance, there is the littoral that only turns into the literal on condition that this turn may be taken in the same way at any time."

So, what is the littoral? This littoral appears so enigmatic, to the point that some people made it the title of a review, a little as if it were *Ornicar?*, as if it were the enigma, littoral. Littoral designates exactly the border that separates the letter, *(a),* from knowledge [*savoir*], reducing the pair $(S_1 S_2)$ to S_2 for simplicity's sake.

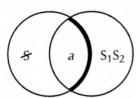

The littoral is represented knowledge and, indeed, the letter that comes to inscribe itself in that place makes one edge distinct in its function from the other edge.

There are not two signifiers; there are two things that are of two distinct kinds. The effect of sense, noted by S_2, and the place of jouissance mean that between the two there is no longer a frontier but a line that is everywhere heterogeneous. It is this line that in *Encore* Lacan will approach in terms of compactness. One could reproach him for the importation of this mathematical concept into psychoanalysis, but I would nevertheless emphasize that it is an extremely sound way to bring forth a separation that is not a frontier and, above all, not a frontier between an interior and an exterior.

It is here that we find in the text the critique of a perspective brought about by biology, where the interior and the exterior, the subject and the object, are separated. Here, you see that with alienation and separation, if one takes these formulas from which Jacques-Alain Miller has established the schemas, in fact the frontier, the littoral enters the interior of psychic reality. This is not a frontier between the interior and the exterior—it is within the subject.

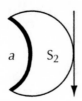

This is the point of the apologue that Lacan adds to "The Purloined Letter." In "The Purloined Letter" he made the place of consciousness apparent; however, it is still too exterior. Here, he points out that the division between unconscious knowledge and jouissance is carried out on the side of the subject and, as noted by Jacques-Alain Miller in "The Seminar of Barcelona" in 1997, Lacan makes a radical jump in refusing the Freudian opposition between the pleasure principle and the reality principle and in considering them as distributed around a topology of the interior and the exterior.

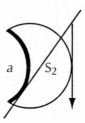

The Unary Stroke of the Brush

Lacan only accepts this opposition as being at play in the interior of the subject, like in this apologue of the trait [*trait*] that operates in the desert, without indicating that what he sees there, secretly, is the stroke [*trait*] of the calligrapher. Here the reference is less to Japan than to Shih-t'ao and to what he had read of the major lesson of chapter V of Shih-t'ao, which François Cheng translated in his book *Le vide et le plein* (p. 84).

Shih-t'ao, who was writing in the seventeenth century, had the particularly original theory that the painter and the calligrapher proceed by what he calls the unary stroke [*trait*] of the brush. This is a Chinese word that François Cheng translates by "unique" in his book; however, it would be better to translate it by "unary," which is what Lacan did in his *Séminaire XIV, La Logique du fantasme*, where he makes reference to this find of Shih-t'ao. He says the following: "The indistinct function of Yin and Yun—it is chaos, not Yin and Yang—constitutes original chaos. And if it is not by way of the unary stroke of the brush, how could one disentangle original chaos? . . . To carry out the union of the Ink and the Brush is to resolve the distinction between Yin and Yun and to undertake the disentangling of chaos. . . . In the midst of the ocean of Ink, to firmly establish the spirit [*l'esprit*]; at the tip of the brush, that life might assert itself and surge forth; that on the surface of the painting is the metamorphosis; that at the heart of chaos the light is installed and springs up! . . . From the One, the Multiple is divided; from the Multiple, the One is conquered, the metamorphosis of the One produces Yin and Yun—and behold! all the virtualities of the world are accomplished" (op. cit., pp. 84–85).[4]

As Cheng notes very well, it is a conception in which there is no opposition between the subject One, and the world that it represents. Creation for the Chinese painter is not opposed to him; he pursues it, he adds himself to it. Far from being a description of the spectacle of creation, painting is an addition that allows a disentangling, to open the way, to add, not to a world conceived as exterior, but to a world conceived as an object.

This approach to Chinese painting, which has been dominant for twelve hundred years, is very specific. The painting of the calligrapher is not a question, as in Renaissance painting, of describing the world, of ordering the internal chaos, but of ordering by way of the stroke [*trait*] of the paintbrush, of operating by making a trace. This is where the gesture of the painter, the gesture of Shih-t'ao, meets up with the gesture of the infant throwing his bobbin to enact the *fort-da*, to shape the anguish of *l'Achose*. It is not only the phonemic opposition of the 'o-a', *fort-da*, but the gesture itself that counts, bearer that it is of the inscription of this trace.

From this distinction, where the real is not in opposition, is not exterior, a littoral is deduced: wholly interior, between the sense, the effect of sense, and the place of jouissance.

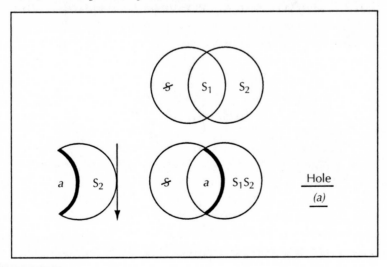

The Tao of the Psychoanalyst

Hence, the last part of Lacan's text can be understood, following these two apologues, one on the Western letter, the other on the Oriental letter, with some considerations that can be centered around a reflection on the conditions "of a discourse that would not be a semblant". From the perspective that Jacques-Alain Miller had thus established, in what conditions could a discourse truly touch jouissance and its littoral with the signifier?

Lacan draws on many discourses. He considers, on the one hand, science and, on the other, psychoanalysis, avant-garde literature and the Japanese subject. In a disparate fashion, he broaches this question so as to designate and articulate what must be called the *tao* of the psychoanalyst, his way [*voie*].

How might the analyst situate himself in relation to these effects of sense? If we refer to the transcription made by François Cheng of his dialogues with Lacan, and to what he noted, precisely enough, it seems, to have been able to subsequently make a transmission of it in *L'Âne* No 48, we find that this was precisely what Lacan was looking for the most with him: the Chinese way in which sense, and not *l'Achose,* but that which has a name and that which doesn't have a name, come to be articulated.

There is a very beautiful passage in the transcription that François Cheng has provided, and who, after having situated the way [*voie*] in Lao-Tzu, isolates the passage that had gripped Lacan: "the way insofar as it is that which is nameless, and that can all the same name itself."

So, I am quoting it because it corresponds exactly with the summary that Lacan made of this problematic at the bottom of page 10 of "Lituraterre."[5] It is from chapter 1 of the *Livre de la Voie et de sa vertu:*

> The Way that can be enunciated
> Is not the Way forever
> The name that can be named
> Is not the name forever
> Without name: from which Heaven-and-Earth proceed
> The name: mother-of-all-things

The *Voie/voix* [Way/voice], insofar as it is, first of all, nomination, and then effect of nomination, makes something come about, but what? For where it is not Greek; the question is no longer one of bringing into

Being, but of acquiring a certain usage. Chinese is not an Indo-European language; it has no verb "to be." At the place of the copula there is this invention proper to Chinese, which is that the word *tao* means at the same time "to do" and "to say," "to enunciate." It is one of the most extraordinary stories of thought that is revealed by the history of thought in China, where Chinese thought has succeeded in accommodating the Being transmitted by Buddhism in the mode of the void because it spoke Sanskrit, an Indo-European language, thus implying Being and non-Being. The Chinese took, all the same, eight hundred years to make *tao* meet up with the Buddhist void. It took a long time, and caused a lot of friction in the different Chinese schools, to adjust two notions that had nothing to do with each other, and to make of it a creation of discourse, which would be transmitted to Japan, with the Buddhism that we call *Zen*. The 'Chan' sect devised, in fact, a rather sophisticated version of this combination of the Hindu void and the Chinese *tao*.

Here we have the *Voie/voix* insofar as it is prior to nomination, and Cheng says that while reading this text, Lacan notes, "it is wonderful!" He stops Cheng and produces the following little schema:

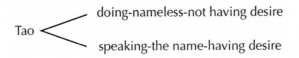

He says to him: there you are, here is the *tao,* so we make two registers. Thus, Lacan produces this little schema, but straightaway he says that "it is now a question of knowing how to hold on to its two aspects, of what Lao-Tzu proposes in order to live with this dilemma."

What use to make of it? This is the question that Lacan poses. How to make these things hold together? When we read this interview from the perspective that Jacques-Alain Miller has traced, once one has isolated the real, the symbolic, and the imaginary, the real, sense, and outside-sense; or these are some dimensions, this is what is at stake— but how to live with them, how to live with this dilemma?

What interested Lacan in speaking with Cheng was the proposed solution, and in Cheng's testimony we read this: "without thinking about it too much, I responded: 'by the Void-median'. Once this term 'Void-median' was pronounced, we did not stop until we had elucidated the reality of this most fundamental of all notions." After having examined the sources closely and verified the interpretations, they were able to establish that the three, in Lao-Tzu, was nothing other than the Void-median. And yet, according to Cheng, who is here the specialist, whereas, until then, the three had not really occupied the specialists of Chinese thought, who stopped at two, at the opposition of Yin and Yang, this interpretation was henceforth adopted by all the sinologists as well as by the learned Chinese themselves. (Cf. *L'Âne,* op. cit., p. 53.) They took great care to observe the multiple usages of the Void-median in the concrete domain at the heart of a person—it is very precious, the Void-median, at the heart of a person—in a couple, between two tribes (with reference to Lévi-Strauss), between actor and spectator in the theatre, and so on.

So this is where, concretely, the void is situated. How to articulate the void is what interested Lacan: the correct use of the void, of this Void-median that is a kind of version of the littoral, that which separates two things that between them have no way of holding together, or any way to pass from one to the other.

In following this inquiry into the Void-median with Cheng, Lacan finds that, all in all, Chinese poetry, the Chinese mode of reasoning, is altogether invaded by metaphor, that everything is metaphorized. And there, he says to Cheng, what strikes him is that, in Chinese thought, metaphor and metonymy are not really opposed. "All in all," he says, "the more there is metaphor, the richer the metonymy. In other words, metaphor and metonymy result from one another, they mutually engender each other, man being the metaphor *par excellence*"—he refers to his own classic definition from *Booz endormi; Sa gerbe n'était point avare ni haineuse* [His sheaf was neither miserly nor spiteful]—"man being the metaphor *par excellence,* his relation to the world—another metaphor—would be, I suppose, but a universal metonymy."

$$\frac{\text{Sheaf}}{} \quad \frac{\text{Other}}{\text{man}}$$

Sheaf
Other
man
---
x

"Shih-t'ao, did he not speak of Universal Circulation?," he continued. "That explains perhaps why the Chinese privileged the notion of subject/subject to the detriment of that of the subject/object, since, as the subject is completely metaphorized, what is important in their eyes is what happens between subjects, rather than the subject itself in terms of being a separate or isolated entity. Here without doubt, concludes Lacan, "the Void-median again intervenes."

This is the summary of a long exchange that situates well the problematic in question, since it is neither with the help of the opposition between metaphor and metonymy, nor with the help of the old system of the bar, that we can best situate the metaphorized place of the subject, but in its relation, in the interior of itself—the relation subject/subject—that is at the same time the relation to another subject or the relation to itself in terms of addressing itself to the Other.

So we can understand from this perspective why the end of "Lituraterre" is concerned with the mode of address of the Japanese subject. Considering the way in which the Japanese subject comes to say "you," how can he prop himself up on the "you," how can he separate what comes back to him—that is, his place as subject—from the Other, insofar as he is a deposit of jouissance, insofar as he is the partner, the "you" to which the subject addresses himself?

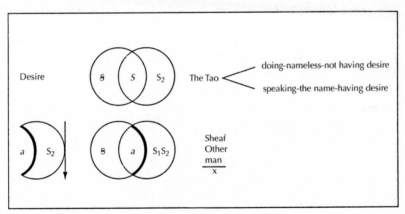

What has to be read, moreover—I will not do it here in detail—in "L'adresse au sujet japonais" concerns the Japanese mode of language [*lalangue*], the way in which this fixes a mode of the littoral separating of jouissance and signifying articulation. It is, again, necessary to consider the discourse of science—Lacan puts a damper on this discourse—insofar as it would come to absorb entirely the real without symptom, a mathematizable symptom.

A Lacanian Ecology?

Here we have the indication of a sort of Lacanian ecology that is yet to be fully developed and is engendered from the following sentence, written in 1971: "Physics finds itself, is going to find itself, brought back to the consideration of the symptom by the pollution of the environment." It must not be forgotten—to the extent that the discourse of science seemed to be without remainder, without any littoral between signifying articulation and jouissance—that what we are going to find, he says, is pollution, the big pile of waste that science fabricates for us and that is becoming more and more difficult to eliminate from the surface of the planet, provoking an interrogation. We are beyond interrogating the links between science and conscience, beyond the moral quandaries of the atomic bomb inventors in their different versions. The scientists of today are no longer seen as grand consciences; besides, it is no longer demanded of them, nobody believes in it any more. The torments that occupied the postwar years, where these grand scientific consciences managed to have an effect of sense, the moral wranglings of Oppenheimer, of Einstein or of Sakharov, mattered, but now everybody knows very well that for a scrupulous biologist, who would stop such and such research, having caught sight of terrible consequences, there would always remain ten or a hundred others to continue the research. No problem—that makes one less competitor, everybody is delighted, and that's all. Things are different now, however, on the other hand, the problems of responsibility, of pollution that are at the heart of our relation with science matter—like the story of contaminated blood—insofar as it concerns, very precisely, a relation to the symptom: we know something about it now, one can no longer say that the discourse of science does not produce a certain number of leftovers.

Avant-garde Literature

There is this other figure that Lacan takes into consideration, that of avant-garde literature. Well, it must be said that Lacan evoked a most contemporary problematic for the intellects who were very lively in those years, in broaching the social bond from the point of view of avant-garde literature, from communities such as surrealism, the

Collège de philosophie, Acéphale, then *Les temps modernes* and *Tel Quel,* and so on, communities founded precisely on a certain relation to outside-sense, to the affect of panic, to jouissance and not to the useful.

In the seventies, Philippe Sollers could still write the single sentence, without punctuation, of his *Paradis;* there was that and then there was a literature that was looking to making a community of readers in the outside-sense, which was transmitted according to certain channels, and this was what Lacan puts in question, in asking this literature on what grounds it is to be distinguished: "Is it possible for the littoral to constitute such a discourse that is characterised by not being issued from the semblant?" For Lacan, it is not because this avant-garde literature is itself made of littoral that it can claim to prove something other than the fracture of which it itself is an effect. As for the fracture itself, avant-garde literature cannot produce it—only a discourse can do it.

The Psychoanalytic Discourse

Now we come to the fourth diagram that is ordered by the relations of the semblant and of sense. It arises from the psychoanalytic discourse in which the letter is grasped in the effects of reading the signifier that it allows.

It is what Michel Leiris illustrates with his exclamation *"reusement."* It is what comes to mark his first memory, the screen memory of his life, which marks his relation to happiness, or, more exactly, his relation to unhappiness and his relation to the woman who corrects him. He chooses the toy soldier he loves, a soldier is going to fall, he only just catches him, he says *"reusement"* and his mother says to him, "No, we don't say *'reusement'* we say *'heureusement'*." Thus, there is this memory that he places at the forefront of his writings, at the forefront of his book, and from there one knows that he has experienced unhappiness, full stop. He had analysis after an extremely serious suicide attempt that occurred in the course of a night spent with Bataille; they had pushed it a bit far on the unhappiness of living, and so on. In addition, he constructed a literature that is of an extreme purism; that is, he never again allowed anybody to say to him: "No, no, we don't say *'reusement,'* we say *'heureusement','* he never allowed that again. It is he who distributed the deformations, who was able to invent codes, deform the usages, and that is wonderful—"we don't do such things, but yes we do, but, yes, old chap!"

Reusement

We can see here what he lodged of jouissance in secret. We can also see that writing is not primary; what is primary is the signifying exclamation of the chap who says *"reusement"* and who drops the *"heu"*; he will always be a little hung up on the *"heu"* in general.

Reusement
_____
Heureux Heureusement
Heu

Nevertheless, and without doubt for a reason, he produces a signifier. Subsequently, the letter allows a reading which is that, indeed, there was *heureu, heureusement,* and so on, and that there is a part, namely, the *"heu,"* that fell. But what it inscribed, from the moment when the signifier that appeared is read, is the part of lost jouissance, happiness forever lost, from where the subjective position is deduced, which is linked to this relationship with unhappiness, an unhappiness that will always be, throughout all the effects of sense, profoundly a relation with the unhappiness of Being that will accompany the subject. It is not linked to the effect of signification; in the same context, if things had been otherwise, if his mother had been a little happier and without doubt a little more cheerful—she did what she could—if his mother had not been depressive, if instead of saying to him, well, bothering him with this purism, she would have given him a cuddle, and presto!, all would've been back as it was, they would have burst out laughing and after he had said: "Everything is really possible," she would have said, "Ah! it's very funny, I'm going to tell your father about it when he comes back, I'm going to say to him 'you know, he did something amazing, he said *"reusement,"* amazing'," well, everybody burst out laughing. Obviously it does not have the same effect; it does not leave the same trace as unhappiness, does it, so it is not signification; it can be read in many ways, and above all the littoral can be inscribed between the effect of sense and the place; the effect, the affect, of jouissance can be inscribed in many ways.

And there Lacan is able to say that in the analytic discourse what operates is the letter, insofar as it dissolves what gives form. What gives form is the signifier, the semblant, the *"reusement,"* and afterward the letter will break it up, will enable it to be read, to be articulated, to produce a certain effect, to transform what "in the semblant pleased" [*plu du semblant*] insofar as it constitutes the signifier with a play on words: one for the rain [*la pluie*], and one is for what pleased [*a plu*] in the sense of the verb "to please" [*plaire*].

Reading

Here, what in the signifier pleased is subsequently placed in question in the reading of the unconscious made by the analytic discourse. Lacan carries out this reading by respecting the fracture that was produced and in causing or in emphasizing the effect of production of this fracture. This effect is what the analytic discourse inscribes from the discourse of the master.

$$\frac{a}{S_2} \longrightarrow \frac{\mathcal{S}}{/\!/ \; S_1}$$

Once you make this type of distinction, it is necessary to produce the identification: you identified yourself with the unhappy child, you were devoted to unhappiness, the time when your happiness, your *"reusement"* was not welcomed by your mother, well, there is your identification and that is separated from all that is unconscious knowledge linked to this *"reusement"* that remains a memory. Still, it is necessary to tear from the subject, for the subject to produce his identification and this in the name of unhappiness, of the trace, I would say, written forever, of the voice before all domination, of the *tao* of unhappiness that he traced for himself. And there it operates on condition that a certain void is introduced between the identification with the master signifier and the unconscious chain.

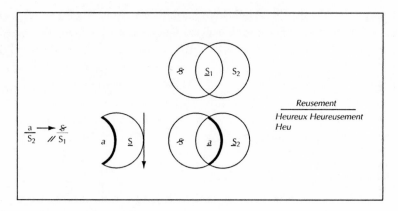

The Void-median ... Making Active

I would like to finish on the handling of the *tao* of the psychoanalyst and the very example that François Cheng gives of it when recounting a day spent with Lacan in 1977.

Cheng wrote his book *La poésie chinoise* in 1977. Lacan asked him to spend an afternoon with him at Guitrancourt. Throughout the whole day, which Cheng recounts wonderfully, Lacan interrogates him on one sole problem, saying to him: explain to me, from this poem, the Chinese conception of time. After having spoken about it for the whole day, and while accompanying him back home in the evening, Lacan said the following: "Dear Cheng, you have known many ruptures in your life. You'll know how to transform these ruptures into an active Void-median linking for you your present with your past, you will, at last, be in your time." It is an interpretation that Lacan allowed himself in the name of friendship. Since it is Cheng who told us this, I am not being indiscreet in making you party to it, and one can see how—with the aid of what is language that was being elaborated, the Void-median meaning something for one and for the other—they knew what they were speaking about. He said to him: "You have known fractures, you have known these frontiers, you have known without continuity a certain number of things, exile, the re-appropriation of another culture," and so on, and the following: "You will know how to transform these ruptures into an active Void-median," with "active" here meaning allowing him to circulate in his history.

All told, the *tao* of the psychoanalyst, if we follow Lacan's indications, is to manage to be able to hold oneself in one's place, there where there was a rupture, there where there was a fracture, there where the letter came to inscribe the littoral, the edge of all possible knowledge, transforming this into an active Void-median. To transform this into a possibility of making what does not hold together hold together, the real and sense, doing and speaking; these registers that were stated in a distinct way by Lacan, but are held together by the place of the psychoanalyst, insofar as, in this place, acting within the rubric of the non-acting [*non-agir*], within the rubric of the active-Void, which is another way to formulate the non-acting of the psychoanalyst, is to manage to do this, to hold oneself at this point where, ultimately, someone can circulate within what, for him, returned.

Notes

1. Although the English translation "flight of sense" would seem to make reference to the theme of flight that runs throughout the text, the original French *fuite de sens* makes no such direct reference.

2. The neologism *"papeludun"* is a homophone of the French *pas plus d'un,* which could be translated in English as "not more than one."

3. The neologism *"Hun-en-peluce"* is a homophone of the French *un en plus,* which can be translated in English as "one more" or "one extra."

4. The page numbers here correspond to those of *Ornicar?* No. 41.

5. J. Lacan, *Seminar III, The Psychoses* (London: Routledge, 1993), p. 228.

References

S. Beckett, *Endgame* (London: Faber, 1964).

F. Cheng, *Le vide et le plein, Le langage pictoral chinois* (Paris: Seuil, 1977).

F. Cheng, *L'écriture poétique chinoise* (Paris: Seuil, 1977).

F. Cheng, *Entretien, Le magazine freudien, L'Âne,* No. 48, Paris, 1991.

F. Cheng, *L'espace du rêve: mille ans de peinture chinoise* (Paris: Phébus, 1980).

F. Cheng, *Shitao* (1642–1707), *Le saveur du monde* (Paris: Phébus, 1998).

J. Lacan, *Le Séminaire V, Les formations de l'inconscient* (Paris: Seuil, 1998).

J. Lacan, "Lituraterre" in *Ornicar?* No. 41 (Paris: Navarin, 1987); also available in *Autres écrits* (Paris: Seuil, 2001).

J. Lacan, "The Agency of the Letter in the Unconscious or Reason since Freud" in *Écrits: A Selection* (London: Routledge, 1977).

J. Lacan, Le Séminaire sur 'La lettre volée' in *Écrits* (Paris: Seuil, 1966).

J. Lacan, "L'Étourdit in Silicet" No. 4 (Paris: Seuil, 1974).

J. Lacan, *Joyce-le-symptôme* in *Joyce avec Lacan* (Paris: Navarin, 1987).

J. Lacan, *R.S.I.* in *Ornicar?* (Paris: Lysse, 1975).

J. Lacan, *Le Séminaire XIV, La logique du fantasme,* 1966-1967, Paris (unpublished).

J. Lacan, *Seminar XI, The Four Fundamental Concepts* (London: Penguin, 1977).

J. Lacan, *Seminar XX, Encore,* 1972-1973 (London & New York: Norton, 1998).

E. Laurent and J.-A. Miller, *L'Autre qui n'existe pas et ses comités d'éthique,* a course held at the Department of Psychoanalysis, Paris, 1996-1997 (unpublished).

M. Leiris, *Biffures* (Paris: Gallimard, 1975, collection 'L'imaginaire').

C. Lévi-Strauss, *Anthropologie Structurale* (Paris: Plon, 1958).

J.-A. Miller, *Ce qui fait insigne,* a course held at the Department of Psychoanalysis of Paris VIII, Paris, 1987-1988 (unpublished).

J.-A. Miller, "The Seminar of Barcelona," *Psychoanalytical Notebooks* No.1, London, Autumn 1998.

Shih'tao, *Propos sur la peinture du moine Citrouille-amère* (Paris: Herman,1984).

PART II

From the Analytic Symptom
to the Sinthome

The Sinthome, a Mixture of Symptom and Fantasy

Jacques-Alain Miller

I did not mention the word "insignia" last time, even though it is a word that stands as the emblem of this year's course, its vector.[1] This is all it took for some to think that I had turned the page on this subject. This clearly demonstrates the use to be made of insistence in teaching. Lacan indicated as much: there can be no teaching without insistence.

I was wrong not to utter this word, and I affirm that the insignia is still what constitutes my object and my theme. I remind you that its function must be circumscribed by two terms that are, on the one hand, the one, the S_1, or even, as indicated in an older and more specific way of writing this term, the big I, the initial of the ego ideal, the mark of the unary trait, and on the other, little a.

$$1$$

$$S_1 \quad a$$

$$I$$

I will add that when it comes to the insignia, there cannot be one without the other, nor the other without the one. The insignia is not only the unary trait. To provide a workable definition of the insignia at once, let us say that it is the unary trait plus object a.

Since this year's theme is not only the insignia, but rather what constitutes an insignia [*ce qui fait insigne*],[2] and in order to make sure that we are within our subject, I submit that what constitutes an insignia has to do with the relation, the articulation between these two terms, and that the first term can be written in different ways. This is what constitutes an insignia in the subjective economy.

$$1, S_1, I a$$

Here we must make an effort of precision to recover or even to reconstruct the notion of the insignia, a notion that some of Lacan's writings, forged for other ends, lead us precisely to misunderstand.

There is no impeccable writing. There is no omnivalent writing. As soon as one chooses to write certain functions, others are obscured. For instance, the writing of the four discourses, which, by virtue of its convenience, has become teaching material, almost textbook material—especially in the Department of Psychoanalysis—is not primarily designed for the purpose [of highlighting the notion of insignia]. Indeed the matrix of the writing [of the four discourses] is the discourse of the master that, from the very first, makes object a as product fall outside the signifying articulation.

At first sight, this discourse does not seem apt for validating what I am formulating here on the insignia, and all the more since it interposes a third term between S_I and little a, S_2, which thereby appears to be an obligatory mediation. And this to the extent that the signifier seems, in effect, to confiscate the representation of the subject—this is what the discourse of the master inscribes.

You should not believe that in saying this, and in what I am going to propose today, which is a manner of inversion and implies a pivoting of perspectives—perspectives that I have myself fashioned at length in the past—I am thinking of making an objection to Lacan. After all, if this was the case, I would say so. I do not make objections to Lacan, except, as is my style, starting from Lacan himself.

To support my point of departure today, I found a fragment of a schema that I took from Lacan's 1967 Seminar, where I found a working version of the ternary that I take as a reference point. This ternary, a fragment of Lacan's schema, is a triangle. One of the sides is inscribed with the barred subject and is completed by two inscriptions, that of little a and that of big I, on the other two sides.

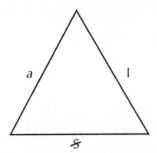

So we will work with this ternary, and this will entail a number of consequences that will become apparent, and which are not small. In this ternary the subject is framed by two terms that relate back to the subject as $\mathcal{S}$, as crossed out, inexistent, the subject we encounter in the analytic experience. This subject has been "wiped clean," just like the board is wiped clean before I enter this classroom. This wiping clean is preliminary to the emergence of a necessity for discourse. Axiomatics (namely, that everything that will be used for the purposes of a demonstration is explained) does nothing more than formalizing this wiping clean—in other words, inexistence is posed as the condition for necessity to emerge. This is what every analytic session reiterates for its own purposes.

The necessity for discourse reflects the omnipotence of the signifier, the omnipotence that supposes inexistence at its origin and even retroposes it. The signifier postulates inexistence as prior to itself. What are we writing when we write $\mathcal{S}$? We are going to ask ourselves once more. In fact, we write two things, not just one thing.

First—and this is usual for us—we write the subject of the signifier. We write the subject as without a name, anonymous. We write any subject. We write the subject without a signifier, on condition that we understand that we write it as equivalent to a missing signifier.

We can also write the subject with the small *s* of the signified. Lacan used this letter in this way and not just at the beginning of his teaching. He started out by writing the subject as an effect of signification produced by the signifier. Then he wrote it as a missing signifier, $\mathcal{S}$, but not without continuing to write it, all the same, from time to time, when the need arose, as small *s,* especially when writing it as subject supposed to know.

To write [the subject] as a missing signifier is to write it as an empty set: in other words, however empty it may be, it is under the domination of the signifier. This set must indeed be drawn so that one can say "there, there is not" [*là, il n'y a pas*].

It is thus—I am repeating myself—a subjective inexistence marked from the first by the signifier. I consider that this has now been acquired—who by? by all of us—on the basis of Lacan's elaboration and of the choice we made in developing this aspect of the barred subject.

To take [the subject] in this way, as the subject of the signifier, as a signifying void, immediately introduces the necessity for a signifier to come to fill the lack, namely, this initial mark. This is what we are often commenting here on the basis of $S_1/\cancel{S}$—the subject is represented by a signifier, and so on. We make this necessity graspable through our definition of the subject itself. It is a subject who is in itself the effacement of a signifier. Then we deduce the necessity for a signifying representation that comes from the Other, and we deduce the necessity of the Freudian identification. We consider that this is the alienation of the subject—to use Lacan's terms—in the initial identification that forms the ego ideal.

I already said that this identification is to be distinguished from any resemblance in the imaginary order, from any specular identification. In fact, Lacan concludes *The Four Fundamental Concepts of Psychoanalysis* on the point of the ego ideal, from where the subject sees itself as seen by the Other—I have already insisted at length on this *from where—from where the Other sees me, in the form in which it pleases me to be seen.*

By writing the subject in this way, and by giving it this sense, we underline the necessity of the Freudian articulation of identification by posing that the subject so defined calls for a signifying complement. This identification, here, is representation.

This value of $\cancel{S}$, which is so operative, and so well emphasized in the schema of the discourse of the master, is not the only one, even if it is the one that Lacan may have appeared to bring to the fore.

This is why I will name the second value of $\cancel{S}$, the value that is not that of $\cancel{S}$ as the subject of the signifier. I would hesitate to do it, after all, if the expression itself had not, once or twice, been used by Lacan. If it is appropriate to call it thus at all, then it is here, where there is the possibility of the least misunderstanding.

Second, in writing $\cancel{S}$, we write the subject of jouissance.

I only intend to move things on by a few millimeters. You will see that we can shift a great deal with these millimeters. If there is a very small divergence in the initial perspective, and we follow it up, in the end we depart further and further away from what we are used to seeing.

I want to apply the logic we use in relation to the subject of the signifier to the subject of jouissance—namely, that there is also something missing on this side, and that there is also a call for what might complement this loss.

If the subject of jouissance is written S, it is because it is designated as voided of jouissance. In the same way that, when we treat it as subject of the signifier, it is not insofar as it is full, but on the contrary insofar as the signifier has been the object of a 'wiping clean'. In the same way that we can say that the bar on the subject, the bar that indicates that something is missing [*cette barre d'en-moins*], is an effect of the signifier, it also conforms to what Lacan articulates: namely, that the voiding of jouissance is an effect of the signifier.

This accounts for the necessity, concerning the subject, of a complement that would not be a signifier. In my opinion, this is what justifies Lacan in having once drawn this triangle on the board, which indicates that there is not just one complement for the subject. There is not just the complement constituted by the ideal. There is another one.

But of course, you tell me—*But we already know that there is a fantasy for the subject*—Lacan writes it ($S \lozenge a$).

I have already asserted, and more than once, that identification, as a signifying representation that articulates the symptom with the subject in the place of truth (this place at the bottom on the left),[3] calls for an articulation with the fantasy. I have even made this a theme, which has become an anthem—*From symptom to fantasy*.

Yet I believe that I am moving things on by a few millimeters here. For if I place the term "subject of jouissance" there, and the call for a complement that ensues, it is well to emphasize that there is not only the fantasy that can respond to it. Here we must expose a much more general relation, of which the fantasy is merely a modality.

This ternary contains the writing of a relation of the subject to object *a*, *and* a relation of the subject to jouissance that is not reducible to fantasy.

The fantasy is doubtlessly a relation to jouissance on the imaginary mode. But we are also speaking of a relation to jouissance when we talk of the drive, this time in the dimension of the real. This means that it is only an approximation or a partiality to treat the relation to jouissance, which is necessarily called for by the second value of S, [only] in connection with the fantasy.

I think it is illuminating to bring fantasy and drive together under the hat of the relation to jouissance, and to oppose the subject's relation to the signifier to the subject's relation to jouissance.

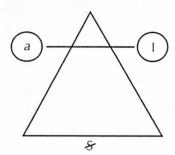

Here we find the two sides of the insignia inscribed.

The duplicity of the signifier and jouissance is also applicable to the concept of the Other, this Other that—axiom—we call the place of the signifier, but which Lacan also formulated as the body insofar as it is voided of jouissance, a desert of jouissance.

I would like to demonstrate how the correlation of S_1 and a literally runs through Lacan's teaching and that it is a question that drives his teaching.

If we read it with this key, we can see the question of their articulation in relation to the subject—who is the subject of the signifier and that of jouissance—emerge from beginning to end of his teaching.

We could already say, taking a shortcut, that the problem in grasping it is that we have a single term for the subject and its two values, while we have two when it comes to what complements it.

To use another shortcut, we can say that Lacan tries, at the extreme edge of his teaching, to introduce a single writing for S_1 and a, a single writing for this complement of the subject as subject of the signifier and subject of jouissance.

The symbol that guides me today, and perhaps will next time as well (this could take some time), in this function, is the sigma of the symptom, Σ. This is my thesis. What Lacan introduces with the renovation of the concept of the symptom, which he sometimes signals with a new writing, *sinthome,* is the effort to write both signifier and jouissance in one sole trait.

$$\frac{\Sigma}{\mathcal{S}}$$

If we want to use the old modes of writing, this is the one I am proposing.

Now that I have shown you my aim, which alters the lines of perspective, I must show you at what point this comes forth in Lacan's teaching and in the analytic experience, since not only does this teaching comment on the analytic experience, it also invents it for us.

First, I must remind you that the two operations of alienation and separation, which are clearly distinguished through a temporal ordering, correspond exactly to the double value of the subject of the signifier and the subject of jouissance. I already pointed out that S_1 and a come to be successively inscribed in the same place on the schema of these two operations. I will not comment on these operations again, but simply remind you of them.

Alienation foregrounds the subject of the signifier, just as separation foregrounds the subject of jouissance.

alienation   separation

Alienation is a representation. It means exactly what it says. It follows that the subject is, as such, distinct from it.

We could localize the subject as barred subject in this part of the set. It is distinct from S_1 and S_2. This is what the formations of the unconscious show, since in these formations we see the faltering and stumbling that occur between S_1 and S_2, and that indicate that the subject remains distinct—this implies that the subject is only represented. We can also say just as well that it is there as truth, since we accept that what reveals itself in the slip of the tongue is a truth. This schematization is appropriate to figure this representation.

In separation, the second operation, we cannot say that the subject is represented. All that we can say of the subject is that it is little a. The subject asserts itself as object a. The positivization we have here with little a comes from the use that the subject makes of its own lack as subject of the signifier, by fitting itself to the Other's lack. There is no representation. There is an identity as little a.

This means that we must at the same time distinguish and articulate identification by representation (which fixes the subject in relation to S_1), and identification with the object (which places us before an identity of the subject, before its being). This articulation both brings out and dissimulates the fact that here little a comes in the same place as S_1. This place is in evidence in these schemas. Yet the fact that it is the same place is not problematized by Lacan in his commentary. It is the same place, but only on the schema, we could say, because, after all, the lack is here, and it can be found again there. Is this structurally the same place? This is not what this schema attests to. But it calls the one into question. It evidences that there is cause to think the relation between S_1 and little a, that there is cause to know what the relation between the signifying representation of the subject in connection with the unary trait and his being of jouissance is.

Coming back from this point, we realize that the same question is taken up by Lacan in his schema of the four discourses.

From the discourse of the master—that is, from the discourse of the unconscious, which is the other name for the discourse of the master— to the discourse of the analyst, we can see that S_1 and little a can come in the same place.

$$S_1 \ S_2 \qquad a \ \ S$$
$$\mathcal{S} \ a \qquad S_2 \ S_1$$

You see that I am only handling abstractions today. I want to get to the point of the symptom and, to get there, demonstrate to what extent this problematic insists in various moments of Lacan's teaching—including in the four discourses where this time there is no temporal ordering. Here we have an ordering of permutation, but one in which the same element is in question as I indicated for alienation and separation. What is it that appropriates S_1 and little a so that they might be liable to accomplish what I used to call castling, namely, to replace one another in an inversion?

I find yet another indication of the insistence of the question in the commentary that Lacan makes of the Freudian schema of identification, at the end of his seminar on the *Four Fundamental Concepts*. Lacan translates what, in Freud's schema, figures as lines that join up with an object placed as common denominator and the function of the ego ideal for each subject, through which the taking up of subjects in a series is accomplished (at 272). And what terms does Lacan use, but the following terms—conjunction, superposition, confusion, of the object *a* and the ego ideal, in other words, of little *a* and big I. This is what he finds the opportunity of formulating in relation to Freud's schema, in order to say, evidently—*this is the formula of hypnosis, which is indeed interesting. We say to ourselves—Hold on, this is the formula of hypnosis; it can always come in handy.*

The point is precisely to not be hypnotized by the fact that Lacan tells us *here is the formula of hypnosis,* but to perceive the logic that is present in this definition. In relation to identification and hypnosis, Lacan formulates that the object *a* can find itself superimposed in the same place as big I. The object *a,* as impossible to swallow as it might be in the order of the signifier—Lacan defines it at the time as being what always remains stuck in the gullet of the defiles of the signifier—can nonetheless superimpose itself in the same place as an essential signifying coordinate, big I. And here a confusion is liable to occur between these two terms.

This is yet another call that is logically legible. We cannot help thinking that there is a certain homogeneity between these two terms, a homogeneity that implies that they are liable to come and confound themselves in the same place. And, prefiguring his four discourses by many years (the discourse of the master is the inverse of the discourse of the analyst), Lacan formulates the possibility of psychoanalysis as the distance between big I and little *a.* Separating big I from little *a* is the condition of possibility for analysis.

The third point I am making concerning S_1 and little *a* allows us to grasp, as a fourth point, the economy of Lacan's graph in connection with the relation between big I-little *a,* for the graph is designed to indicate it.

What does the graph imply on this point? It implies that the normal issue of transference is identification, insofar as the very economy of transference is founded on suggestion. As soon as the subject engages in speech to the Other—and in the initial, primary form of speech that is demand—the issue of his trajectory is identification with the Other. As soon as he addresses the Other as the omnipotent Other of demand, what he ferries during his journey—and this is where it ends up—is an identification. Transference, in this respect, brings demand to identification.

It is the schema of the discourse of the master that is there on Lacan's graph, a schema that includes alienation as the essential operation, namely, signifying representation, which Lacan modulated in diverse ways in his four discourses or in the operation of alienation.

How is the discourse of the analyst inscribed on the graph? It is inscribed by virtue of its operating in such a way that demand may go all the way to the drive.

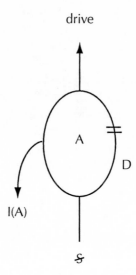

This is what distinguishes transference as properly analytical. This is where the desire of the analyst makes the difference, in Lacan's own terms. While transference brings demand back to identification by taking it away from the drive, the desire of the analyst, operating in big A, opens the way to the drive.

So what does Lacan formulate at this point? What does he suppose happens when the demand of the subject goes toward the drive, attains it? He says something very curious and even opaque in its formulation, which he did not really take up again as such—*then, the fantasy becomes the drive.*

The notion that the fantasy, once the plane of identification is crossed, would become the drive is very strange. Is it not precisely the possibility of formulating that *the fantasy becomes the drive* that justifies that both the fantasy and the drive are brought together by virtue of the common trait that both qualify a relation with jouissance? This implies that, so long as the subject is before or within the plane of identification, the drive is masked by the fantasy. The subject's relation to the object *a* must be mapped out for the fantasy to cease masking the drive. In other words, the crossing of the plane of identification is only possible—this is what Lacan formulates—by means of the separation of the subject in the experience, that is, by passing through the point where he confounds himself with the object *a*. This means that although the formula of the fantasy unquestionably writes the relation of the subject to jouissance, it does so in an imaginary form since, as soon as the subject finds his bearings with respect to little *a,* the fantasy becomes liable to confound itself with the drive.

Identification, as written I (A), implies that the drive is masked in the fantasy. This is difficult to read on Lacan's graph because the graph evidently stems from an earlier part of his teaching. There the object *a* figures only at the level of the fantasy. The only relation to the objet *a* that is written on the graph is thus that of the fantasy.

This constantly throws the reading of Lacan off course, because this object *a* is even more prominent when it comes to the drive, although it does not figure on the graph. This is even where it would be legitimate to write ($ \mathcal{S} \lozenge a$). *a* is italicized on the graph because Lacan wants to indicate that it is imaginary. We could write it in normal script to indicate that it concerns the drive. We could even write it thus: (a → $\mathcal{S}$). There is something akin to a diagonal on this graph between I (A) and little *a,* which opposes, which puts at both ends, both terms, the signifier of identification and object *a.*

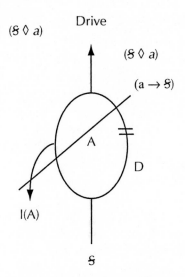

We find that this conjunction, this articulation S_1—little *a,* is essential to the theory of transference. It is not only that the issue of transference is identification, but that the very medium of transference is the ideal signifier S_1. And this to the point that in 1969—although of course he already situated the place of object a in transference in his seminar on the *agalma*—Lacan is still writing that *Transference seems to be already sufficiently motivated by the primacy of the unary trait*. This shows the extent to which the basic structure of transference does not imply object a. The basic structure of transference implies the primacy of the unary trait. It is the very condition that makes it possible to think of defining transference in connection with the subject supposed to know, since it implies a definition of transference starting from the signifier, starting with an effect of the signifier.

This brings us to the fifth point, to the subject supposed to know.

You know how Lacan introduces the subject supposed to know. He introduces it as an effect of signification of an S_1, which, in the event, takes on the name of the signifier of transference. He writes it—signifier of the transference over its effect of signification (which the subject supposed to know is). He writes it like this, as an effect of signification, in order to say—I am asking you to write down only the phrase—that it is a signification that holds the place of a still latent referent. I have already taught you to read this phrase in the past. It implies that, in effect, little a will come to this ideal place.

$$\frac{St}{s \to (a)}$$

Little a will act as the referent of the affair. The fall of the subject supposed to know implies the replacement of this signification by object a. If we read it as it should be read, it is yet another mode of conjunction between S_1, here the signifier of transference, and little a, supposed to come in the place of the signification induced by this signifier.

So in the very theory of the subject supposed to know, there is implicitly the notion of a conjunction between S_1 and a—the point at which this effect of signification is liable to be replaced, if you want, by a real product.

Since I have drawn the ternary: the problematic of the subject supposed to know is articulated between the signifier of transference and little a, and here the subject is written as an effect of the signified.

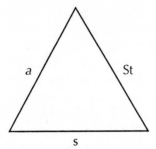

In flicking through Lacan's teaching in diverse places, we can see that the question of the articulation between S$_1$ and little *a* is posed at every turn.

We are finally moving on to the sixth mode, precisely in connection with the theory of the symptom.

One might think that analysts would agree that symptoms, in psycho-analysis—at least 'analyzable' symptoms—are interpretable. If a symptom is interpretable by the Other, it is because it counts as a message to the Other and, as communication is fundamentally inverted, the symptom is fundamentally a message from the Other. This is Lacan's starting point, a point one could call Freudian, on the symptom.

Of course, he had to draw the consequences of the way in which he defined the unconscious, since the symptom is articulated with the unconscious. Any definition of the unconscious given by an analyst will rebound and have an impact on the definition he gives of the symptom.

Once the unconscious is defined as structured like a language, the definition that Lacan gives of the analyzable symptom is that it is *supported by a structure that is identical to the structure of language*. Why not say *supported by the structure of language*? That's also true. To say that it is identical to the structure of language is to say that the elements that can hold a function [*être mis en fonction*] can just as well be borrowed from the body. So there is a little shift here.

Lacan formulated the idea of the structure of language—you will find it on page 444 of *Écrits*—by way of reference to the distinction between signifier and signified. This implies that the symptom is not simply a signification, but also the relation of a signification to a signifying structure. This is what you find to be implied by the schema of the graph, where the place of the symptom is to be found at *s* (A), signified of the Other. But this signification is not enough to constitute the symptom.

Let me add that, when I say symptom, the same goes for the identical structures of the dream, the *lapsus,* and the *Witz,* namely, everything that Lacan called a formation of the unconscious.

The possible interpretation of the symptom, that is, in retro-position, in retroaction with respect to the fact that it is analyzable, the sole fact that it may be interpreted or, better, that it can be read, implies that it is itself articulated in a process of writing. Lacan will not pay much attention to this word "writing," which appears in his writings as early as the fifties, until the end of his teaching.

Why does this signification not suffice to produce what the symptom is?

You know how Lacan articulated it on his graph, close to Freud. For there to be a symptom, the fantasy must come to interfere with the effect of signification that originates in the passage of demand to the Other.

Let us rapidly go over the argument again. Here we suppose a subject equipped with need. He must formalize this need under the guise of the demand to the Other, and in the process a certain effect of signification is produced, among which there may be love, for example. We could also have, and particularly, misunderstanding, displacement, and so on. It is in agreement with the Other that this effect of signification is produced.

For there to be a symptom, another element must come into play. This is where Lacan writes the fantasy. Another element must come to interfere with this signification, which has nothing to do, in itself, with this signification. What is produced by the whole circuit, which passes through the drive and masks the relation to the drive, must come here. The symptom is a composite element in this regard.

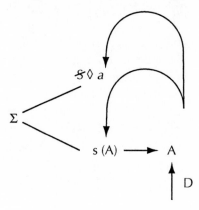

I am not illustrating things. I am showing you that what I am going to develop is founded in multiple ways in Lacan's work.

The symptom, as it is put into place on Lacan's graph, is made of two elements. It is made of a signification that is an effect of the signifier and of an element that is called the fantasy here, but which we have already clarified as being the subject's relation to jouissance.

Already the symptom is only thinkable as an articulation between a signifying effect—we could even call it an effect of signification or an effect of truth—and the relation of the subject to jouissance.

We can understand why that seemed appropriate to Lacan at the time. How can it interfere? Two elements are concerned, nonetheless imaginary, the fantasy and signification, that join up with each other in the symptom. We can see here what is meant by the construction of the fundamental fantasy, which causes a lot of worries in analysis—*Am I constructing my fundamental fantasy properly?* The construction of the fundamental fantasy is strictly dependent on interpretation insofar as it trims the symptom down. Interpretation trims the symptom down by virtue of enumerating or leading the subject to enumerate the set of master signifiers, the swarm [*essaim*]⁴ from which signification arises.

The construction of the fundamental fantasy occurs on the rhythm of the interpretation of the symptom—in other words, the rhythm at which the effects of truth of the symptom are progressively linked back to the S_I that induces them. And, by way of consequence, object *a* is isolated; in other words, the fantasy is des-imaginarized. The construction of the fundamental fantasy is the same thing as its reduction to the drive.

What is already implied in Lacan's graph? It already contains a certain knot of the symptom, where object *a* and an effect of truth, object *a* and a signifying effect are engaged at the same time. One cannot misrecognize the question that is posed here. Or, rather, one can misrecognize it because object *a* only appears in the graph as taken up in the fantasy. And it is barely there as object *a* on the graph, for it still is the little other that one stages in the fantasy as imaginary. It is only progressively, including in the formula of the fantasy, that Lacan brings out object *a* as surplus-enjoyment [*plus-de-jouir*]. One can easily misrecognize what is at stake. A relation to jouissance is in fact implicated in the symptom at the same time as the effect of truth. But one should not misrecognize the question of the implication of jouissance in the symptom, and that the symptom is doubtlessly articulated by means of a signifying structure.

How can we think the jouissance that is caught up in it? And what is the inscription, the writing in which jouissance interferes?

In order to find this theme once more developed as such by Lacan, we have to wait for his reflections on the pass, where he defines the symptom as follows—I mentioned it before—that it is a truth, s (A), which resists knowledge, that is, deciphering, because of jouissance. It is a truth that plays on the side of jouissance.

This leads Lacan to draw another triangle, the triangle of jouissance, knowledge, and truth, at the same time as he constructs the ternary that I drew earlier, S, little a and I.

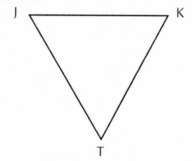

This is the very problem that the so-called negative therapeutic reaction discovered by Freud brings to the fore—namely, the jouissance of the symptom. Even when it is interpreted, there is a jouissance in the symptom that continues to resist.

We must realize that, if we put the accent on the jouissance that is in the symptom, that is, if we discover that, beneath what is here called fantasy, what is at stake is the 'complementarizing' relation of the subject of jouissance, then the distinction between fantasy and symptom can be thrown into question; it can be overcome.

These two terms can be encompassed by a third one: this term, which came at the end of Lacan's teaching to encompass the symptom and the fantasy, is the *sinthome*.

This is why he could at the same time highlight the jouissance of the symptom and say, *You only enjoy your fantasies*. This was to indicate that, if one is to recenter things on jouissance, then there is a mixture of the symptom as effect of truth and of the relation to jouissance, which is, properly speaking, the sinthome.

I went a little quickly last time, when I told you straightaway that Lacan, with regard to inexistence, said of the symptom that it was conditioned both by the inexistence of truth and by the inexistence of jouissance. I was quoting from memory from his articulations in his seminar *Ou pire.* I checked. He didn't put it exactly like this. Indeed, in his seminar *Ou pire,* he is still just before his invention of the sinthome. He speaks of the inexistence of truth—that is, of 𝔖 in the place of truth or of *s* (A)—as the essence of the symptom, and of the inexistence of jouissance as the essence of repetition-compulsion. *Inexistence is the essence of the symptom, the inexistence of the truth that it supposes, even though it marks its place, while repetition-compulsion brings to the light of insistence the inexistence of jouissance.* It is not part of a great development—he said this in passing.

You see that, in this type of proposition, he is still situating the symptom only as *s* (A), effect of truth, and that he distinguishes the relation to jouissance that is present in repetition-compulsion. We are just a step away from the one he will make two or three years later.

This guides all his research of that period—and nobody saw it coming, myself included—which precisely aims to give a definition of the symptom including both truth and jouissance, the signifying effect and jouissance, and so including repetition-compulsion in the symptom.

And indeed, he tries to write the symptom and repetition-compulsion in a single trait with this great thing he calls *RSI* and his seminars on knots. This is why he could formulate *The symptom is what does not stop writing itself.* In order to be able to say that *the symptom is what does not stop writing itself,* one can no longer define the symptom in connection with the effect of truth, which certainly is not something that does not stop writing itself. Symptom and repetition-compulsion must also have been defined in the same stroke.

This is when he lays his cards on the table in his *RSI,* in the effort that it contains, in other words, Lacan's last problematic, when he can say that he defines the symptom—I already said this last time—as *the way in which each subject enjoys his unconscious insofar as the unconscious determines him.* This definition turns everything upside down; it entirely changes the perspective. When he says *insofar as the unconscious determines him,* Lacan expressly designates S_1, the imperative signifier, the primary statement [*dit*]. He defines the symptom as a mode of jouissance of the unconscious, precisely a mode of jouissance of S_1.

His last effort bears on what I have just enumerated for you today, that is, this conjunction—which one finds throughout his teaching—this superposition of S_I and little a. And here he goes so far as to define a jouissance of the signifier.

The jouissance of the signifier displaces all the perspectives. This is why at the time—and this seemed opaque to me then—at one point Lacan substitutes a reflection on the sign for his reflection on the signifier, that he opposes sense and sign. Whereas the basics we thought we knew were precisely that the sign had given way to the signifying articulation. He speaks of the sign (in *Television,* e.g.) in the place of the signifier, precisely because he is looking for a term in which the signifier is complemented by jouissance.

This is also why he substitutes a problematic of deciphering for the problematic of interpretation. Interpretation does not have its antonym, while deciphering has its antonym in ciphering. He employs the term "ciphering" and "cipher," not just to vary his vocabulary but to try to think the signifier and jouissance in the same movement.

This is where he brings out the function of the symptom. What does he make of the symptom? The symptom, precisely because it is at once little a and big I, at once the signifying function and the function of jouissance, designated by a single symbol Σ, is what is, more than anything else, capable of writing the proper name as particular to the subject.

This is why Lacan said Joyce-the-symptom. He made a number of comments—which have remained rather opaque until now—aiming to designate the true proper name of James Joyce by calling him *Joyce-the-symptom.* By saying that he was saying that what constitutes an insignia for the subject is his symptom.

Notes

1. This is a translation of the transcript of the thirteenth session of "Ce qui fait insigne," *L'orientation lacanienne* (Department of Psychoanalysis, Paris VIII). The text was established by Catherine Bonningue from the notes and recordings of Fabienne Henry, Michel Jolibois, and Bernard Cremniter.

2. *Ce qui fait insigne* can be heard both as that which constitutes an insignia and that which makes a sign to the subject [TN].

3. A reference to the structure of the discourse of the master, in which the subject occupies the place of truth [TN].

4. *Essaim* in French is homophonic with S_I [TN].

Two Statuses of the Symptom: "Let Us Turn to Finn Again"

Jean-Louis Gault

I reflected on the treatment of psychosis. I asked myself how to define the practice of the psychoanalyst with a psychotic subject, and on what it might rightly be founded. We could probably speak of the psychoanalysis of psychoses. We could, but we hesitate to do so. When we broached this theme [in the past], we preferred to do it under the title of the psychoanalytic experience of psychosis. In any case, we would have to distinguish it from the psychoanalysis of neuroses, and give a new sense to what we mean when we speak of psychoanalysis in the case of psychosis.

Lacan uses the term "treatment"—at least he does so to qualify the objective of the practice with a psychotic subject. In this practice we encounter the symptom, but with psychoses the point is neither to interpret it, nor to decipher it. What the psychotic subject can expect of a psychoanalyst is a treatment by means of the symptom. The experience of psychoses paved the way for the discovery that the symptom is a mode of treatment, and this is what Lacan develops in the second part of his teaching by encountering a new symptom, different from the Freudian symptom: the Joycean *sinthome*.

Once again Lacan lets himself be taught by psychosis, and in 1987 Jacques-Alain Miller drew attention to this by emphasizing the value of the experience of psychosis. The status of the symptom in psychosis rightly inscribes the psychotic subject in the psychoanalytic experience, in that the psychotic symptom, as sinthome, tells the truth about the neurotic symptom. In his "Interpretation in Reverse,"[1] Jacques-Alain Miller drew conclusions that led him to ask us to start from the sinthome in order to orientate ourselves in the treatment of neurotics. He deduced a new regime of interpretation from this, formulated as follows: "A practice that targets the sinthome in the subject does not interpret like the unconscious." Jacques-Alain Miller made it clear: in analysis, the idea is to redirect the neurotic subject to his truly elementary signifiers, against the grain of the interpretation of these signifiers provided by the unconscious. Since the elementary phenomenon, which manifests the primary state of the subject in relation to *lalangue,* is stripped bare in psychosis, it follows that neurosis can be thought of as starting from psychosis. I rely on this consideration to define the status of the psychoanalytic experience of psychosis.

If we take Lacan to the letter of his *écrit,* there is a possible treatment of psychosis for him. During the course of "On a question preliminary to any possible treatment of psychosis," Lacan becomes more specific and considers the objective of this treatment. It is remarkable that, having placed himself in a psychoanalytic perspective, Lacan should introduce the term "treatment." He does so in connection with the problem of psychosis. It is not a word he ever uses in connection with neurosis, and he never speaks of the treatment of neurosis. He wrote two texts in 1958. One of them, already mentioned, tackles the treatment of psychosis. A few months later, Lacan produces a second text, which bears on the direction of the treatment. "La direction de la cure,"[2] it is clear throughout the text, concerns the direction of the treatment in neurosis.

The word *"cure"* designates an analysis, with its beginning, its duration and its end. The direction of the *cure* implies a politics as to its end, a strategy of transference and tactics of interpretation. In this sense, the *cure* is that of a neurosis. The term "cure" is classically used in the vocabulary of psychoanalysis, and so Lacan uses it at the beginning of his teaching. Thus, in 1955, prior to the 1958 text, he wrote a text entitled: "Variantes de la cure-type" [variations on the typical treatment]. The term *"cure"* recurs in Lacan's writings even though the expression *"cure-type"* had been imposed on him, and despite his rejection of it. It is only after 1958 that he abandons the term and replaces it with that of psychoanalysis, simply. In fact, the substitution of one word for another occurs in the 1955 text, in the course of a sentence: "a psychoanalysis . . . is the cure we expect from a psychoanalyst." This turning point of the text contains another shift, which is decisive for the later work. This other shift consists in taking the emphasis away from a formalist definition of the *cure* and placing it on an interrogation on the desire of the analyst.

An analysis, in the case of neurosis, begins when a patient meets a psychoanalyst to complain of a symptom, and the analysis consists in the deciphering of this symptom. At the end, an analysis claims to go beyond the fantasy that supported the symptom, in order to reach the real of the drive that is lodged at the heart of the jouissance of the symptom. Thus, the analysis of a neurotic subject goes from the symbolic constituted by the formal envelope of the symptom, to the real of the drive.

In his "Lituraterre," Lacan derides the advice once given to Joyce to go into analysis. He considers that Joyce would have gained nothing from it, since the artist, in a direct way, achieved the best that can be expected from the end of analysis. Lacan continues in this vein, underlining that Joyce reached the possibility of attesting to the jouissance specific to the symptom, without having to resort to the experience of analysis. This remark takes on its full value if we bear in mind that Lacan refers to Joyce as a case of psychosis. The [logical] conclusion should be that there is no need for analysis in psychosis.

What is expected of an analysis is that the subject, beyond his identifications, should obtain a glimpse of the real of his being as waste. Lacan shows that Joyce reached this point without any analysis. He illustrates it, following Joyce, by playing on the equivocation *letter/litter: letter,* the letter as symbol, and *litter,* the letter as waste. The writer, beyond the letter as *semblant,* is in direct relation with the real of the letter as waste. The formidable creative power of Joyce stems from the fact that he is not held back by any of the connections that the letter has with the symbolic and the imaginary. He is in relation with a letter that has severed all its identifications, which is not attached to any stable signification. His work pays the price of this extraordinary freedom by being, for the most part, unreadable.

Joyce described the process of his literary creation. He collects words from shops and posters, from the crowd that walks past him. He repeats them to himself over and over so that in the end they lose their signification for him.

These words read, heard, present themselves in the dimension of the elementary signifier, detached from any signification. The word becomes the thing that it is. Joyce raises the mutation of *letter* into *litter* to the dignity of an epiphany. It is not really a hallucination, unless we reconsider the sense of hallucination. Lacan defines the epiphany as a direct knotting of the unconscious to the real. This formulation is to be compared with "the irruption of a symbol into the real," which is how he defines the hallucination "sow" in 1958 [in the "Preliminary question"].

The words are not addressed to Joyce, and he does not tend to attribute them to a subject either. For him, what is in question is a relation to the elementary phenomenon of *lalangue,* prior to any subjective implication, whether that of the Other or his own. It is rather *lalangue* as Other, *lalangue* as first partner of the subject, as Jacques-Alain Miller underlined in his "Ironic Clinic."

Joyce treats this elementary phenomenon, returned to its literal value. He interprets it in a very particular way. After his wandering, once his harvest of epiphanies accomplished, he goes home and assembles the words and phrases that have no meaning. Every day, over many long years, he pursues this *work in progress,* he becomes the Artist.

Lacan proposed considering *Finnegans Wake* as a fundamental language to the extent that it does not mean anything, and it does not say anything. It does not speak. It is a language, and, more precisely, a language made up of scattered scraps of the English language, but equally plucked from forty or so other languages. It is the language of a new world, a 'newspeak' that nobody can speak, which is made only to be written and which is made in being written. It is only reached through writing, but it can be used, and Lacan tried with some success.

Lacan showed that the translinguistic homophony used in *Finnegans Wake* is supported by just one letter that conforms to the spelling of the English language. Joyce exploits translinguistic homophonies of this type: the word written as *who* in English can be heard as the French *où.*[3]

Counterpoised to Joyce's use of the letter, we can situate the use a French-speaking neurotic subject makes of the letter. This subject uses up his existence in the mute fascination held for him by X-ray images [*radio*graphies] that he scrutinizes from morning to night for the necessities of his professional activity. Riveted to the letter on its transparent support, he remains frozen in the infinite jouissance that fixes him to the old radio [*radio*phonie] whose modulations covered the sexual frolics of the parents. This professional choice, raised by the subject to the dignity of a symptom that maintains the fiction of the writing of the sexual rapport, enjoys the benefit of an equivocation. The radio-machine can be radiophonic or radiographic. At the end of one of these multiple days that leave him feeling crushed, he says in a session *"je suis avide—à vide."*[4] Picking up on the equivocation, he adds: "I don't know how to write it, in one or two words." Commenting these two spellings, he associates them with a child present in a dream. He recognizes the young person as the child he himself had been, a child avid for knowledge, notably mathematical, scientific, or technical knowledge. But this avidity cannot be satisfied because the child gets tangled up in the use of the mathematical letter. He gets stuck in the writing of algebraic equations that he cannot resolve and encumbers himself with a letter too heavy with the significations of his father, who is a brilliant engineer. So he exhausts himself in the hackneyed reading of specialized works, in vain. He would have to empty this letter of its leaden weight so that, lightened at last, it could serve a new avidity. He will only succeed by way of a new symptomatic relation to knowledge, which will no longer be characterized by the aboulia and apathy that weigh him down today.

Let us go back to an example of psychosis, with the way in which Wolfson deals with the resonant material of the English language. He does it with the aid of a little symptomatic instrument of his own making. The phonetics, lexicon, and spelling of four languages are brought in to contribute to the transformation and the defusing of the sounds of English. These four languages are French, Hebrew, German, and Russian. This linguistic transmutation relies on the letter. Thus, the sound of "early" in English can be deactivated by its transposition into the French *sur le champ*. This operation relies on the two letters "r" and "l," which can be found in the respective spellings of "early" in English and *sur le champ* in French. This is a transliteral operation. The simple translation of "early" by *de bonne heure* would not be sufficient because the point is to really attack the word or, more precisely, its sonorous substance, while nonetheless retaining its literal skeleton. Some words are very difficult to treat: for example, it took Wolfson forty pages of writing to deal with the word "believe."

So the following question arises: since, in psychosis, the subject reaches the point that is situated beyond a psychoanalysis, what can be expected of an analysis in the case of psychosis? Nothing, said Freud. He thought that analysis was impossible in psychoses because there is no transference in the sense of transference-love, and because transference-love is the condition of possibility for analysis.

On this point, Lacan disagrees with Freud insofar as he considers that psychoanalysis should not step away from psychosis. By the same token, the question is displaced. Freud noted that an analysis relying on the subject supposed to know was impossible in psychosis. Lacan adds that in any case it is presumptuous to propose an analysis to a psychotic subject, since he has already obtained the best that can be expected of analysis. However, having placed aside the possibility of analysis, Lacan maintains that the analyst must confront psychosis. So the question is formulated as follows: what can be expected of an analyst in the case of psychosis if it is not an analysis?

Lacan thinks that the psychotic subject could expect something from an analysis, and it is in this respect that he introduces the term "treatment." He considers that psychosis calls for a treatment, and he considers that this treatment was possible, although subject to the following preliminary question: is it possible to handle psychotic transference?

Freud noted that there was no transference to the subject supposed to know in psychosis. For all that, Lacan adds that there nonetheless exists a psychotic transference, though it is of a particular kind: it is an erotomaniac and persecutory transference. With the subject of his doctoral case study, Aimée, aptly named in the event, Lacan experienced this transference. This transference is an obstacle to the action of the analyst. Analysis is only conceivable if the transference can be handled and its nature changed. Lacan also experienced that this was possible, precisely in the case of Aimée. When he had to deal with her, he was not for her the agent of a persecutory erotomania, but the reader of her writings, and her secretary. On the basis of this experience, he deduced that it was possible to envisage such a shift in the transference in the case of psychosis, so that a transference could be established that is neither love addressed to knowledge, nor erotomaniac transference, but a transference addressed to an Other. This opens the possibility of a relation with an analyst that allows for his intervention. On occasion, Lacan defines some of the positions of the Other and their transferential form. There are different registers of the imaginary, symbolic, or real partner that the analyst can incarnate for the subject to allow him to operate in psychosis. The notion of partner-symptom introduced by Jacques-Alain Miller leads us to approach the question of knowing what we can be for the psychotic subject in the analytic experience from a new perspective.

So a treatment of psychosis could be possible, but what could be expected of such a treatment if the subject in a case of psychosis has already reached the end of the road of analysis? What can be expected is in fact totally different from what one can attain through the analysis of a neurosis. It is even the exact opposite.

In neurosis, the point is to decipher the symptoms, moving from the symbolic to the real. It is this deciphering that the very word "analysis" aims at. In psychosis, on the contrary, the idea is to go from the real to the symbolic, and to construct a symptom. This is where the term "treatment" is justified. The treatment indicates the modality of action of the symbolic on the real where the point is to treat the real with the symbolic by means of the constitution of a symptom. The dictionary, besides the medical use of the same word, lists a series of significations of the word "treatment" that could designate the operation of the symptom. To treat is, for example, to subject a substance to the action of a physical or chemical agent so as to modify it. Treatment is used to designate the process allowing the modification of a substance. Thus, one speaks of the treatment of a mineral, of the thermal treatment of a metal, or even of the treatment of radioactive waste to deactivate it. There is also the treatment of information, which involves the application of a logical or mathematical operator to raw data in order to exploit them following a program. So the symptom can be conceived as a mode of treatment of the enjoying substance by means of the symbol, in order to modify it, deactivate it, and render its usage possible for the subject.

The only illness we suffer from as speaking beings is the one introduced into the living by the parasitism of the signifier. Lacan spoke of language as a cancer and evoked the virulence of *logos*. He defined the unconscious as the effects of speech on the subject, and he showed that the Freudian clinic developed the incidences of the illness of the signifier.

The primordial tear inflicted by the symbol on life is experienced by the subject as an unbearable jouissance. The writer Mishima described the burning pain he experienced as a child, and which was due to the corroding effect of language. So for the subject the idea is to equip [*appareiller*] this jouissance, and this is where the term "treatment" finds its use. To equip jouissance is to treat the effects of language on the living.

Mishima explained how he set about defending himself against the suffering caused by words. He was four years old at the time, and although he already knew how to speak, he did not yet know how to handle writing. So it is in thought that he develops the habit of composing short fables or brief stories with the words that make him suffer, and he strives to memorize them by repeating them. These are the fragments that will form the material of his future literary fictions. For Mishima this is his own treatment of the jouissance of *lalangue*.

The subject obtains the equipment [*appareillage*] of jouissance through discourse and fantasy if he is neurotic. He gets there through delusion if he is psychotic—at least, if he is paranoiac. For the schizophrenic, for whom the whole of the symbolic is the real, this recourse is excluded. This is a reply of Lacan's to Jean Hippolyte, to whom he specifies: "In the symbolic order, gaps are as significant as the nonvoid; it would seem . . . that the gap of a void constitutes the first step of all [its] dialectical movement. . . . This would seem to explain the insistence of the schizophrenic on reiterating this step. All in vain, since for him all the symbolic is real." Then Lacan counterpoises the paranoiac subject, for whom he demonstrated, he says, the possibility of integrating these pre-signifying elements that the elementary phenomena are in the discursive organization of a delusion.

In the course of his teaching, Lacan explored the different ways of capturing excess jouissance in psychoses. They range from Schreber's transsexual practice to Joyce's use of the letter. In all cases of psychosis, we have to elucidate such attempts at treatment as well as the place and the part the psychoanalyst is liable to take in it.

It is from then on possible to understand the difference between a psychoanalysis, taken as the *cure* of neurosis, and the treatment of a psychosis that is expected from an analyst. A neurotic is a subject who has found a solution to defend himself against the real. This solution relies on the Name-of-the-Father and the fundamental identification that goes with it. The response through the paternal *semblant* is never totally satisfying because it ignores the real of the drive. The ideal identification to which the neurotic subject clings always involves a repression of drive-jouissance. This is the problem in neurosis, and this is what brings the neurotic subject to analysis. The neurotic solution is noticeably insufficient, in that it leaves the subject prey to, on the one hand, a claim of the drive that he does not want to recognize and that nonetheless continues to want to exercise its rights and, on the other hand, an ideal, contaminated by the return of the drive-jouissance.

The psychotic subject rejects the solution of the Name-of-the-Father. Consequently, he is defenseless against the real. While the Name-of-the-Father is a valid solution for all, the psychotic subject who, in the name of his irreducible singularity, rejects this universal solution, is led to invent a unique solution. There is no place for an analysis of the symptom in psychosis. The problem is different; it amounts to finding a solution, a solution for the treatment of excess jouissance precisely by means of the symptom. Two paths in the analytic experience are opposed in relation to the symptom: analysis of the symptom in neurosis, treatment by means of the symptom in psychosis.

Some subjects find their own solution, on their own. They are, for example, Schreber, Joyce, and Wolfson. We meet other subjects who have elaborated similar symptomatic solutions. It can be in the event of difficulties arising in connection with some dramatic circumstance of their existence that reveals the insufficiencies of the equipment that supported them until then. The subject then needs to restore order to the world. In other cases, we see the subject immediately, at the moment when he is confronted by the immensity of the task of having to defend himself against the real. The analyst can contribute to help the subject to construct a symptom. An analyst has a place in the attempt at treatment because he is supposed, as an analysand, to have acquired the knowledge of structure. He can therefore occupy a place that allows the subject to orientate himself. Jacques-Alain Miller brought out something essential in this relation of the subject to structure, which he condensed in this formula: the rights of the structure. From this point of view, an analyst is a subject who, through his own analysis, has learned what the rights of structure are. It is only in this way—namely, in remembering that he was an analysand—that the analyst can respond to the demand of a psychotic subject. Here we rejoin the address to the psychoanalyst with which Jacques-Alain Miller concluded his "Ironic Clinic": "Remember that you yourself were once an analysand." With the psychotic subject, situated like him on the same side of the wall of language, the analyst has to find a way for the structure to have its rights respected. To do so, in every case a certain mutation of the subject must be obtained.

The primordial rejection of the Name-of-the-Father cannot go so far as to ignore the rights of the structure. This is where the untenable character of the position of the psychotic subject resides. He begins by rejecting the signifier, then he comes to reject the effect of castration introduced by the signifier, and he ends by believing that he can be the master in the city of the signifier.

This position is fallacious, and for the subject it is the source of considerable difficulties. The subject cannot be the master of the signifier; he is always an effect of *logos,* and this is one of the rights of the structure. Joyce ends up conceding it when, in order to qualify his *work in progress,* he declared: "I obey laws which I have not chosen." Like the neurotic subject, the psychotic subject has to deal with what he nevertheless pushes away. What he rejects in the symbolic returns and presents itself to him as a real that persecutes him. The condition of the treatment is that the subject should keep note of the effects of his position. Eric Laurent showed that if the subject accepts to assume authentically the consequences of his position, he is able to erect himself as guarantor of the order of the world. At the beginning, the point is to rectify the subject's relations to the phenomena of psychosis, and this leads him to accept responsibility for what happens to him. The extraordinary work of elaboration accomplished by Schreber on the nervous illness he suffers from is such an example. The great literary creation of Joyce is another, and so are the writings of Brisset or Wolfson.

Notes

1. J.-A. Miller, "Interpretation in Reverse" in this volume.
2. The French title of "The direction of the treatment" is "La direction de la cure." "Cure" is translated into English as treatment since the word "cure" has specific connotations in English, at odds with the aims of psychoanalysis. We use the word "cure" in relation to neurosis in this text so as not to obliterate the distinction that J-L. Gault is at pains to clarify [TN].
3. In English: "where" [TN].
4. *Avide*—"avid"; *à vide*—"empty" [TN].

Hysteria and Sinthome

Marie-Hélène Brousse

I took my starting point from the theme of your work for this year, the clinic of hysteria. Things are such that, on the one hand, the analyst learns from Freud, Lacan, and a few others who have known how to invent in psychoanalysis and, on the other hand, from those patients whose speech [*parole analysante*] constitutes a real that is pregnant with knowledge for the analyst. For some years now, I have been taught by a hysterical patient about the relation between the hysterical symptom and the feminine position. The particularity of this case lies in that it demands a reflection on the question of the definition and limits of the hysterical symptom, while remaining articulated to what represents its structure—namely, the question of the woman.

The Freudian and Lacanian clinic, a structural clinic, rests on the structural opposition between neurosis, psychosis, and perversion: here the hysterical symptom finds the conditions of its mechanism and of its function. Yet, in the mid-1970s, Lacan ceases to take his bearings solely from the differential clinic and introduces the perspective of the borromean knots, with the consequent production of new statements on the symptom. Lacan even reverts to an ancient spelling, that of "sinthome," to conceptualize what of the symptom cannot be reduced to structural determination—that is, to a determination "of language" [*langagière*].

Because of the type of symptom that prevails in her psychical organization and in her treatment, one of my patients led me, by way of a working hypothesis, to envisage the possibility of introducing the sinthome in a hysterical problematic.

Lacan introduces this concept apropos of Joyce, and so in connection with psychosis and writing in the clinic of knotting. Is it possible to introduce it in the clinic of hysteria, defined by the parameters of the structural clinic? What openings are allowed by this introduction in the hysterical question about the feminine, as no longer articulated merely to the phallus, but also to the not-all?

I will start by giving you a few coordinates on the evolving definition of the symptom.

We can reduce this discussion to the essential: on the one hand, we have the symptom as ciphering and deciphering of the unconscious, namely, as articulated by the signifiers that form the chain constituting the subject. These signifiers, through ciphering in the symptom, fulfill a function of fixation of jouissance. This is why Lacan says, following Freud, that there is a jouissance in the symptom—phallic jouissance in the hysterical symptom in hysteria. This first definition articulates the symptom with the function of the signifier in neurosis. So this definition is grounded in the functioning of the signifying chain and, in this sense, it may be more accurate to speak of 'psychotic phenomena' in the case of some manifestations of psychosis, instead of 'psychotic symptoms'. This is in fact how Lacan expresses himself in Seminar III. The symptom as ciphering, articulated to the signifying chain $S_1 - S_2$, is an ordering of the signifier, and sometimes an extraction or a substitution of a privileged signifier that allows for a localization of jouissance and opens it to signification. The deciphering of the symptom is correlative to a jouissance linked to the appearance, to the emergence of the signification of this symptom. This jouissance is of the same type as the jouissance in slips of the tongue or witticisms. The symptom is of the same order, but it pinpoints the particular mode of enjoying the signifier of a subject. It is therefore receptive to interpretation, which has the same texture and plays on the same equivocation of the signifiers, on their elision, on their substitution. A symptom is constructed like a metaphor.

In the mid-1970s, in the seminar *R.S.I.* in particular but also in all the very difficult writings devoted to Joyce, Lacan speaks of the symptom in a way that is not without relation with this first definition, and yet is slightly different. He speaks of it as a function and writes it f(x), a function that no longer refers to a signifier or a signifying chain, but to a letter. If we write the symptom as he does at that time, (x) is what can be translated of the unconscious by a letter. You see that a letter is of the order of writing, whereas the signifier is of the order of the spoken and implies the possibility of equivocation that produces the jouissance I mentioned earlier: the jouissance of deciphering, the jouissance of sense. The letter excludes this. As soon as you write down a pun, it vanishes. So, (x) is what can be translated of the unconscious by a letter. In the letter, 'self-identity' ['*l'identité de soi à soi*'] is isolated from any quality.

The symptom is what enables the subject to write her identity as not defined by significations and not correlated to a sense. Such is self-identity, which precisely implies an identity without having to go from S_1 to S_2 to $S_3 - S_4 - S_5$. It is self-identical: one. At this point, there is no possible sliding, if you like. But, by the same token, the link is a kind of progressive opaqueness [*opacification*], of solidification of being. This is why Lacan speaks of it as a knotting that tightens up, and not as circulation of sense, as is the case in a metaphor. It is a *one* that fixes the subject as self-identical. Lacan adds that the letter writes the *one* of the unconscious, that is, the *one* of a signifier that, transformed into a letter, has an effect of condensation of a jouissance that is not a jouissance of deciphering this time, but rather a jouissance of fixity. With the letter, we take account of something that is no longer ciphered/deciphered in the unconscious, that something that precisely escapes ciphering/deciphering, and rather emerges in the Real. So it is in connection with Joyce—Lacan puts forward the hypothesis that Joyce has a psychotic structure—that he produces the definition of the sinthome evidenced in the clinic of supplementation [*suppléance*]. This amounts to a reversal of the symptom as metaphor of the Freudian hysteria. Yet, in neurosis also, all is not reducible to the response of the Other. What I call the response of the Other is the fact that the unconscious is ciphered/deciphered. If it is ciphered, it is obvious that there has to be an Other in play, a code, and this coded Other is the name of the unconscious. We can say that, in neurosis, the symptom as I first defined it is the ciphered message of the response of the Other to the question of the Subject, to the question the Subject asks him- or herself about his or her existence or gender. It is a response of the Other that implies the function of the father and so phallic jouissance. In the last analysis, the hysterical symptom, articulated in relation to the father, can be reduced to a phallic signification that confers the power of equivocation on it. But in *L'Étourdit,* Lacan emphasizes that the [hysterical symptom] is not all response of the Other. Something in the hysterical symptom sends Lacan back to the definition of the symptom he is elaborating for Joyce in relation to the psychotic structure. In the hysterical symptom also, the part that escapes from the response of the Other is a response of the Real.

In neurosis, the response of the real can still be articulated to an Other that implies castration, whereas in psychosis this response of the

Real does not include castration—that is, an empty place. The symptom is not all response of the unconscious (of the Other); it is also a response of the Real. This Real is articulated with S($\bar{A}$), with an Other of the empty place, of castration, or, as Lacan says at the time, "of castrations."

In a conference entitled "La troisième," Lacan also affirms that "we cannot speak of castration in the singular, but only of castrations in the plural." Admittedly, we can interpret this formulation as accounting for the difference between symbolic, imaginary, and real castrations, namely, for modalities of castration. Yet the fact of pluralizing castration implies a relativization of the very strict opposition between foreclosure and repression. I am not saying that the difference between neurosis and psychosis is of no use. It is absolutely crucial, but a number of problems that arise in the clinic call for the possibility of varying our models [*modélisation*] to be able to account for certain aspects of the clinic of neuroses and psychoses. In "La troisième," Lacan proposes such a writing in the framework of the clinic of knots.

Phallic jouissance is situated at the junction of the symbolic and the real and Lacan places the symptom, in the new sense he just gave to it, in continuity with this circle. The symptom has to do with what moves from the symbolic to the real. The response of the real differentiates the new definition of the symptom from phallic jouissance, which interpreted the symptom in the classical metaphoric sense. We are dealing with what links S and R, whereas in the classical hysterical symptom the direction was from S to I, toward the imaginary in the sense:

- Of the body in somatic phenomena.
- Of significations, of the jouissance of significations in the deciphering, with significations being more in the imaginary register.

On the contrary, in this model [*modélisation*] the symptom leans toward the Real. This is what I wanted to set up as framework for the case I am going to discuss. My question is the following: if Lacan says that it is a letter—(x) in the formula f(x)—that condenses jouissance for a given subject, in the case of this patient it is an image. Under what condition can an image be a letter?

The patient in question is a young woman now in her thirties who, impelled by a certain number of sentimental and professional difficulties, has been coming to see me for the past four years. She could not get over her failure at a competitive examination, and her love relation was becoming unbearable. She was imprecise about her symptoms, apart from saying that for some time now she had not been able to reach orgasm [*jouir*] with her partner. The clinical picture is dominated by anguish that seizes her mostly at nightfall. She then has to go home or be in company. I am only going to give you a few elements of this case, those necessary to circumscribe my clinical question.

This young woman has two brothers and is the only daughter of a North African Jewish family that emigrated to France. She herself is born in France. She initially describes her father in two simultaneous ways: he is an extremely religious man, very strict on the principles of the Jewish religion. At the same time, he cheated on his wife all his life, leading a hectic extrafamilial love life characterized by the fact that his mistresses, whom he fairly regularly introduced to his daughter, were not Jewish. The father was very violent with her, as well as with the mother, and she still remembers being beaten by him with a belt. She recalls lively debates at the table; so vibrant was the discussion that one could never eat without a dictionary. She was constantly criticized by her father for being fat and ugly. In the course of time I realized that her father was probably paranoiac. His fits of violence were sufficiently strong for him one day to have wanted to kill her and her mother with a shotgun.

As for the mother, she is a woman with whom the patient has an easygoing relationship. She is a rather kind woman, completely crushed by her husband. The particular point is that when there is a crisis between the father and the mother (from the beginning), he attacks the body of the mother. He would not refrain from describing, in no matter how crude and violent words, the horror she arouses in him: she is "dirty," "filthy," she is a "gaping hole." The house is caught in the same context: it is never clean enough. The tyranny of the father over the mother bears as much on her body as on the housework.

I want to insist a little on the relation to the father. In the session of January 1975 of *R.S.I.*, Lacan comes back to the question of the father in terms that must be related to what Lacan says about the father in the last part of the "Preliminary question," a crucial text for the structural differentiation between neurosis and psychosis since it develops the notion of the foreclosure of the Name-of-the-Father. And yet, already in this text of *Écrits*, Lacan evokes the paternal ravage in roughly the same terms as in 1975.

What is at stake here is not the Name-of-the-Father—that is, the paternal function—but the father of, let's say, reality. Lacan evokes the father of the psychotic and says that the relation to the father is ravaging when this father incarnates or seeks to incarnate the Law; when he, as a living person, is identified with the ideals.

This short passage from *Écrits* is extraordinarily lyrical. Lacan enumerates all the paternal ideals. His hatred for the ideals of salubriousness, health, and moral hygiene, for 'virtuous Fathers' [*Pères-la-vertu*]—Schreber's father is evidently the model—is palpable. This father figure, the father incarnating the living and ferocious ideal, the father in his mode of jouissance or, again, the singular 'version' of a paternal jouissance, is taken up again in *R.S.I.* There Lacan returns to the fact that some "versions of the father" have "foreclosing effects." We can sustain the difference between the general foreclosure of the Name-of-the-Father and the foreclosing effects of a version of the father [*père*], that is, of a version of his jouissance, precisely not *père*-versely oriented. These foreclosing effects are the consequence of certain particular forms of paternal jouissance. They affect the subject without touching on the quilting point of the function. Perhaps we could juxtapose the expression "foreclosing effects" with the expression that pluralizes the Names-of-the-Father, and consider psychical spaces differently affected by these effects.

For the patient in question, the father had a similar—localized—effect. That the effect was localized probably stems from the fact that, in the face of the ideals he pretended to incarnate, he nevertheless showed her a contradiction: ideals of 'Judaicity' yet *gentile* mistresses. In the face of jouissance, of his incarnation of the Law, the hidden door of a desire outside the law subsisted.

The analytical work considerably modified the conditions of this patient's life: there are therapeutic effects manifest at the level of her work-inhibition, for today she has interest in the creative work she is engaged in: she writes and is published, which was previously both desired and impossible. She got married and so was able to inscribe her relationship to a man in a symbolic frame—although in very specific conditions—whereas she was previously fully organized by her fantasy that made her identify man with torturer. From the point of view of 'love and work', she is more satisfied. Yet there is an element that did not shift. It concerns a particular phenomenon that is at the origin of the anguish that seizes her at nightfall, and which she confessed after a year of analysis by way of a digression during a session. This, let us call it a symptom, is the following: in the street, in the gutters, on the pavement, and also at home, she sees dead animals. These cadavers are a considerable cause of anguish. No signification is associated with them, and the visions remain perfectly enigmatic.

She was able to refind the origin of this symptom that affects the perception of reality. It was the year in which she was preparing herself for a very difficult examination, very important to her father and she therefore considered it as the way to be recognized by him. One winter morning, when it was still quite dark, she was on her way to a preparatory class and she saw the cadaver of an animal spiked onto the rails of a fence in a square. It turned out to be a dog run over by a car. Although she did not linger over it, the dog gave her the impression of being merely a fleshless skin, a fur. Having glanced at it, she ran off in horror. Since then, although in an irregular fashion, but particularly after her failure at the said examination, any obscure and vague shape at nightfall—such as strips of fabric used to direct water in gutters, cardboard, or paper leftovers glimpsed on a pavement or a street—is susceptible to give rise to a similar vision. Notwithstanding any element extracted from the subject's history, I would like to show why these visions are not psychotic hallucinations, even though Lacan's formulation "what did not come to life in the symbolic appears in the real" ("Réponse au commentaire de Jean Hyppolite sur la *Verneinung* de Freud" in *Écrits,* p. 388) seems perfectly suitable—indeed the patient evidences an effect of the real through both her anguish and the void of signification that accompanies the vision.

There are, however, two points worth mentioning: there is no other implicated in the phenomenon, neither *semblable* nor persecutor. It could be argued that the reference to the other is easier to bring out when the hallucination is verbal, as the effects of subjective attribution organize the signifying distribution. So here it is more appropriate to refer to the paradigm of the visual hallucination of the Wolf Man. From this point of view, the visions of cadavers, dead and deflated animals, like the cut finger of the Wolf Man, would have to be placed in the perspective of a possible assumption of castration contaminated by foreclosure. And, in fact, the sexual signification is no longer manifest; what is manifest is rather an imaginary capture of the primordial trauma, precisely as in the case of the Wolf Man. Yet the structure of the vision is different: the mute vision of his own finger cut by the subject himself situates castration outside the possibilities of symbolization by the subject, outside speech, and with no mediation being directly inscribed on his body, in a topological regression to the visual form of one's own body. In the case of our patient's vision of the dead animal, her own body is not concerned, the body remains out of play. Nor does it concern an absence or a mutilation but the presence of an object, a contaminated living that is not a *semblable* and which, as we will see, can mobilize signifiers. In the case of another patient, the apparent similarity with the Wolf Man is even stronger. She told me the tale, kept silent so far, of a childhood memory: one day at Mass, in a subjective atmosphere of elevated mystical spirituality, she saw, in the thurible balanced by the priest, the body of a dead child—an enigmatic vision she nevertheless found repellent at the time for its cruelty, and which she preferred to keep secret lest she be thought mad. In both cases the vision is one of death, involving an object distinct from the body of the subject, an object that does not target the subject, for it is precisely annihilated by the signifier and therefore belongs, in this capacity, to the symbolic order. Still, it nonetheless constitutes an invasion of the field of reality by the Real, which, as such, breaks in. Her vision does not include a persecutory other, leaving her own body out of play. At the time of the first vision, it was clearly a skin [*peau*] that was at stake, an animal skin framing a void: neither mutilation nor *semblable*. The associations can probably bring up some phallic significations of the phenomenon.

The triggering is situated in relation with, on the one hand, the ego ideal (in this case the image she wants to impress on her father by succeeding at the exam) and, on the other hand, it involves an encounter with a real that we will be careful not to understand as being naturally propitious to the triggering of horror. It seems to me that the associations are the only reliable guide. They take place on several axes. The patient is led to speak of all these elements, including those of the triggering of the trouble, at a time when, precisely, this trouble no longer occurs in the street but only at home, in the same conditions regarding darkness, but in a phase of literary creation for her, so linked to her work of writing. She notes this alternation of inside–outside, home–street. Yes, but what is she writing? Poetry, which resonates with the *peau* [skin] that covers and separates an inside from an outside. It is precisely the question of the skin covering, or not, the flesh, that she was faced with at the time of the first encounter with the cadaver of the dead animal, and which she rejected in an "I don't want to know anything about it." In fact she points out that all her adolescence unfolded against the backdrop of skin [*peau*] problems that caused her much suffering, undermining her image at that time. Lastly, the poetical texts she then wrote are entitled *Meat,* and are an attempt to knot, if we can chance saying so, soul to flesh: the flesh which in the animal is never guilty.

Some of her other associations about some contemporary poets show them evoking the importance of the moments of contemplation of corpses in the morgue for their work. All these axes go toward the circumscription of a signifying pair, skin/fur on the one hand, and meat/flesh on the other. The disturbance of perception is therefore organized by the signifying chain, and shows some possibilities of metaphorical equivocation. At times of poetical creation, the visions, although they remain scary, are experienced with less anguish, and so are endured more easily to the extent that they come as a counterpoint to a process of writing that transforms these vague perceptive forms into letters. The vagueness also seems linked to a disturbance of vision that could then be medically detected. The medical diagnosis, which puts an organic problem into play, accounts for the chiaroscuro moments in which the visions appear, but does nothing to explain their content.

Apart from I(A), the ego ideal implied by the father, the visual perceptions imply the signifying pair: *skin* [*peau*], a signifier referring to $i(a)$, the narcissistic image of the signifying and unified body, and *flesh* [*chair*], evoking sexuality in the form of fornication in its least idealized aspect, namely, in the guise of the prostitute $(-\varphi)$ at the same time as an unnameable object veiled by skin (object a). Indeed, the circumstances of the development of this disturbance as of its first occurrence have to do with her love relationship with a man, which was quite a complex one. For the part concerning the idea that this young woman has of her friend, she associates him, to her great sorrow and great fascination, with the commerce of prostitutes, and poses through him the question of her own relation to the other woman, namely, the prostitute [*prostituée*]. Of course we stress the *tué* [killed] contained in the signifier *prostituée,* which the flesh of the dead animal comes to imaginarize.

These 'visions' are not without relation to the symbolic, and are partly organized according to the principle of the return of the repressed as it is realized by these associative chains. So they are partially linked with repression and the law of the Name-of-the-Father.

In fact, they are linked to the father in the form of his fault: the whole childhood of the patient was marked by her encounters with the father's numerous mistresses, whom he always chose in opposition to the most sacred principles, and even in contradiction with the bigotry he imposed on his whole family. This fault inscribes the father in a relation to the law that is after all quite banal in neurosis, placing his daughter in a position of rebellion and hysterical defiance in the face of the lie of the paternal order that she nonetheless supports absolutely.

And yet, something resists a phallicization that would reduce this vision to a metaphor by producing a surplus of sense [*plus de sens*]. The persistence of the phenomenon, despite the work of association and interpretation, attests to this.

In a text of *Écrits,* "La psychanalyse et son enseignement" (p. 452), Lacan makes this beautiful statement apropos of the hysteric: "In her relentless quest for what it is to be a woman, she can but fool her desire, since this desire is the desire of the other, for she failed to complete the narcissistic identification which would have prepared her to satisfy the one and the other in the position of object." Here the difficulties posed by the patient's narcissistic identification are patent: refusal of her own image, anger and immediate rejection of any audacious person who dares to speak to her of her image, who shows, even in a discrete fashion, why it interests him. He is either immediately referred to his rudeness or taken for a short ride, after which he becomes an object of disgust concerning this or that part of his body, and is expelled from the field of desire [*mis hors désir*]. Incidentally, sexual desire is particularly fragile for her and does not come into the relation with her husband at all.

And yet she takes good care of her image; she is very beautiful and elegant and seems wholly committed to incarnating the phallic mystery in her image.

The way in which the patient's father related to the mother of his children was such that the patient was sometimes caught in it: she has, with her mother, been the object of a rejection that, as far as she is concerned, manifested itself on at least one occasion in the form of a death threat. In addition, for this man the mother is defined as fundamentally dirty, messy, in her housekeeping as well as in her own appearance; the family has lost count of the scenes in which the father would have a go at her on the subject. Those scenes sometimes ended up in very threatening violence. According to the repeated statements of her father, the body of her mother is a "stinking hole." Under the skin there is meat—this is the flipside of the phallic image. It is on this point that the hypothesis of the 'foreclosing effect' could be made. For the father, there is no access to the feminine through the fantasy. At each triggering of a crisis, he attacks the body of his wife as if it was his.

In these conditions, the mother could not be placed in the position of object-cause-of-desire by the father. There is only a void surrounded by fur, a beast, as no desire has come to humanize the feminine object.

I am hypothesizing that this singularity, this singular version of the father, had foreclosing effects for this patient as to her possibility of symbolizing the feminine. Of course, the signifier of the woman is foreclosed, but this does not prevent the imaginings and metaphors of the feminine; quite the contrary: it fosters them. Perhaps we could say that the impossibility for the father to humanize the feminine— that is, to give it the status of object *a* over $-\varphi$—had the consequence for the patient of barring her access to her body by the signifier. The vision is linked to her incapacity of representing herself in a body. And, for this patient, these images are linked to what matters more than anything else in the world for her: to write and publish poetry. I think I have already said that her texts revolve around the signifiers 'meat–flesh–carrion' and that she carried out research on a poet whose inspiration, he said, regularly impelled him to visit the morgue. The Medusa head is for her 'killed [*tué*] animal', 'nonlicentious flesh' [*chair non-dévergondée*]. Her visions are linked to her 'sinthome', writing. The foreclosing effect is to reject in the real the object she is for the other.

But the literary work comes, by way of writing, to give her a body capable of being named: f(x), x being her poems (*peau-aime*) and her verses. The search in poetry for a woman's name that identifies her serves as a supplementation [*suppléer*] to the incapacity of the Name-of-the-Father to transmit a desire that would call the feminine as object into question. What is at stake for her is a solution to a problem that does not have one. By way of the sinthome, she seeks to find the letter that would give her a feminine self-identity, and this is impossible to find.

In this way, she counterbalances her visions that mobilize the image of a not-all phallicized body. Thus, vision—symptom—and writing—sinthome—complement one another, and, sure enough, she noticed it, since these images of death are never more potent than when she is just about to write. For some time now, she has been directing films on writers, but she finds this side of her activity interesting only insofar as the image is employed in the service of the written. So the vision is what of the body was not phallicized for her, and the writing attempts to elevate this unsymbolizable point to the [status of the] name.

Identification with the Symptom at the End of Analysis

Esthela Solano-Suárez

In order to speak of identification with the symptom at the end of analysis, we have to accept the hypothesis that the analytic experience can produce, at its end, an unprecedented bond with the symptom in terms of identification.

Lacan mentions this proposition only once in his teaching, on 16 November 1976, and then only as a question. But Lacan himself taught us that we do not ask questions to get answers but that the question arises as a consequence of the answer that logically precedes it. So we might assume that, with his question, Lacan is sharing something he found in his analytic practice. In this perspective, if identification with the symptom at the end of analysis becomes a question for us, it is perhaps because of the answer that precedes us.

The answer can only originate from what the analytic experience teaches us. In this respect, Freud showed the way with his inaugural step. He invented psychoanalysis and in so doing paved the way for a new type of social bond. If the analytic discourse was able to emerge, it was because Freud, docile to the hysteric, started to believe that the symptom was saying something. He then verified that not only did it speak, but also that it fulfilled an aim of satisfaction. Psychoanalysis is an epistemic consequence, an elaboration of knowledge produced by the emergence of the symptom. And this elaboration can be deduced from the treatment of the symptom, a treatment that belongs to a practice. In this sense, we can say that people come to analysis through the door of the symptom.

Each time an analysis begins, this inaugural step has to be taken again. Why do people come to analysis? Because they are suffering from something that they would like get rid of. What they suffer from is carried as a complaint, a foreign body, that disturbs, binds, constrains. It is something they experience, notice, enact, and suffer from, that is imposed to what is most intimate in the sense of self as what is most exterior to the self. It is a disturbing extimacy, an intrusive will in me, more than me, since "it's beyond my control!"

Still, the complaint, which is addressed to the analyst as demand, must be circumscribed in its particularity as symptom. Isolating the symptom as such is a preliminary step that gives the analytic practice its orientating principle. In some cases we will have to promote the orientation toward the real, and in others we will have to not disturb the semblants that the subject can make use of in the guise of identification. We will only consider the first situation here, since the identification with the symptom at the end of analysis is the result achieved by the analytic treatment of a neurotic symptom.

To treat the symptom within the framework of the analytic experience means deciphering it. As Freud demonstrated, neurotic symptoms have a sense. The sense of the symptom, *der Sinn,*[1] turns the symptom into a language entity [*entité langagière*]. The symptom speaks, insofar as it "says something."[2]

For Freud, there is another side to the symptom, that of the *Bedeutung* through which the symptom accomplishes "a new mode of satisfaction of the libido." This "real satisfaction" is "unrecognizable to the subject who . . . feels the alleged satisfaction as suffering and complains of it."[3] Lacan distinguishes the symptom's "relation to the real"[4] on the side involving drive-satisfaction. And now the problem is even more complex: people request analysis because they suffer from a symptom; but a will to jouissance is accomplished through the symptom, perhaps even drive-satisfaction. How can we manage, through analysis, not only to decode the symptom's meaning, but also to touch its "relation to the real"? This question requires us to interrogate the relation of the symptom to the satisfaction it involves once it has been treated by analysis.

In other words, what is the destiny of drive-satisfaction at the end of analysis? This is the question Freud asks in his text "Analysis Terminable and Interminable," because we must know, he says, if "it [is] possible by means of analytic therapy to dispose of . . . a pathogenic instinctual demand upon the ego, permanently and definitively?"[5] Under consideration here is a symptom that has been treated by psychoanalysis—what remains of its exigency, what ceases to suffer from it, what one can separate from and what one can no longer get rid of. What can possibly happen for there to be identification with the symptom at the end of analysis when it initially represents what is most alien to the subject?

Compulsion of Thought

Let us start from a particular symptom, the one that characterizes obsessional neurosis. In this neurosis, compulsion characterizes the symptom, as compulsion of thought. Obsessionals suffer from their thought, "a thought that burdens the soul" said Lacan.[6]

But it is rare for the obsessional to disclose his thoughts straightaway. It is easier for him to speak of acts he feels compelled to carry out; first he talks about his embarrassment, his difficulty in choosing, loving, doing. He speaks of his generalized suffering, his anxiety, his sadness, his inhibition. But transference is needed before he can recognize that it is his own thoughts that are the symptom. This is why it can be difficult to get the analysis started with an obsessional patient, that is, to get a change in the subjective position so that he surrenders his thoughts and gets down to work. Often such patients come driven by a subjective emergency and speak freely, deploying their talents and charm to put us under a spell of fascination, fascination for the *Gestalt*. The obsessional wants to be the "marvel that dazzles us,"[7] unfolding discursive treasures before us and refusing the institution of the metaphor of love, which implies having to do with lack.

The obsessional offers us his armor first, his soul, because it is bound up with the symptom. This is a case in which the symptom, as Freud said, "is found to be useful in asserting the position of the self and becomes more and more closely merged with the ego," to the point that obsessionals are those who can derive a narcissistic satisfaction from "systems which the obsessional neurotic constructs [to] flatter his self-love by making him feel that he is better than other people because he is specially clean or specially conscientious."[8] This is why, according to Lacan, obsessional neurosis is conscience.

In the strategy of the obsessional subject, man or woman, the ego occupies a privileged place. We recognize here 'the fortifications *à la Vauban*'[9] that Lacan speaks of. This imaginary prevalence pertains to the One of the body image in which the obsessional drapes himself as a defense against the effects of division. But his attire and parade do not protect him from his parasitical thoughts. And for a reason! Obsessional thought is dysfunctional; it goes round in circles. This circularity may be characteristic of thought, but in obsessional cases thought demonstrates its essence as speech-parasite.

Following Lacan, we can say that thought is not a cause—it is a consequence. We think because someone has spoken to us. This is what gives thought its extimate character, which becomes extreme in the case of the obsessional imperative, where the subject gives himself orders in the second person, for example, for the Rat Man: "Kill yourself, as a punishment for these savage and murderous passions!"[10]

As a result of living in *lalangue,* we are speaking beings, getting this being only from speech. *Lalangue* also produces all sorts of effects on the body, effects of cutting, effects of jouissance, effects of affect. So the body, *lalangue* and what *ex-sists* of them as real are knotted in the speaking being. Thought is one of the effects of *lalangue* on the body. *Lalangue* traverses the body, and it results in the body imagining itself as a unity, and this unity imagining itself thinking.[11] Thought, as an effect of *lalangue* on the body, and if it becomes a body-event acting as symptom, can be situated at the level of affect. This is why we can be affected by thought, suffer from it. This amounts to saying that *appensée* [*a*-thought] is jouissance. We are enjoyed by our thoughts. So we can imagine the difficulty posed by the obsessional symptom because of its being of thought. Let us try to move on at the level of the particular of this symptom. What does the deciphering of obsessive thought teach us? We can always find the meaning of obsessive thoughts in analysis, however absurd that meaning may be. This is the first lesson Freud draws from the case of the Rat Man. Freud teaches us about the complexity of his scaffold-like construction resulting from false connections, inversions, ellipses: we are dealing with a drawer-like structure, where within drawers are found yet other drawers—ad infinitum. This has to do with the nature of the signifying chain. But the specificity of this thought is to "cover its tracks" through an operation that consists in isolating bits of the chain, breaking off the signifying implications, and replacing them with a series of disconnected consequences.

It is possible that we will end up finding a sense to it. In fact the obsessional subject would be delighted. He lends himself gladly to the game; meaning is all he wants. He can enjoy deciphering; he adores the subject of the signifier. Yet we see that the more meaning he adds, the more he associates, and the more he is mortified [*cadavérisé*], petrified.

Effectively, it reassures him that there are only signifiers; he can leave his body in the wings and play the angel. At this level, he can play the game without risk. In the treatment of the obsessional, the point is to get the subject to engage his body in the analysis; the effect of anxiety is guaranteed.

This is a condition for the analysis to get at the jouissance. The other question is that of the treatment of the effects of meaning. This is a question that occupied Lacan a lot during his last teaching. Starting from the idea that in analysis one works from the effects of meaning, he wondered what was the effect of meaning required in analysis in order to get at the jouissance effect of the symptom. How can one obtain an incidence on the jouissance of the symptom as 'outside meaning' [*hors-sens*] through the effects of meaning that result from the signifying articulation produced in language? In other words, if the effects of meaning have to do with the incidences of the symbolic on the imaginary, how can we operate in analysis to touch the real, which eludes this dimension? It means that interpretation has to go beyond speech[12] and toward the real, which is crucial when dealing with an obsessional symptom.

A Passion for the Impossible

This practice, as a practice of language—Lacan says so—is shown to work efficaciously via the *Witz*.[13] To make use of equivocation implies using the sound of words to bring out the use-value of an unprecedented meaning, a meaning that is outside of its regular use. In this way it is possible to reduce meaning to bring out the *jouis-sens,* or enjoyed sense.

In these conditions, the obsessional subject can hear the hatred resonating at the heart of his nicest and best-intentioned statements, of his thoughtfulness for the other, or the death wish prevailing at the core of his behavior, to the point of exposing the function of the symptom that is rooted into the impossible. The obsessional is impassioned by the impossible. He makes the impossible his fundamental partner. He can only subjectivize this partnership if he leaves the impotence to which he is doomed by his thoughts.

We know that obsessional subjects experience a precocious sexual awakening during childhood. This awakening is guided by a curiosity that urges these subjects to want to know, to solve the enigma of sexuality. Obsessional subjects are particularly sensitive, in their research, to signs coming from the parental couple, looking out for the relation between jouissance and semblants. They look for and find the lie of behavior, the imposture of the ideal, the inconsequentiality of function. In short, a contingency stresses the irremediable failure of the father, leaving obsessional subjects defenseless in the face of the unlimited jouissance of the mother. Consequently, they see themselves sucked up by the limitlessness of the hole of S($\cancel{A}$). They respond with a strategy consisting in wanting to reduce the $\cancel{A}$ to the One by means of their thoughts.

The failure of the paternal function leaves the obsessional subject defenseless, without recourse to semblants in the face of the impossible. He does not, like the hysteric, have the armor of love of the father to defend himself against the real at his disposal. So he resorts to thought to treat the impossible—hence his predilection for topics of thought that are unthinkable, such as paternity, life's duration, and life after death.[14] Through this thought that acts as exception [*fait exception*], the obsessional thinks *ex-sistence* in order to supplement [*suppléer*] the One of exception, to preserve the All of thought correlated to the phallic function.

This is where the phallicism of the obsessional stems from. To plug with the One consists in keeping watch constantly on the presence of the phallus, at the risk of making himself the representative of the phallic enterprise. Anything can be used, his body, his image, his thought, his work, his exploits. We know the phallic value that thought can take in the obsessional, who can play with and enjoy his thoughts as if it were an organ. The eroticization of thought for the obsessional is the consequence of an irruption of phallic jouissance into the imaginary. If the obsessional subject is a woman, the phallic strategy prevails for her as well. Her relation to castration differentiates her from the obsessional man. Nevertheless, the particularities of her penis envy [*Penisneid*] render her relation to the phallus more complex. She does not want the phallus in order to play the man—she knows she hasn't got it—but her duty is to adorn herself with the phallus, to invest herself in the phallic masquerade to fill the lack in the Other.[15] The more she wants to make believe that she *is* it [*l'est*], the more she hates it [*l'hait*]. And this, insofar as she tends to believe that this phallus finds more consistence in a man, not at the level of his having but at the level of his being—hence the type of entanglement that characterizes her relation to lack. Her partner will incarnate for her the misunderstanding of phallic rivalry, while she will make love *ex-sist* through the man of her thoughts to the point of engaging in an erotomaniac trance of thought.

The Other's Inconsistency

All the same, for the obsessional, the problem—a logical problem—is not so much the Other's incompleteness as its inconsistency. Hence his strategy—full of hatred—that consists in degrading the Other to the level of a devalued object, reducing it to the One. On this point, we recall the insult the Rat Man addressed to his father: "You lamp! You towel! You plate!"[16] If the insult targets 'being', it then makes the Other consist via the object. It is more of a problem than a solution, because the maneuver liquidating the Other harms the subject's desire, and irremediably shuts him up in the boredom of the One. From this we can deduce the necessity for the subject of supporting the Other by means of protection, and even of answering for it. Additionally, reducing the Other to the One implies always having to start again, since there will always be another signifier associating with the One, making the interval between the One and the Other appear. In this case the obsessional must wear himself out in order to annul the second signifier by taking up the first, or exhaust himself by counting in order to fill up the gap between the two signifiers with the One, as in the case of the Rat Man who counted and counted, between lightning and thunder.[17]

The necessity for the obsessional symptom of making One [*faire Un*] with the Other *does not cease to be written*. The symptom is inscribed as cipher designed to ward off the structural impossible [*chiffre conjuratoire de l'impossible de structure*]. The impossible, as such, *does not cease to be written,* as cipher liable to make One with the two [*d'eux*] of sex.

The obsessional has a chance of getting out of his union with the One though love. Love, under the guise of transference, makes him come out of the One and leads him toward the barred Other. First, because he must speak. The Other of speech can prevent him from centering himself on the One of the autism of his thought. But this is not enough because it is not uncommon for an obsessional subject to fall into the autism of speech. The operative value of the Other of love in transference is measured at the level of the possibility, introduced by the analytic act, of giving value for the subject to the barred Other as being the One-that-lacks [*l'Un-en-moins*].

The function of transference-love allows the obsessional to overcome the vertigo he experiences in the face of the signifier lacking in the Other. As a consequence, he has a chance, through transference, of encountering the modes of the possible and the contingent. On this condition, he can give up the jouissance of the symptom and stop thinking in order to dam up the Pacific. Thus, through analysis, the obsessional can find a way out of the tyranny of necessity. Thanks to the analysis, a remolding comes about, at the end of which real, symbolic, and imaginary are ordered and distinguished. As a result, the phallic function shrinks back to its place, between real and symbolic, freeing the imaginary of the task of having to supplement it in an effort of thought. A considerable alleviation ensues, due to the lifting of inhibitions and the disappearance of anxiety, both liberating the body from its chains. The subject can henceforth dispose of his body, because of the disjunction and distinction that took place between the consistency of the imaginary on the one hand, and the *ex-sistence* of the function on the other. In the same way, the symbolic is emptied of the duty of filling up the unthinkable of its own hole through the necessity of thought. It follows that the jouissance of the impossible, as an exercise kept alive by the parasite of thought, ceases. By placing itself outside the symbolic, the real constitutes its limit. This outcome is the one through which the limitation and the tightening up of the limits of the symptom are accomplished. Indeed, "it is by knotting itself to the body—that is to say to the imaginary—by knotting itself to the real also, and to the unconscious as third party" that the symptom encounters its limits.[18] The obsessional can get to the end of his analysis. He will not have transgressed the real, he will not have traversed the nontraversable zone of the impossible that occupied his thoughts. Nonetheless he will have found the means to do better with his thoughts, within the limits of the possible. Leaving the entanglement of his thought behind will allow him to not be in a permanent state of embarrassment at the level of his acts and decisions. He will be able to manage without deferring everything until the next day, and to authorize himself to make the Other of permission exist.

In the same way, now that he knows the lining of jouissance concealed beneath his virtues and qualities, he will be able to be more virtuous without feeling meritorious, accept pleasure, and abandon the reign of obligation. His will, disjoined from the imperative, will find itself in agreement with desire. But he will know that this economic remodeling, as limitation to the symptom, does not imply that he might be done with his symptom. The obsessional subject will have had the opportunity of noting that his symptom is no longer foreign to him, that he is familiar with it to the point of knowing that the symptom is his permanent mode of being, inescapable, nontraversable. Wherever he goes, whatever he does, he will carry it with him. It is not a mask; it is his own face. His semblant of being is nothing other than the symptom with his knot-like being [*cet être de nœud du symptôme*], which knots his body, his way of speaking, and the real. So he concludes that he is nothing other than this scaffold that knots him and holds him together.

If the obsessional subject is a woman, then she will know that this knot does not merely hold her together, and that it also binds her not only to those others who are interested in her, but more singularly with an other who has made her his partner. She knows what her function as partner-symptom consists of, thanks to the love that acted as encounter between two sets of unconscious knowledge [*deux savoirs incons-cients*], as is always the case. She may also know the formula of the contingency of the encounter, then of the necessity of the symptom, in terms of libidinal element. And she will know how to make do with the symptom that she is.

For a woman, the identification with the symptom at the end of analysis goes against the grain of what the hysteric refuses to be when she is interested in the Other woman, a man's symptom. This solution also goes against the grain of the obsessional woman's refusal, who would like to be equal [to a man] in order not to be herself symptom. On the other hand, identifying oneself with the symptom—related to a man's body—implies knowing how to make do with femininity in other ways, accepting to only get one's being as woman by accomplishing oneself, qua Other, as symptom.[19]

The identification with the symptom at the end of analysis comes down to accepting the enjoyment [*jouis*] that underlies the "I am" [*suis*], purifying the sinthome. We can say that this identification opens onto the horizon of the possible, beyond hope. For we know that we will always have to deal with the impossible, getting on as best we can thanks to a good use of the symptom. Once the limit of the impossible is found, the subject can play his hand with the limitless of $S(\cancel{A})$. This is, the subject can engage with the exigency of having to circumscribe a bit of the real, over and over, by making use of a thought henceforth freed from sin.

This piece of work is a remainder of my experience as analysand, as 'passante', and also as member of the cartels of the pass. It finds its place in the work accomplished by the school on the end of analysis, and in the Lacanian orientation sustained by Jacques-Alain Miller.

Notes

1. S. Freud, *Introductory Lectures on Psychoanalysis,* lecture XVII, SE Vol. XVI.
2. J. Lacan, "Conférences et entretiens dans des universités nord-américaines" in Scilicet No. 6/7, p. 46. See also J.-A. Miller, "The Seminar of Barcelona on *die Wege der Symptombildung*" in *Psychoanalytical Notebooks* No. 1 (London, 1998), p. 28.
3. S. Freud, op. cit., lecture XXIII, pp. 365–366.
4. J. Lacan, "Geneva Lecture on the Symptom" in *Analysis* No. 1, trans. R. Grigg (Melbourne: Centre for Psychoanalytic Research, 1989), p. 17.
5. S. Freud, "Analysis Terminable and Interminable," 1937, SE Vol. XXIII, p. 224.
6. J. Lacan, *Television* (London & New York: Norton, 1990), p. 6.
7. J. Lacan, "Proposition of 9 October 1967 on the Psychoanalyst of the School" in *Analysis* No. 6 (Melbourne: Centre for Psychoanalytic Research, 1995), p. 7.
8. S. Freud, "Inhibitions, Symptoms and Anxiety," 1925, SE Vol. XX, p. 99.
9. J. Lacan, *Le Séminaire IV: La relation d'objet* (Paris: Seuil, 1994), p. 487.
10. S. Freud, "Notes upon a Case of Obsessional Neurosis," 1909, SE Vol. X, p. 188.
11. J. Lacan, *Seminar XX: Encore* (London & New York: Norton, 1998), p. 139; see also J. "Conférences et entretiens dans des universités nord-américaines" in *Scilicet* No. 6/7, p. 40.
12. J. Lacan, *Le Séminaire XXII:* R.S.I., 1974–1975, unpublished.
13. J. Lacan, *Le Séminaire XXIV: L'insu que sait de l'une-bévue s'aile a mourre,* 1976–1977, unpublished.
14. S. Freud, op. cit.
15. J. Lacan, *Le Séminaire IV: La relation d'objet,* op. cit., pp. 449–456.
16. S. Freud, op. cit., p.205.
17. Ibid.
18. J. Lacan, "Joyce le symptôme" in *Joyce avec Lacan* (Paris: Seuil, 1985), p. 29.
19. Ibid., p. 35.

PART III

A Psychoanalytic Clinic of Psychosis

From the Elementary Phenomenon to the Enigmatic Experience

Herbert Wachsberger

The term "enigmatic experience" designates a fact of psychosis recently introduced by Jacques-Alain Miller that is yet to be received in the Freudian field under this name. It has been recognized by Lacan in comparable terms at different moments of his teaching. Thus, in his article in the *Encyclopédie française,* Lacan designates as the fertile phase of a delusion those moments when "objects, transformed by an ineffable strangeness, are revealed as shocks, enigmas, significations";[1] in his thesis in medicine he notes the "enigmatic character" of the initial experiences that have determined the delusion;[2] in his third public seminar he remarks that the enigma, produced by a given phenomenon of mental automatism, could only be truly formulated with the affirmation of the initiative of the other (as distinguished from the Other);[3] and in his writing on psychosis the "enigmatic void," which affects signification, is isolated as a factor in delusional intuition.[4]

Occurrences of this problematic signification are to be placed in their context. From Jaspers's conception of 'process' to the function of speech, from the laws of speech to those of language,[5] Lacan makes a number of adjustments rendered necessary, first by the "insertion of the unconscious into language,"[6] then subsequently by further redefinitions of the unconscious. The elementary phenomenon, initially implicated in these elaborations, will finally be left behind in favor of the enigmatic experience. At least, that is the thesis being put to the test here.

The "question preliminary to any possible treatment of psychosis" puts the enigmatic experience in its rightful place,[7] but this text is not final; it should be read in the light of Lacan's "Présentation" of the Memoirs of President Schreber[8] and his later considerations on Joyce.

These advances, made in contrasting leaps and bounds, never lose the thread of their ambition: to grasp, in the psychotic phenomenon, "the purest phenomenon" in which the structure that it indexes can be glimpsed.

The Moment of the Phenomenologists

In his medical thesis[9] Lacan holds to the principal doctrinal current of his time: the tendency to isolate the elementary disorders of psychosis, following the hypothesis of an original lesion preceding the delusion and recognized as "primordial fact,"[10] *Grundstörung,*[11] "original or primary delusional experience,"[12] "disorder generative of the delusion."[13] The thesis of a primary psychotic fact distributes the theories between those that conceive the delusion as being in continuity with the former personality and those that situate it as the consequence of an irruption, a perturbation, a "subduction of personality."[14]

Initially accepted by Lacan, the notion of psychical process[15] modeled on an organic process and transposed onto mental activity is supposed to account for this alteration of mental life that in principle is definitive.

The elementary phenomenon condenses all these facts in itself.[16] It is primary and initial, without exterior cause; the factors that determine psychoses are expressed in it, it is the principle of their triggering. It is less certain, on the other hand, that the delusion is organized and fixed in an organic link with this phenomenon, and according to secondary affective reactions and rational deductions. Its parasitic, irruptive character, heterogeneous to personality, draws it closer to the phenomena of xenopathic thought that characterize mental automatism, or to the phenomena of the syndrome of external influence.

The enigmatic inflection, inspired by Jaspers's phenomenological approach to the facts of psychosis ("events mean something, but do not mean anything specific"), that Lacan attributed to the elementary phenomenon had already been highlighted by numerous authors as a phenomenon typical of paranoia. Before Jaspers, Marguliès had identified perplexity, undetermined agitation, the sense of an approaching catastrophe, and a tone of anxiety, as signs of an inaugural perturbation to be situated in the sphere of affects.[17] Tiling had noted a confused and indefinable anxiety, or a feeling of being cornered, at the origin of the search for clarifications of the subject.[18] After Jaspers, Westerterp will insist on the strange primary modification of the environment.[19]

The subject's certainty of being personally targeted by the phenomenon, "a remarkable subjective certainty," Jaspers wrote, had been isolated by Clemens Neisser[20] under the name of the experience of personal signification (*Eigenbeziehung*) [self-reference] as a primary symptom of paranoia.[21]

The clinical traits of the elementary phenomenon will allow Lacan to consider interpretations, states of passion, illusions of memory, intuitions, and so on as elementary phenomena, and likewise, concerning the case of Aimée, feelings of transformation of the moral atmosphere, feelings of strangeness, of déjà vu, and of thought divination.

The elementary phenomenon includes in itself the anomalous mental structure characteristic of psychosis itself.[22] But this foundation remained imprecise, and Lacan's cautious 'morbid x', if it referred to the Jasperian process, also promised further elaborations.

From the Laws of Speech to the Laws of Language

Lacan's recognition of psychotic phenomena as phenomena of language modified the doctrine.

The notion of process, now obsolescent, is replaced by that of structure. A new definition of the elementary phenomenon ensues: a phenomenon is elementary in the manner of a leaf, which reveals the structure of the plant.[23] The phenomenon has the structure of language. The imago, which was at the center of Lacan's exposé on psychical causality,[24] is sidelined in favor of the signifier, and the notion of personality is displaced by the subject as subject of the signifier.

In short, the clinical value of the notion of elementary phenomenon has evolved alongside the advances of doctrine. The elementary phenomenon, essential to the status of the process, has been eclipsed by the importance that Lacan gives to the 'fertile moments' and to the paranoiac knowledge [*connaissance paranoïaque*] that structures them;[25] then, once its relation to the signifier has been defined and its insertion into the subject's relation to the Other clarified, the elementary phenomenon refinds its place in the field of language. Such a definition is nondefinitive because it is dependent on the displacement of the subject's positions in its relation to the Other: first as Other of recognition, then of speech—the elementary phenomenon is thus raised to the status of paradigm of the psychotic fact—and finally as Other of language, which sounds the death knell for the elementary phenomenon, the absence of which in the "Preliminary question" is noteworthy.

These steps clarify the root of the precariousness of the Other in psychosis: the failure of the Other (as Other of recognition or Other of speech) in the seminar on psychosis; the fault in the Other (as Other of language) due to signifying foreclosure in the "Preliminary question." In this article, hallucinations are brought to the forefront of psychotic phenomena. Starting with the text of the hallucinations, Lacan distributes them between phenomena of code, relative to the Other, and phenomena of message, which emphasize the pole of the subject.

To the code phenomena, to which the hallucinations of Schreber's *Grundsprache* belong, Lacan adds phenomena of intuition,[26] those "primary delusional experiences" studied by Jaspers (immediate significations, or transformed significations of the ordinary signification of things, sudden intuitions, experiences without an adequate content) that he had used in his semiology of elementary phenomena. Would the phenomena of intuition now account for what Lacan had until then attempted to grasp through the elementary phenomenon—which did not, for its part, resist the linguistic analysis of psychotic phenomena? In effect, from the seminar on *Psychoses* to the "Preliminary question," the co-ordinates of the incidence of the signifier in the psychotic fact underwent a modification parallel to the revision of the status of the Other.

Two types of phenomena, "in which the neologism outlines itself," are studied in the third book of the Seminar: delusional intuition, which gets its character as a fulfilling [*comblante*] experience from the plenitude of the neologism; and the stereotyped formula, which contrasts with the former with its worn triteness. Both have the effect of a close-up on "signification as such," attributable to the signifier. The effects of signification for which the signifier is responsible clarify its status and its incidence in the phenomenon. Isolated from its chain, pure non-sense, it weighs the neologism down, conferring its density on it: it creates the enigma for which it is the key [*mot*]. This presence of the signifier in the real, through the defection of the Other, produces effects of signification; suspended signification, referred first to itself; then, reducible to another signification: the enigma's key is found, and it produces a feeling of ineffable understanding of an unprecedented experience; then, it is emptied of its signification.

In the "Preliminary question," consideration of the text (of the hallucinations) rather than of the phenomenon (the neologism) modifies the contour of signification effects. It is less the presence of the signifier in the real, its "high tension," that is experienced first, than its absence in the Other. And the enigmatic feeling no longer depends on the realization of a signifier outside the chain but on the decompletion of a chain that the encounter with the signifying absence in the Other provokes: an effect of signifying equivocation that obviates common meanings. This absence initiates an intransitive "it means/it wants to say" [*ça veut dire*], an unaccomplished signification—enigmatic emptiness, s_0, degree zero of signification—soon to be doubled by an 'it means/wants to say something' [*ça veut dire quelque chose*]—signification of signification, $s(s_0)$—where the certainty of the subject that it is implicated in its being through this phenomenon is anchored. Delusional interpretation, which calls for a figure of the Other to detach itself from the darkness, finds its very condition in the psychotic structure.

One will have noticed that the intuitive phenomenon and the neologism, dealt with together in Book III of the Seminar, are distributed in two registers, belong to two different moments. The inaugural, intuitive phenomenon reveals the fault of the structure, the 'primary lesion' (Minkowski) that the psychiatrists had guessed at, the initial morbid fact that no longer has the name of elementary phenomenon. The neologism, for its part, follows its own trajectory; it is emptied of its "high tension" and becomes a mere twittering: a deflation that throws certain subjects into a frantic effort of signifying creation. The enigmatic experience is informed by structure, but it involves a diachronic dimension:[27] effect of signification, signification of signification, neologistic invention—a 'kind of weight', like 'lead in a fishing net' [*plomb dans le filet*]—which in the subject's discourse[28] arrests signification.

The examples given by Lacan to illustrate the elementary phenomenon are subject to the revision introduced to Book III of the Seminar by the "Preliminary question." For example, the delusional belief in the "perplexing *soul murder*,"[29] this fact that Schreber did not understand and yet to which he referred with certainty the outbreak of his psychosis; the neologistic term, *Seelenmord,* with which he had indexed this onset in order to formulate the unformulable moment of his fall into psychosis, became, retrospectively, the index of his inaugural encounter with the effects of foreclosure, namely, this hole in phallic signification that is written Φ_o. This experience was certainly enigmatic, affected with a signification of death that infiltrates certainty, the outcome of which will be damaging: "a disorder caused at the most personal juncture between the subject and his sense of being alive."[30]

The insult "sow," likewise, localizes and identifies a non-inaugural phenomenon, evidently secondary to the primitive experience in which the subject experienced the unspeakable effects of the phallic elision and of the subjective catastrophe that it prefigured. The said insult is an attenuated reedition of it.

In his commentary, Lacan shows the libidinal effect of the signifying lameness in the locus of the Other, and the subject's defense correlative to it: "In the place where the unspeakable object is rejected in the real, a word makes itself heard."[31] The "rejecting intention," *Verwerfung* in the Freudian sense, and the enigmatic encounter with that jouissance, will be conceptualized only after Lacan follows the "Preliminary question" up fully by situating Schreber's god as the Other who enjoys his being reduced to passivity [*son être passivé*].[32] In the experience of jouissance as enigmatic experience, the fullness of the invasion of jouissance further accentuates the emptiness of signification.[33]

Toward a Differential Clinic of the Enigmatic Experience?

The delusional intuition (whose types have been designated in classical psychiatry as ideas of reference, delusion of supposition,[34] delusion of signification,[35] early disorganized interpretations[36]) has, so far, only been considered within the category of paranoia. Is the enigmatic experience, which ties them together, observable in schizophrenia?

The crises of irreality that appeared in Renée[37]at the age of five allow for the beginning of a reply. Only after a few months did her experience of modified reality (loss of signification of surrounding objects and of the harmony between them, emancipation of each object, sense of artificiality, etc.) settle into a delusional conviction: the wind is going to acquire a particular signification. Renée supposes it to be the bearer of a message that she has to guess and that she will soon grasp the signification of: the wind is trying to make the earth jump. The initial experience is of a profoundly transformed reality, fragmented, opaque, in which each object, having no relation to the others, is reduced to its signifying skeleton, the pure non-sense that an abstract signification will resolve, without either the Other, as common denominator of significations, or the subject, whose belief there is no trace of (in the sense of personal signification), being detectable. Schizophrenic psychoses include moments of ineffable anguish, of incomprehension of the present where the idea of an approaching death is floating, without the core of a delusional belief taking root in a figure of the Other, as it is the case in paranoia.

Notes

Since many of the terms used by the author in this text have long disappeared from British psychiatry, the reader is referred to the first chapter of Lacan's third seminar on psychoses for context and elucidation.

1. J. Lacan, *Les complexes familiaux dans la formations de l'individu* (1938) (Paris: Navarin, 1984), p. 80 ; also in *Autres écrits* (Paris: Seuil, 2001).

2. J. Lacan, *De la psychose paranoïaque dans ses rapports avec la personnalité* (1932) suivi de *Premiers écrits sur la Paranoïa* (Paris: Seuil, 1975), p.147.

3. J. Lacan, *Le Séminaire, livre III, Les psychoses 1955–56* (Paris: Seuil, 1981), p. 220; *The Seminar of Jacques Lacan, Book III, The Psychoses, 1955–1956* (New York & London: Norton, 1993), p. 195.

4. J. Lacan, "D'une question préliminaire à tout traitement possible de la psychose" (1959), *Écrits* (Paris: Seuil, 1966), p. 538; "*On a question preliminary to any possible treatment of psychosis*" in *Écrits. A Selection* (London: Routledge, 1977) p. 185.

5. J.-A. Miller, *Scansions dans l'enseignement de Lacan,* course of 2 December 1981 (unpublished).

6. J. Lacan, "De nos antécédents" in *Écrits* (Paris: Seuil, 1966), p. 71.

7. J.-A. Miller, *De la nature des semblants,* course of 4 December 1991 (unpublished).

8. J. Lacan, "Présentation des Mémoires d'un névropathe" in *Autres écrits* (Paris: Seuil, 2001), pp. 213–217.

9. *De la psychose paranoïaque dans ses rapports avec la personnalité,* op.cit.

10. J.-J Moreau, known as Moreau (de Tours), *Du hachisch et de l'aliénation mentale,* 1845, reprinted in 1970, vol. II, p. 100.

11. J. Berze und H. W. Gruhle, *Psychologie der Schizophrenie* in *Monographien aus dem Gesamtgebiete der Neurologie und Psychiatrie* (Berlin: Verlag von Julius Springer, 1929), p. 66.

12. K. Jaspers, *Psychopathologie générale,* French translation of the 3rd ed. (1922) (Paris, Librairie Félix Alcan, 1938), chapter I, section 1, §1, pp. 86, 87, *General*

Psychopathology, vol. I and II, trans. by J. Hoenig and Marian W. Hamilton (Baltimore: Johns Hopkins University Press, 1997).

13. E. Minkowski, *Contribution à l'étude du syndrome d'automatisme mental* in *Annales médico-psychologiques,* No. 85 (12e série, t.1), Paris, 1927, pp.104-119.

14. E. Minkowski, *Du symptôme au trouble générateur* (1928), reprinted in *Cahiers du groupe Françoise Minkowska,* December, 1965.

15. K. Jaspers, op. cit., chapter V, section 4, §2, p. 439.

16. Lacan claims to have taken the elementary phenomenon from de Clérambault, although it is difficult to discover this term in the latter's work, at least in the volume of his collected papers; however, one finds a 'primordial phenomenon', an 'initial disorder', a 'molecular disorder of elementary thought'. 'Elementary phenomenon' is, on the other hand, present in Jaspers in op. cit.

17. A. Margulies, *Die primäre Bedeutung der Affekte im ersten Stadium der Paranoia* in *Monatsschrift für Psychiatrie und Neurologie,* No. 10, 1901, pp. 265-288.

18. T. Tiling, *Zur Paranoiafrage* in *Psychiatrische Wochenschrift,* 1902, No. 43, p. 432-435; No.44, pp. 442-445.

19. M. Westerterp, *Prozeß und Entwicklung bei verschiedenen Paranoiatypen* in *Zeitschrift für gesamte Neurologie und Psychiatrie* 91, 1924, pp. 259-380.

20. C. Neisser, *Erörterungen über Paranoia vom klinischen Standpunkte* in *Zentralblatt für Nervenheilkunde und Psychiatrie* 15, 1892, pp. 1-20.

21. On this point, cf. F. Sauvagnat, "Histoires des phénomènes élémentaires. A propos de la signification personnelle" in *Ornicar?* No. 44, Paris, 1988, pp. 19-27.

22. J. Lacan, "Exposé général de nos travaux scientifiques" in *De la psychose paranoïaque,* op. cit., p. 401.

23. J. Lacan, *Le Séminaire, livre III,* op .cit., p. 28/*Seminar III,* op. cit., p. 19.

24. J. Lacan, "Propos sur la causalité psychique" in *Écrits,* op. cit., p. 188.

25. J. Lacan, Ibid., p. 180.

26. J. Lacan, "D'une question préliminaire à tout traitement possible de la psychose," op.cit., p. 538; "On a question preliminary to any possible treatment of psychosis," op. cit., p. 185.

27. According to J.-A. Miller's remark that a clinical prescription, that a structure, must allow the inscription of the temporal factor, in *De la nature des semblants,* course (unpublished) of 3 June 1992.

28. J. Lacan, *Le Séminaire, Livre III,* op. cit., pp. 43-44/*Seminar III,* op. cit., p. 33.

29. J. Lacan, *Seminar III,* op. cit., p. 343/305.

30. J. Lacan, *Écrits,* op. cit., p. 558/201.

31. J. Lacan, *Écrits,* p. 535/183.

32. J. Lacan, "Présentation," op. cit., p. 214.

33. C. Soler, *L'expérience énigmatique du sujet: de Schreber à Joyce,* exposé à la Section clinique le 22 avril 1992, *La Cause freudienne,* No. 23.

34. Perplexed uncertainty, delusional doubts (Tanzi) characterize this form of delusion of interpretation according to P. Serieux and J. Capgras, *Les folies raisonnnantes. Le délire d'interprétation* (Marseille: Lafitte, 1909/1982), p. 168.

35. K. Jaspers, K., op.cit., p. 89.

36. I. Meyerson and P. Quercy, "Des interprétations frustes" in *Journal de psychologie normale et pathologique,* No. 17, 1920, pp. 811–822.

37. M.-A. Sechehaye, *Journal d'une schizophrène* (Paris: P.U.F., 1969; 1950); Marguerite Sechehaye, *Autobiography of a Schizophrenic Girl: The True Story of 'Renée'* (New York: Signet Books, 1951; reprint edition Meridian, 1994).

Three Enigmas: Meaning, Signification, Jouissance

Eric Laurent

"Je ne suis pas ce que je suis, car, si j'étais ce que je suis, je ne serais pas ce que je suis."[1] This is an enigma proposed in *Le Moniteur* and the solution to the enigma is a "servant" who, if he did not follow his master, would not have to be a servant and be what he follows.

What is the thing that one receives without thanks, which one enjoys without knowing how, that one gives to others when one does not know where one is at, and that one loses without noticing? It's life.

This is shared experience, that of the enigma that presents itself as a question. The enigma according to Littré is "the definition of things in obscure terms but which, taken together, exclusively designate their object and are given to be divined."[2]

The enigma, this definition of things in obscure terms, has for a long time been an elective path for the discourse of the Master. We are told that among the first Babylonian kingdoms, the first city states, the masters exchanged enigmas between them and stole from one another the soothsayers skilled in their fabrication or resolution. The Bible tells us how the Queen of Sheba, having heard about Solomon's great reputation, came to Jerusalem to experience his great wisdom, armed with enigmas. Such is the path she took to find out whether he was a man, a real one.

Why should one choose to pursue the study of paranoia and schizophrenia through the enigma? Is psychosis not par excellence the domain in which what is present is certainty, delusion, where everything is explained according to an order of reason, giving substance to the classic adage: "The madman has lost everything but reason." Why this title then, since it is rather neurosis that pertains to an enigmatic experience? Oedipus was chosen by Freud as the emblem of all human beings, of himself, and of neurotics. As early as 15 October 1897, this is what Freud wrote to Fliess: "I have found, in my own case too, falling in love with the mother and jealousy towards my father, and I now regard it as a universal event of early childhood, even if not so early as in children who have been made hysterical. (Similarly with the romance of parentage in paranoia—heroes, founders of religions.) If that is so, we can understand the riveting effect of *Oedipus Rex,* in spite of all the objections raised by reason against its presupposition of destiny . . . . Each member of the audience was once, in germ and in fantasy, just such an Oedipus, and each one recoils in horror from the dream-fulfilment here transplanted into reality, with the whole quota of repression which separates his infantile state from his present one." [3]

What is *Oedipus Rex,* if not the story of the deciphering of an enigma, as well as of the impossibility for the one who had deciphered it of knowing what it implied for his destiny?

We note that, from the outset, Freud knots paranoiac delusion, founding hero of religion and the Oedipal question. (I draw your attention to the fact that in the French version of the letters to Fliess, "romantization" is used for "delusion of filiation.") Whether it concerns neurosis or psychosis, psychoanalytic work rests on the establishment of a meaning, a *Deutung,* an interpretation.

Meaning

In the Freudian study of the *Memoirs* of President Schreber, the second part follows the explanation of Schreber's path and the recall of his biography. This part, which is entitled "Attempts at interpretation," begins as follows: "There are two angles from which we could attempt to reach an understanding of this history . . . and to lay bare in it the familiar complexes and motive forces of mental life. We might start either from the patient's own delusional utterances or from the exciting causes of his illness." [4]

Freud adopts the first angle: "It is perhaps worth giving a more detailed illustration of this procedure . . . the so-called 'miracled birds'. . . . They cannot understand the meaning of the words they speak, but they are by nature susceptible to similarity of sounds." [5] Thus, Freud travels along what he calls the explanation of the universe produced by the paranoiac in these terms: "patient has withdrawn from the people in his environment and from the external world generally the libidinal cathexis which he has hitherto directed on to them. Thus everything has become indifferent and irrelevant to him, and has to be explained by means of a secondary rationalisation":6 he has to explain the universe to himself. And the paranoiac reconstructs the universe by means of his delusional work. There is thus a production, by the paranoiac subject, of a whole world, using phenomena of meaning as starting points, their transformations, their distributions. If Freud emphasizes this positive, productive side of psychotic phenomena, he evidently does not ignore their foundation in the negative, and he adds: "the process of repression proper consists in a detachment of the libido from people. . . . It happens silently; we receive no intelligence of it. . . . What forces itself so noisily upon our attention is the process of recovery, which undoes the work of repression and brings back the libido again on to the people it had abandoned."7

Freud articulates this experience of silent detachment as part of a series of different phenomena: confusion, perplexity, and so on. This is where the experience of an enigma is situated for the paranoiac, since for him the whole world becomes a world of obscure things, organized in a way that has been lost and that has to be reconstructed so that they eventually come to designate something.

These two movements, reconstruction and preliminary loss, are summarized by Freud in his 1911 text in an aphorism: "What was abolished internally [aufhebt] reappears from without."8 It is with the same mechanism that thirteen years later, in 1924, after having introduced the id and the superego in "The loss of reality in neurosis and psychosis," he will conclude his text: "Thus we see that both in neurosis and psychosis there comes into consideration the question not only of a *loss of reality* but also of a *substitute for reality.*"9 These two sides, loss and reconstruction, are intimately linked for Freud without, however, the structure of the experience of loss ever being distinct, in his work, from that of reinvestment.

In Freud's work, there is no idea of an experience of decomposition of the ego functions, or again of a hierarchical regression of the different functions according to the definition given by Ribot of depersonalization in 1894, a definition taken up again by Dugas. Ribot will retain his idea until 1915, throughout the sixteen editions of his treatise, and will keep to this approach in academic psychopathology.

Freud refused to separate the experience of loss from that of return, considering both to be taken up in what he called the distribution of libido, which he entirely describes as a phenomenon of meaning. It is exactly on this point that Lacan's thesis will take up the opposition between abolition of meaning and dissolution of functions. Lacan's thesis of 1932 is preceded by his article "The structure of paranoid psychoses" in the *Semaine des Hôpitaux* in 1931. This thesis, he says, expresses a conception that is founded "neither on the *sentiment* of personal synthesis, such as one sees disturbed in the subjective troubles of depersonalization . . . nor on the psychological unity given by *individual conscience* . . . nor on the extension of memory phenomena"[10] but, on the contrary, on *relations of comprehension* . . . and further on, "Let us define the characters specific to *delusional interpretation* . . . it presents itself moreover as a *gripping* experience, as a specific *illumination,* a character that early authors, whose scrutiny was not veiled by any psychological theory, had in mind when they designated this symptom with the excellent term of phenomenon of *"personal signification."*[11]

This thesis, constructed against any idea leaning against the dissolution of a synthesis or the continuity of a personality and a constitution, places, on the contrary, all the emphasis on the emergence of a new signification, a productive phenomenon certainly, a phenomenon that is not deficient, but nonetheless proposes itself to the subject as an enigma to be deciphered. This signification, if it is articulated, is not immediately articulable, and the subject will deploy it for the duration of his delusion. Lacan thus proposes an investigative method inspired by Jaspers; a method of investigation that starts with the most comprehensible psychoses and moves on to discordant psychoses.

We will now distinguish three parts in Lacan's approach to this question of the enigmatic experience in psychoses. The first part will be "Propos sur la causalité psychique," or enigma and meaning. The second part will be "Function and field of speech and language in psychoanalysis" up to *Seminar III, The psychoses,* which could be entitled: from enigma to signification. The third part goes from the text that Lacan wrote as a preface to the writings of President Schreber in *Cahiers pour l'analyse* in 1967 to "Joyce-le-symptôme" (1975).

Enigma and Meaning

Let us start with "Propos sur la causalité psychique," in which Lacan takes up his thesis again after the war for the first time, having abstained from publishing during the war. One forgets how singular a position that was, not to publish during the war; eminent spirits such as Merleau-Ponty and Sartre had continued to do so. Lacan made it clear that he would wait for "the disappearance of the enemies of mankind from the soil of his fatherland" to take up the thread of his thinking. He had chosen to express himself in 1949 before the public of *L'Evolution psychiatrique,* composed of young psychiatrists whom he calls a "young academia," and there he exposed anew the advances present in his thesis, simply stripped of the respect due to the authors he had to explore and oppose at the time. He recalls that "madness is lived entirely in the register of meaning. . . . The phenomenon of madness is not separable from the problem of signification for being in general, that is to say from language for man."[12] Faced with the organo-dynamic thesis that aims to isolate a first experience of loss, of dissolution—however one calls it—whose cause would be organic, and which is then followed by a psychic reconstruction, Lacan maintains there is a unique psychic causality. He exposes, on the one hand, a phenomenon of rupture that he notes to be a decision, "unfathomable decision of the being through which it understands or misrecognises its liberation,"[13] and on the other an experience homogenous in its structure of the reconquest of being, which will be the unfolding of madness itself.

Thus, he can say that all the phenomena of psychosis "whatever they be, hallucinations, interpretations, intuitions, and with whatever extraneousness and strangeness they may be experienced by him, these phenomena target him personally: they redouble him, reply to him, echo him, read in him, just as he identifies them, interrogates them, provokes them and deciphers them. And when he comes to lack all means of expressing them, his perplexity still manifests to us an interrogative gap in him."[14]

How best to isolate the enigmatic experience in psychoses, paranoia, and schizophrenia, since Lacan does not distinguish them on this point? He evokes *psychosis,* since he can designate it in the singular whereas he isolates *phenomena* in the plural, *psychosis* is played out in the register of meaning. Under the heading of madness, he specifically underlines this unity in front of the attentive ears of those present, members of *L'Evolution Psychiatrique* whose project it was "to accustom" French psychiatry to the concept of schizophrenia. He knew that his choice to continue approaching psychosis from the angle of paranoia rather than from that of schizophrenia, and to conserve the name of madness, amounted to affirming his distance.

Having defined this madness entirely in terms of phenomena of meaning, he could add that his discussion aimed at nothing less than "the heart of the dialectic of being." This is the term he uses and it is on this point that the essential misrecognition of madness lies. It is from this perspective that the ego can be defined as a central system for the formations of misrecognition and not as a synthesis of the relational functions of the organism. Lacan criticizes what links "the organicist illusion to a realist metapsychology,"[15] the link between the organicist illusion of the loss of relational functions to a realist metapsychology through which these relational functions would ensure a relation with the real. This critique of realist metapsychology is still relevant today since one of the effects of science on our world is certainly to dissolve the naive realism according to which an organism and the world would adapt themselves to each other. It makes the real retreat ever further, to express myself like Despagnat, an epistemologist whose position has been amusingly termed "depressed realist" in his books—for example, in his work entitled *In search of the real.*

Enigma and Signification

Lacan will transform the notion of madness as taken up entirely in phenomena of meaning by insisting on the fact that madness is taken up entirely in a phenomenon of language. As early as in "Function and field in speech and language," Lacan introduces a new term, which had not appeared in "Propos sur la causalité psychique," that of symbolic function, with which he now designates phenomena of meaning and their support. He says that it is "in the *name of the father* that we must recognize the support of the symbolic function."[16]

In this text he gives a new definition of madness as "negative freedom of speech that has given up trying to make itself recognized . . . [with] the singular formation of a delusion which . . . objectifies the subject in a language without dialectic."[17] From then on, the distribution of meaning phenomena takes place differently, and the experience of the enigma will be centered differently by Lacan. We will see it in his 1958 text, "On a question preliminary to any possible treatment of psychosis," in which he shows that it is the very nature of the signifier that becomes the object of communication in psychosis. The phenomena of meaning in Schreber's psychosis will be distributed between message phenomena and code phenomena. Schreber's fundamental language teaches him, instructs him on how it is done, on what the new signifier that comes into the world to reconstruct it is made of. This phenomenon allows Lacan to add that it is the very signifier that is the object of communication. "We are presented here with phenomena that have wrongly been called intuitive. . . . What is involved here is in fact an effect of the signifier, insofar as its degree of certainty . . . assumes a weight proportional to the enigmatic void that first presents itself in the place of the signification itself."[18] So there the enigmatic void of signification is knotted in a new way to the raising to the power of a second stage that certainty provides. So first, there is elision and void, then there is certainty. The emptier the void, the greater the certainty. In this text, Lacan will take up the whole series of phenomena that he had established in "Propos sur la causalité psychique": interpretation, hallucinations, perplexity, all that and also the "tensions, the lapses, the phantasies that the analyst encounters . . . it should be added, by means of elements of the particular discourse in which this question is articulated in the Other. . . . their chain is found to survive in an alterity in relation to the subject as radical as that of as yet indecipherable hieroglyphs in the solitude of the desert."[19] The presentation of delusion itself, and of its experience, will be that of a deciphering of these hieroglyphics in the subject's attempt at answering the production of these new significations.

To qualify the position of the psychoanalyst, Lacan says: "We must listen to the speaker when it is a question of a message that does not come from a subject beyond language, but from speech beyond the subject."[20] What would seem possible there nevertheless remains enigmatic in the degree of effectiveness of speech on the structuration of the subject, since what is being listened to is a speech that comes from beyond him. In a way that is perhaps enigmatic for the reader, Lacan refers back to the work of President Schreber, who could declare with relief that all non-sense annuls itself, *alles Unsinn aufhebt.* The path traced there by Lacan for analytic action remains enigmatic in this text and will only find a solution much later with Joyce. Let us simply remember that from the moment at which madness is centered around language phenomena, Lacan displaces the emphasis from sense to non-sense. The two are distributed according to the instance of the letter, which is fundamentally outside of sense.

In Seminar III, which preceded "On a question preliminary . . . ," Lacan insisted on the point, that, contrary to what Wernicke had claimed, a delusion is not the explication of a primitive experience. He strongly underlines that elementary phenomena already have the structure of the delusion, and that delusion has exactly the same structure as the elementary phenomenon.[21]

This page of the Seminar goes back exactly to what had been said in a page of Lacan's thesis, where he grounded the homology of structure on the metaphor of the leaf and the tree: "this striking structural identity between the elementary phenomena of delusion and its general organization imposes an analogical reference to the type of morphogenesis materialized by the plant."[22]

This is why it is possible to speak of an enigmatic experience in Lacan, an enigmatic experience in the elementary phenomena that precede the triggering, and that it is without doubt legitimate to speak of nontriggered psychosis. When Lacan says that delusion and elementary phenomena have the same structure, it does not mean that between someone who has entrenched phenomena that remain limited to that for thirty years, and a fully deployed delusion, we are speaking about exactly the same thing. It means that it is exactly the same thing from the point of view of the structure of meaning. That said, its full weight must be given to the discontinuous experience of triggering, an experience that underlines the conception that Lacan took from Jaspers who, beyond a nosographic definition, called schizophrenia a conception of psychosis that marks a discontinuity. "This term theoretically designates all the mental illnesses whose process begins at a definite moment."[23]

Enigma and Jouissance

From 1967, in the preface he writes to Schreber's *Memoirs,* Lacan reformulates "Freud's operation" on psychosis. He notes that, if Freud turns President Schreber's memoirs into a Freudian text, it is because he introduces there "the subject as such, which means not evaluating the madman in terms of deficit and of dissociation of functions."[24]

This is what he recognized as Freud's merit, and it is what he had himself recognized in his "On a question preliminary. . . ." But at this point he adds, "To give credit to the psychotic would amount to nothing more in this case than what would remain of any other treated just as liberally: to force an open door has absolutely nothing to do with knowing onto what space it will open."[25] It is a critique. It is a critique, or at least a complement that Lacan wants to bring. He will underline the importance of jouissance phenomena in Schreber, approached in this short preface from the perspective of the object *a*.

Over ten years ago, driven by Jacques-Alain Miller's compelling introduction, the year's work of the clinical section was dedicated to the introduction of the object "petit *a*" in the reading of President Schreber. That year we were able to reread the precious indications given by Lacan on the question of jouissance in psychosis, and on the place to be given to the singular term in this text of "subject of jouissance," as distinct from "subject represented by the signifier."[26]

This expression, which had not been taken up again by Lacan, had the merit of clarity for the audience, who nonetheless completely missed it at the time. Still, eventually, fifteen years later, the clinical section took it up. This is the delay that Lacan considered to be normal for the reading of his texts.

The whole consideration of Schreber's text could be that of an enigma in a third sense, not only the enigma of meaning, not only the enigma of signification, but also the enigma of the jouissance of God. What is enigmatic for Schreber is that God or the Other should enjoy his passive being and that he should support this. What surprises him is that it is sufficient that he should abandon himself to "thinking of nothing," *nichts denken,* for God, this Other made of an infinite discourse, to slip away and that from "this torn text that he himself becomes, a scream should arise,"[27] a scream that no longer had anything to do with any subject. He experienced himself as an isolated subject, One, in relation with a jouissance full to the point of becoming the point of jouissance of the universe. He becomes this subject who experiences the mystery of seeing himself as the repository for all the little experiences of jouissance of the souls of the universe, which allows Lacan to add "which will allow us to come up with a more precise definition of paranoia as identifying jouissance in the locus of the Other as such."[28]

Here we witness the emergence of a central distinction, on the basis of jouissance, between a signifying mechanism common to the psychoses, foreclosure, and the diverse destinies of jouissance. This is what Jacques-Alain Miller pointed out in a course on schizophrenia and paranoia, noting that in this 1965 definition we have a perfectly valid definition of paranoia, while that of schizophrenia remained to be found. We find it in *L'Étourdit* in 1973, when Lacan, referring to, dialoguing with, and rectifying the position taken the year before by Deleuze and

Guattari in their *Anti-Oedipus,* speaks of the schizophrenic's relation to the organ. It so happens that Deleuze and Guattari had found it useful to distinguish a "body without organs" in schizophrenia and that this seemed to them to be a major concept, affording a possible liberation from the ascendancy of the signifier. Lacan replies to them in *L'Étourdit.* "What becomes an organ for his body . . . , this is even the starting point for him to be reduced to realizing that his body is not without other organs, and that each of their functions is a problem for him; accordingly, the said schizophrenic can be characterized as being caught without the help of any established discourse."[29] In bringing together the two definitions, the return of jouissance in the Other qualifying paranoia, and the return of jouissance in the body that completes, we obtain a distribution of the enigmatic experiences of jouissance in paranoia and schizophrenia.

So we have quite a distinct distribution across these different periods: phenomena of meaning and their emptying, the place of the excess of signification, and that of the excess of jouissance. However, we had to wait for the new definition that Lacan gives of the symptom in the seminar *RSI,* a definition later developed in "Joyce-the-symptôme," for the insertion of jouissance, the distribution of meaning and of jouissance to occur differently than in "On a question preliminary. . . ." In this text, Lacan could speak of the role of fantasy in President Schreber insofar at it was distributed between two poles: that of transsexual jouissance, that of the future of the creature. The place of the fantasy is still defined according to the effects of signification. The fantasy is taken as an effect of signification interfering in the chain going from the signification of need to the Ideal. In *RSI* and "Joyce-le-symptôme" this is no longer the case. The symptom is produced in the same register as the miracle of the scream isolated in 1965, which no longer had anything to do with any subject. The symptom, or sinthome, as underlined in the introduction to the volume *Joyce avec Lacan,* is introduced so that the "symptom does not say anything to anybody: it is ciphering and it is pure jouissance of writing," to use J.A. Miller's expression.[30]

The symptom is then no longer defined in relation to effects of signification, or even to a signification outside of dialectic, but in the register of writing, which is the way in which each subject enjoys the unconscious insofar as the unconscious determines him or her.

This new definition of the symptom affects that of the fantasy, which it puts in another place. The fantasy finds itself no longer an intersection in a chain directed toward a subject, but it echoes, as distinct from the symptom, a way of enjoying the unconscious that is no longer determined by it. We can find a clinical translation of this in noticing, in the context of extremely varied psychoses, the presence of perverse experiences, of fantasies acted with a great ease that contrast in this very ease, in this *laissez-être,* with the rigor of the delusion.

It is from here, from this introduction of the letter insofar as it abolishes the symbol, that we can now return to what Lacan had underlined in Schreber: Schreber's relief at being able to note that all non-sense annuls itself . . . *alles Unsinn aufhebt,* this is Schreber's central enigmatic experience, or the *Unsinn* with which he is confronted. This is precisely what can be abolished in the experience of constructing his delusion, a construction that owes everything to the letter, to writing, and so little to speech. It is the construction of a delusion that endeavors to be its own reference. It is what renders attempts at interpretation derisory—as if the productions of writing led to a subject. Lacan does not interpret the production of President Schreber; he shows its coherence, its consistency. Similarly, Jakobson, as a linguist interested in the productions of Hölderlin, does not aim to do the least exegesis of the poet, distinguishing himself on this point from Blanchot. He simply aims to explore why Hölderlin's later poems were better than those written before the breakdown. These were in the same vein, but they were even simpler, or more self-conscious about their poetic effects.[31]

The delusional work can be conceived thus: to construct the letter with the aid of the letter to the point where it can abolish the symbol and so really raise it to a second power. This is what will make its coexistence compatible with the absence of support, not of an established discourse, but of any established Name-of-the-Father.

Notes

1. In French "je suis" could either refer to the verb "to be" or the verb "to follow." Thus "I am" and "I follow" are two meanings of "je suis"; hence, the equivocation with which the paper opens: "I am/follow not what I am/follow, for if I was what I am/follow, I would not be what I am/follow" [TN].

2. *Littré Dictionary* (Paris: 1878).

3. S. Freud, "Letter 71 to W. Fliess" (15 October 1897), SE I, p. 265.

4. S. Freud, *Psychoanalytic Notes on an Autobiographical account of a case of para-noia (Dementia paranoides) (Schreber),* SE XII, p. 35.

5. Ibid. at pp. 35-36.

6. Ibid. at p. 70.

7. Ibid. at p. 71.

8. Ibid.

9. S. Freud, "The loss of reality in neurosis and psychosis," SE XIX, p. 187.

10. J. Lacan, *De la psychose paranoïaque dans ses rapports avec la personnalité* (Paris: Seuil, 1975), pp. 43-44.

11. Ibid. at p. 211.

12. J. Lacan, "Propos sur la causalité psychique," *Écrits* (Paris: Seuil, 1966), p. 166.

13. Ibid. at p. 177.

14. Ibid. at p. 165.

15. Ibid. at p. 178.

16. J. Lacan, "Function and Field of Speech in Psychoanalysis," *Écrits* (London: Routledge, 1977), p. 67.

17. Ibid. at pp. 68-69.

18. J. Lacan, "On a question preliminary to any possible treatment of psychosis," *Écrits,* op. cit. p. 185.

19. Ibid. at p. 194.

20. Ibid. at p. 214.

21. J. Lacan, *Séminaire III,* p. 28 ; *Seminar III,* p. 19.

22. J. Lacan, *De la psychose paranoïaque dans ses rapports avec la personnalité,* op. cit. p. 297, note 58.

23. K. Jaspers, *Strindbergh et Van Gogh* (Paris: Editions de Minuit, 1953), p. 38.

24. J. Lacan, "Présentation," *Cahiers pour l'analyse* 5 (novembre/décembre 1966), p. 70.

25. Ibid.

26. Ibid.

27. Ibid.

28. Ibid.

29. J. Lacan, "L'Étourdit," *Scilicet 4* (Paris: Seuil, 1973), p. 30; also in *Autres écrits* (Paris: Seuil, 2001), p. 474.

30. J.-A. Miller, "Préface," *Joyce avec Lacan* (Paris: Navarin, 1978), p. 11.

31. R. Jakobson, "Un regard sur La Vue de Hölderlin," *Russie folie poésie* (Paris: Seuil, 1986).

A Child through the Mirror

Gabriela van den Hoven

Lacan is going to extract a new signification from the experience of an infant in front of the mirror. In the field of psychology this phase has already been observed as part of a progressive and evolutionary stage in the development of a child. Lacan is going to give it a new interpretation. He will bestow on it a new meaning that will not add up to the others, or complete them, but a meaning that will strengthen the importance of the phenomenon at stake. And with it he will modify the idea of the formation of the psychical personality.

At first sight, "mirror stage" appears to be a description of the genesis of the psychological subject. In any case, that is the way it was understood within the field of psychology, the tradition Lacan could not ignore. In 1931, in the *Journal de psychologie,* Wallon publishes "Comment se développe chez l'enfant la notion de corps propre" ("Development of Self-awareness in a Child").[1] Wallon's paper is a psychological one. For Wallon, this phase revolves around the notion of knowing and recognizing reality. It is for him a moment in the cognitive development of a child that will culminate in the acknowledgment of reality. The fact that the child doesn't have the same understanding as an adult is judged by Wallon to be a defect. It is a dysfunction that has to be overcome. Wallon's conception of psychical personality remains tied to a finalist notion. Psychic development is, in his view, a slow but progressive one toward objective knowledge and social life.

However, Lacan does not interpret this phase from the perspective of a positive achievement or adaptation to reality. In his text "The Mirror Stage," Lacan speaks of "the formation of the I as we experience it in psychoanalysis. It is an experience that leads us to oppose any philosophy directly issuing from the *Cogito.*"[2]

The effect of the phenomenon that hits the subject when confronted with its image has an impact that goes beyond any notion of psychological maturation. Lacan says "as we experience it in psychoanalysis," which means that it is only from the patient's discourse, and not through observation, that we will be able to reconstruct and have an idea of how a particular subject has gone through this phase. Only through the patient's discourse will we learn how his ego has been formed. The analyst's interest is not the detailed date and classification of what the child does or does not, but the effects that the image has on the infant.

Lacan explains in "The Mirror Stage" that the human infant, in contrast to the chimpanzee of the same age, is able to recognize as such his own image in a mirror. Not only does he recognize his image, but he also assumes it, in Lacan's terms, "in a flutter of jubilant activity."[3] The fact that the infant finds a source of enjoyment and excitement in the image implies that he has recognized in it something that concerns him. The proof is that the child begins a systematic activity of gesticulation and variation of postures, accompanied by a jubilation that prolongs the first "Ha!" of recognition. The image appears to the infant as a gestalt—the concept Lacan takes from M. Merleau-Ponty and phenomenology. Gestalt is understood in psychology as follows: the complete figure is more than its parts added up. When Lacan uses this term, he emphasizes the importance of the image as complete, to the detriment of the different elements that form it.

He says: "The fact is that the total form of the body by which the subject anticipates in a mirage the maturation of his power is given to him only as *Gestalt,* that is to say, in an exteriority in which this form is certainly more constituent than constituted, but in which it appears to him above all in a contrasting size that fixes it and in a symmetry that inverts it, in contrast with the turbulent movements that the subject feels are animating him."[4]

We are far from Wallon's "faithful reflection of reality" that would make an objective knowledge possible. The infant will experience a tension between the image, the gestalt, and its motor insufficiency. He is not able to recognize himself as one, as a unity, by taking into account his body's multiple vegetative sensations. Adults lack that capability as well. If we try to feel the unity of our body, we will soon realize that it is impossible to achieve a uniform sensation. There is always something that stands out; it can be a pain, an itch, and so on. If people spend so much time trying to feel their body (yoga, massage therapy, meditation, etc.), it is simply because we fail to do so.

I said that there was a tension between the unity of the image and the motor insufficiency. Such a tension implies a rivalry with the image, an aggressive tension. However, what is more important to us is that the rivalry is experienced by infants as a threat of body fragmentation, and it is this fear that precipitates infants to identification. It is as if the child said, "I'd rather be a mirage than a fragmented body." The infant experiences its body as fragmented in opposition to its image. It is then, in relation to the fantasies of corporal fragmentation, that the mirror stage can be read. We find its logic there: it's the law of anticipation/insufficiency.

Lacan says that there is a symbolic matrix in which the ego finds its identification. The symbolic matrix is the mother's desire that gives the infant his place, as imaginary phallus—that is, the imaginary phallus is the image with which the subject identifies. The subject turns to an 'other' that is its image. It is the place of alienation and misrecognition that explains why the subject always demands recognition, given that no one can have the certainty of being one's own image. The demand for recognition is to make the image consistent.

From the subject's point of view, the little others have all the virtues of the image, its unity and good shape. They appear to be equal to their image, seem to fully coincide with it, and, as such, occupy the place of the phallus. We know that narcissism supposes the existence of only one unique place, the place of the imaginary phallus. This implies for the subject a threat to unity that will lead to aggressivity as a way to fragment the other in order to be able to stand in its place. Such a threat, hanging on the subject's ego, is persecutory and paranoiac.

I will now present a case in which a failure of identification can be read.

Victor is ten years old, lives with his mother, younger sister, and grandmother. The school psychologist referred him for a consultation. His parents refuse to believe that something could be wrong with him. Even though his teacher says that he harms himself, and that he is not able to perform any of the expected work, his parents think that this can't be true and the problem is that they do not accept him in his difference.

In a preliminary interview his father said: "I think that he is OK. He is in good shape, and eats well. But he is not like everyone else, he doesn't play football, nor fulfils the expectations people have of him.

That is what the teacher said and that is the reason why we are here. So I have to say that I think we are wasting our time here and that this is a chit-chat."

The father's attitude to treatment appears very hostile. I began to wonder whether I should invite him to come for an interview or wait for his demand.

Victor's mother says: "I want to know what happens to Victor, how to deal with him. He is very different from me. I do not know why, perhaps it has to do with the delivery. He was born with the umbilical cord wrapped around his neck. He was black. I saw him and I thought, is this black rat mine?! They took him away. How could I understand that I gave birth to a black baby? But now, he is *blanco sotano* [which literally translates as "white basement"]. He was black, but then, when he was brought back to me in the afternoon, he was albino."

In my understanding, Victor's mother has a different attitude to treatment. She says that she wants to know. However, I wonder whether she lacks knowledge about her son, or whether it is rather the lack of knowledge that she is not prepared to bear. After this interview, I invite the mother to come once more, before I meet Victor. She accepts.

She says: "I got pregnant in the same month my father died. I chose the name 'Victor' because this was my father's name. He was born a day after my father's birthday. I did not know for a long time that I was pregnant. The doctor said: "When somebody in the family is ill, then others tend to come up with all sorts of symptoms."

She continues: "The kids at school take the piss out of him and discriminate against him. They talk about football and girls, but Victor is not interested in these things. He is infantile, he is between six and seven. He still wants to play. He is interested in designing a bomb that would destroy the world, but not the plants. He speaks about things that I do not understand. He invents things. He believes everything he sees in the cartoons. He is interested in inventing."

We said earlier that the ego identifies with a symbolic matrix, and also that the symbolic matrix is the mother's desire that will give the infant a place as imaginary phallus—an image with which the subject identifies. However, Victor does not seem to be in the place of the imaginary phallus. In fact, I do not hear anything in the maternal discourse that could remind me of any of the gloss that is usually attached to the imaginary phallus. His mother said that for a long time she did not know that she was pregnant.

Lacan says in "Deux notes sur l'enfant" that for there to be subjective constitution, "the relationship to a desire that is not anonymous"[5] is necessary.

Before the infant is born, his mother has all sorts of fantasies and desires that will mark him in one way or another. These fantasies find their material support in words, and are intertwined, constituting a symbolic-imaginary net. When this intertwined symbolic-imaginary is missing, the subject occupies the place of the object *a* in his mother's fantasy. However, to be a subject as subjected to a fantasy, the subject must not be the object of the Other's fantasy.

I decided to see Victor to find out more. Victor's movements are rigid and robotic. He speaks like a character from a cartoon. He doesn't like to play, and says that he wants to invent things.

He says: "This is a laboratory, but do not mention it, do not mention that word."

Analyst: "Which word?"

Victor: "The red fluid." He spells b-l-o-o-d, and adds: "I could pass out. In the year 2003 there is not going to be any water. A comet is going to kill us all. I do not like laboratories, but I am not going to say anything about my experience of it. I'm thinking of other things, I'm thinking of the tramps."

I invite him to do some drawings, but Victor doesn't want to touch anything; pencils can be electrified, and chairs can be traps. He didn't want to sit down. Finally he said, "I do not know how to draw people, I know how to draw plans."

After this first interview, what caught my attention is the peculiar way in which he speaks. He seems to be representing a figure of the cartoon at all times, while at the same time it seems to help him to detach himself from things. His difficulty in drawing human beings anticipated his problematic relationship to his body.

During one of the interviews that follows, he picked up a stethoscope that was in the consulting room and, looking at it, asked me what it was used for. I explained that it is used by doctors to hear heartbeat. He carefully placed the stethoscope on his heart to listen. After holding it for a few seconds he said "It disgusts me," and asked me to let him leave the room. At this point, I suggest that he should try to explain to me what he felt. He replies: "I feel sick, I want to leave, it is better for everybody, I could go mad."

Listening to his heartbeat was a traumatic excess of jouissance in the real of the body whose effect was the vanishing of the imaginary identification. We know that, in psychosis, the image is not consistent, given that it is not supported by a symbolic identification. In the case of this patient, the image that usually covers and interdicts the access to the object fails in its function, and the subject has a direct relationship with its reality as object. It is worth pointing out that the object *a* does not reflect in the mirror. It cannot be reflected, because what characterizes it is the fact that it is lost. The object *a* is not therefore part of the narcissistic image. However, the object *a* sometimes manages to break through the image and make its presence felt in a way that produces an uncanny effect, as we can see in this case. The image can only remain unified when the object is outside. As we know, Lacan writes it between brackets *i*[*a*].

On another occasion Victor speaks as an E.T. that recognizes a human being. We play and I intervene by repeating what he says in different tones of voice, sometimes as human, another time as an E.T. trying to produce a fissure that would allow him to speak with his own voice. My intervention, even though it was based on transference, was not an interpretation. It was made up to be accepted or refused. It was a maneuver through which I intended to detach, to des-identify the subject from the place of the object and to regulate jouissance. I would be the scribe of his 'new symbolic story'.

Victor was for his mother something that disturbs her, something that she was unable to name and place in a lineage: "How could I understand that I had a black baby?," "Is this black rat mine?" He embodies then the object of the maternal fantasy, making it impossible for him to be a subject subjected to a fantasy. How does he deal with it? He stabilizes himself and obtains an imaginary identity through his identification with the cartoon figure. After a few sessions pass, Victor starts to write letters on a typewriter. Sometimes he writes letters, and sometimes words that overlap, without leaving any space between them.

He asked: "Guess what it says?"

Analyst: "I don't understand, can you help me?" With his help, I manage to spell his name.

Victor: "It is in a code. I don't want to be discovered."

He writes again and says with joy: "Victor, Victor, Manuel, Martin, ten years old."

In the next sessions, he continues to write, asking me to circle the scrambled word that I could single out. He writes, for instance: shit, *Xuxa,* cow. I respond doing both: what he asked me to do, which was to single out the jumbled words, and to integrate those words in a sentence "A boy is not a shit," "A boy is not a cow."

Victor's writing suggests to me the idea of the holophrase. It is a space with no holes to which he seems to be attached. There is no articulation of S_1 and S_2. My function will be to offer him a different sentence that contains negation and, in doing so, I pretend to produce something of the order of separation to detach him from the petrified signifiers that come from the Other.

"Words come from the Other. The ego makes that message its message through negation, but when this function and its consequence, the subjective attribution, fails, the analyst believes in assisting the volatilisation of the subject, without realizing that the subject has become real."[6]

Notes

1. H. Wallon, *Journal de Psychologie*, Vol. 27:705–748, 1931.

2. J. Lacan, "The Mirror Stage as Formative of the Function of the I as Revealed in Psychoanalytic Experience" in *Écrits: A Selection* (London: Routledge, 1977), p. 1.

3. Ibid., p. 2.

4. Ibid.

5. J. Lacan, "Deux notes sur l'enfant" in *Ornicar?* No. 37, Navarin, Paris, 1986; also in *Autres écrits* (Paris: Seuil, 2001).

6. Rosine and Robert Lefort, "Psicosis y significantes." *Articulaciones. El Analiticon* No. 3, Barcelona.

PART IV

Jouissance, the Object, Anxiety

Jacques Lacan and the Voice

Jacques-Alain Miller

Jacques Lacan gave a specific place to the voice in psychoanalysis.[1] I will focus my interest on the ways through which he came, in his teaching, to give the voice the status of an object, named object little *a* in what he called his algebra.

It seems to me that this is an innovation in psychoanalysis. Indeed, since Freud, Abraham, Melanie Klein, the psychoanalytic tradition had circumscribed the function of the object but only to stress two objects, nowadays very well known beyond psychoanalytic practice: the oral object and the anal object, supposed to be successively prevalent in the chronology of development—the development of the individual or, more precisely, that of his libido as it is finalized through its convergence toward the genital object.

In other words, the function of the object did not await Lacan to be situated, but these two objects were inscribed in developmental stages. And it is a fact of the history of psychoanalysis that the object voice remained unnoticed as long as the prevailing perspective remained the diachronic, chronological point of view of object relation. The object voice did not appear in psychoanalysis until the perspective was organized by a structural viewpoint.

What is the structural viewpoint in psychoanalysis? It is the viewpoint inaugurated by Lacan—he is not the only one to have endorsed it—giving the unconscious its status through the structure of language as presented by Saussure and developed by Jakobson. This viewpoint consists in canceling questions of genesis from the outset and, in so doing, operating a separation in the theory of the development of libido between, on the one hand, what the genetic viewpoint entails—namely, the theory of stages still in use—and, on the other hand, what the stages covered and cloaked—namely, the two objects that are there, issued from this catastrophe.

So the structural viewpoint also forces us to reconsider the notion of the individual as support of development, and substitute another concept for it, that of the subject—which is not the support of development, not even the support of structure, but which is exactly what the structure supposes. In this way, this subject is the subject of the signifier; it is the only thing that we can know about it: it is supposed by the structure of language. Thus, the theses of genetic development give way to the thesis of the structural causation of the subject. The object is thereby torn away from the diachronic frame where it was initially inscribed in psychoanalysis, to be located within the operations of the subject's causation. The problem of the object is no longer a temporal problem. It is no longer formulated in terms of succession—progression or regression—but in structural terms.

How is the function of the object, as it has been worked through in psychoanalysis since Freud, inserted within the relations of the subject to the structure of language? There are two problematic points to this question.

First, how can the relation of the object to linguistic structure be formulated, given the fact that the object—including the oral and anal objects—is not a element of linguistic structure, since it is neither a signifier nor a signified? If Lacan writes the object with the letter *a,* it is to differentiate it from all his notations of the signifier or signified, for which he uses different types of S—capital, small, italic, and so on. Lacan sets the object apart from the linguistic structure by writing it with a letter that he does not decline.

Second, how can there nevertheless be a relation between this object that is not a signifier, and a subject defined, on the contrary, as what is supposed by the structure of language, that is, as subject of the signifier? This is a matricial problem in Lacan's teaching: he toiled for many years to match up these two requirements that may seem animated by an antinomy.

On the way to posing and solving these problems Lacan encountered what we can name two new objects in psychoanalysis: the object voice and the scopic object, the voice and the gaze that generalize the status of the object insofar as they cannot be situated in any stage. There is no invocatory or scopic stage.

Lacan devoted a development, now famous, in his Seminar *The Four Fundamental Concepts of Psychoanalysis* to the scopic object[2] on the occasion of the publication of Merleau-Ponty's posthumous book *The Visible and the Invisible.* The reason for this is not simply an encounter, even if chance played its part. In actual fact, Lacan, dealing with the object gaze, found the occasion to correct the sense of what he had himself introduced and which is just as famous, the mirror stage.

To the very extent that the specular relation of the "I see myself seeing myself" supports imaginary identifications—and, basically, the mirror is there to materialize the image—it conceals the distinction to be made between vision and gaze: between vision as a function of the organ of sight and gaze, its immanent object, where the subject's desire is inscribed, which is neither an organ nor a function of any biology.

We do not have a comparable development on the object voice in Lacan's teaching. Such a development can nevertheless be outlined on the model of the articulation between eye and gaze—without even needing a mediation such as that of the mirror. The mirror is necessary to produce the 'seeing oneself', whereas the 'hearing oneself' is already present at the most intimate point of subjectivity—or to express it like Husserl, in 'the self-presence of the living present of subjectivity' [*la présence à soi du présent vivant de la subjectivité*].

But on the model of the split [*schize*], the opposition, the antinomy between eye and gaze, why not introduce a split, an antinomy between ear and voice? This already suffices to indicate that at a glance the voice as object *a* does not in the least belong to the sonorous register—just like the gaze as object *a,* in Seminar XI,[3] is very well illustrated by the noise that surprises the voyeur in the analysis that Lacan borrowed from Sartre. I evoke the names of Merleau-Ponty and Sartre—all these constructions of Lacan are unremittingly related to phenomenological analyses.

If the voice as object *a* does not in the least belong to the sonorous register, it remains that potential considerations on the voice—in connection with sound as distinct from sense, for example, or on all the modalities of intonation—can only be inscribed in a Lacanian perspective if they are indexed on the function of the voice as *a-phonic* [*a-phone*], if I may say so. This is probably a paradox, a paradox that has to do with the fact that the objects called *a* are tuned to the subject of the signifier only if they lose all substantiality, that is, only on condition that they are centered by a void, that of castration.

As oral, anal, scopic, invocatory, the objects surround a void and it is in this respect that they incarnate it diversely. Each of these objects is doubtlessly specified by a certain matter, but only insofar as it empties this matter. And this is why object *a* is in fact for Lacan a logical function, a logical consistency that finds its incarnation in what falls from the body in the form of diverse wastes. This means that there is a fundamental criterion to ascribe the letter *a* to some objects; we can formulate this criterion in the terms of the Wolf Man: it has to be a little thing separable from the body.

What put Lacan on to this lengthening of the Freudian list with the objects voice and gaze? The answer is simple: it is clinical experience. It is not, in the case of the object voice, a meditation on the subject's monologue with himself in his solitude. It is a clinical experience in which gaze and voice manifest themselves in separate forms, clearly characterized by their exteriority with regard to the subject.

This means that it is the clinical experience of psychosis that led Lacan to lengthen the Freudian list. We can say that in a certain way these objects were known to psychiatrists and that the theory of the voice and the gaze as objects *a* comes from the crossing of Lacan's psychiatric experience with Freud's theory of stages, under the auspices of the Saussurian structure of language. Lacan extracted the scopic object from the delusion of surveillance because this delusion renders manifest the *separate* and *external* presence of a gaze under which the subject falls. In a similar way, it is from the phenomena of mental automatism—so named since Clérambault, whom Lacan acknowledged as his only master in psychiatry—that Lacan extracted the object voice. Here one speaks of voices, although these voices are all immaterial—they are nevertheless perfectly real to the subject. They are even what he cannot doubt, despite the fact that nobody can record them. Their sonorous materiality is not what would be at the fore here.

This is why, very logically, it is in his writing on psychosis[4] that we find the most developed articulation of the relation between subject and voice. This articulation, like his development on the articulation of the subject and the gaze in his seminar,[5] contains a confrontation with Maurice Merleau-Ponty—it remains implicit in the text—more precisely with his *Phenomenology of Perception* in which there is a fairly developed theory of the motor verbal hallucination.

There is a logical necessity to the fact that Lacan encountered the voice before the gaze since he started from the function of speech in the field of language in order to grasp the analytic experience—this logical necessity would warrant a development of the confrontation between Lacan and Merleau-Ponty on the question of the motor verbal hallucination. I would say that the instance of the voice deserves to be inscribed as a third term between the function of speech and the field of language.

We can start from the fact that the function of speech is the function that confers a sense on the individual's functions. Speech knots signified—or rather the 'to be signified', what is to be signified—and signifier to one another; and this knotting always entails a third term, that of the voice. If we say that one cannot talk without a voice, we can, just by saying that, inscribe the residue, the remainder of the subtraction of signification from the signifier in the register of the voice. And we can, in a first approach, define the voice as everything in the signifier that does not partake in the effect of signification. This is what a very simple schema of Lacan implies.

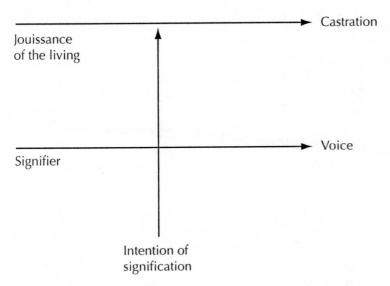

This schema presents the operation of speech in connection with the crossing of two vectors: that of the intention of saying, the intention of signification that can only be realized by crossing the vector of the signifier. The voice is everything in the signifier that does not partake in the effect of signification. The intention of signification is only realized on condition of encountering what is its structure both as lexicon and syntax on the vector of the signifier. This is what the structural viewpoint entails. To inscribe the voice there positions it immediately as a remainder.

The second vector inscribed by Lacan in this schema incarnates the dynamic of the living and, symmetrically, the jouissance of the living that ends up there in the guise of castration for having traversed this structure. There is of course cause to reason about the symmetry of position between the voice and castration.

Not only is the Lacanian voice, the voice in the Lacanian sense, not speech, but it also has nothing to do with speaking. We saw the development of a linguistics of intonation that appears to many linguists as a limit exercise. It seeks to define what the signifiers of intonation would be according to the effects of meaning with which they are loaded. In this respect, the linguistics of intonation has nothing to do with the Lacanian voice that is not the intonation, since its position is fundamentally outside meaning. We could think that what Lacan calls the voice is akin to intonation and its modalities. I do not believe that this is what Lacan aimed at insofar as this linguistics of intonation is only possible on condition that it finds its bearings, in the end, on the effects of meaning that are produced there.

In this respect the voice, in the very special use Lacan makes of this word, is doubtlessly a function of the signifier—or, better, of the signifying chain as such. "As such" implies that it is not just the signifying chain as spoken and heard, but also as written and read. The crucial point about this voice is that the production of a signifying chain—I put it in Lacan's very terms—is not linked to such or such sensory organ or to such or such sensory register.

There is an outline of the phenomenology of speech in Lacan's work, which aims to bring out the paradoxes of the perception of speech. These paradoxes consist in that the subject proves to be *patient* for the most part—that is, that he bears the effects of speech. Without developing my point, I note that this phenomenology must first give way to the analysis of the subject's perception of the other's speech, insofar as every word of the other implies a fundamental basic suggestion. This is quite well illustrated by the fact that anybody can keep quiet all day to listen to the other's speech—listen or sleep. It does not mean that one will automatically obey it. The suggestion occasionally entails the subject's distrust vis-à-vis the other's speech: "He says this, but what does he really mean? He says this, but is it really his?" The distrust is inscribed in continuity with the suggestion, as a fundamental warning of the subject vis-à-vis the suggestion that comes naturally from the other's speech.

And the subject's perception of his own speech also entails a number of paradoxes. One example among the paradoxes mentioned by Lacan is that the subject cannot speak without hearing himself, which is to say that his own speech contains a spontaneous reflexivity, so to speak, a self-affectation that never fails to charm the analyst of consciousness phenomena. But this 'hearing oneself' is different from 'listening to oneself', where the subject's applied attention corrects, comes to recapture this spontaneous reflexivity. On this point, we note that the subject cannot listen to himself without being divided; numerous experiments show that, for instance, if the subject gets his own speech fed back to him with a small delay through headphones, he will lose the thread of his speech if he listens to what he says.

On the topic of the subject's perception of his own speech, we should mention what we owe to psychiatric observation, that is, that the verbal hallucination is linked to slight phonatory movements of the subject—this can be observed on occasion. On the question of verbal hallucination, this observation leads us to assert that the verbal hallucination rests on a misrecognition of his own activity by the subject—this indicates the ascription to the subject, as constituting, of the responsibility for the hallucination.

The structural perspective in which Lacan's concept of the voice is inscribed is completely different. It is the perspective according to which the subject of the signifier is constituted by the signifying chain—not constituting but constituted. It is the signifying chain and its structure that have the primacy. It is then that we can formulate that the voice is a dimension of every signifying chain insofar as a signifying chain as such—audible, written, visual, and so on—involves a subjective attribution, that is, assigns a place to the subject. And this subjective attribution, as a rule, says Lacan, is distributive—it is by no means univocal.

As a rule, a signifying chain assigns several subjective places. This has not eluded a form of linguistics that considers that every discourse fundamentally involves citations, that every discourse is in this respect fundamentally indirect, that there is no discourse where, in the enunciation itself, the subject is not taking a step back, preparing himself, taking position in relation to what he says. As you know, some go as far as making negation into such a citation—there must first be a posing of the term, after which comes the negation of the term that had been posed. This is exactly where Lacan uses the term *voice* in the first place: every signifying chain has several voices—which indeed makes voice and enunciation equivalent.

In his writing on psychosis ["On a question preliminary . . ."], this analysis comes before his comments on a famous verbal hallucination recounted by a patient at Sainte-Anne Hospital, who had heard her neighbor calling her "sow." Lacan stresses that he got the patient to tell him what preceded this insult: the complete sentence "I've just been to the pork butcher's."

What is the crucial point of Lacan's analysis? It is that he considers the set formed by the insult and the sentence as a signifying chain that has been broken, that is, in which a distribution of the subjective assignation has happened. The "I've just been to the pork butcher's" is attributed to the subject who can then acknowledge that she thought it, whereas the word "sow" is snatched from this signifying chain to be attributed to the Other. We can probably recognize here, in the sentence "Sow, I've just been to the pork butcher's," the 'cutting up' fantasy of this patient who in the word "sow" hears the word of her being resonate.

It is the affective—or let's say libidinal—charge of the word "sow" that operates a rupture of the signifying chain's continuity and a rejection in the real. In this respect, what Lacan calls *voice* is an effect of the foreclosure of the signifier that is not reducible, as the vulgate would have it, to the famous foreclosure of the Name-of-the-Father. Insofar as a piece of signifying chain—broken because of what we call for now the libidinal charge—cannot be assumed by the subject, it passes in the real and is assigned to the Other. The voice appears in its dimension of object when it is the Other's voice.

What is important here? Is it the tone, be it insulting? If it had been murmured softly in her ear, it would still have remained an insult. What is important here is that the voice comes from the Other. In this respect, the voice is the part of the signifying chain that the subject cannot assume as 'I' and which is subjectively assigned to the Other.

But, after all, "sow" is also a word, a signifier that produces an effect of signification that we call an insult. So are we still properly in the register of the signifier and the signified? We must not obliterate what we quickly called the libidinal charge of this term. In other words, in words that only slightly shift those that you have so far accepted, it contains a charge of jouissance that cannot be integrated in the signifying chain (here I really make *jouissance* the equivalent of *libido*).

In this respect, the voice comes in the place of what is properly unspeakable about the subject, what Lacan called the subject's "surplus enjoyment" [*plus-de-jouir*]. Castration, which I mentioned quickly, means that one does not hear a voice in the real, that one is deaf to it. Where then is the instance of the voice when I speak? It is not the tone that I adopt—even if I entertain variations according to the effects of meaning that I want to produce. It is not simply that my recorded voice will appear to me to be that of somebody else. The instance of the voice is always present as soon as I have to locate my position in relation to a signifying chain insofar as this signifying chain is always situated in relation to the unspeakable object. In this respect, the voice is precisely that which cannot be said.

It has been said that there is something in the voice that escapes the instrumental effect. Of course I use the signifier in order that the Other would answer—every signifying chain is an invocation—but, more radically, I am waiting for the Other's voice, the one that will tell me what I have to expect, what will become of me and what has already become of my being as unspeakable. And this is precisely what makes me attached to the Other: it is the voice in the field of the Other that makes me attached to the Other.

This is why we can say that the psychotic subject, who is subjected to mental automatism, is the free man. He is the man free of the Other, because the Other's voice is already with him and because the Other has already responded to him.

For those inscribed within it, castration means that they always will be beggars. This is why the objects caught in the demand—oral object and anal object—came to the fore in analysis before the voice, which is an object of desire.

If there is the voice, it is due to the fact that the signifier revolves around the unspeakable object. And the voice as such emerges each time the signifier breaks down, and rejoins this object in horror.

If I had to formulate the invocation of any signifying chain, I would say that it is this: "Do not give me what I am asking you for because it is not what I desire." But perhaps we may put it more briefly under the form of this fundamental injunction to the Other: "Shut up!"

So we do not use the voice; the voice inhabits language, it haunts it. It is enough to speak for the menace to emerge that what cannot be said could come to light. If we speak that much, if we organize symposiums, if we chat, if we sing and listen to singers, if we play music and listen to it, Lacan's thesis implies that it is in order to silence what warrants to be called the voice as object little *a*.

Notes

1. This text was published in *Quarto* No. 54 in a version revised by the author and initially published by *Lysimaque* Ed. (1989) as the transcription of a lecture given during a symposium on the voice in Ivry, 23 January 1988.

2. J. Lacan, *Seminar XI: The Four Fundamental Concepts of Psychoanalysis* (London: Penguin, 1977), pp. 67–119.

3. Ibid., p. 83.

4. J. Lacan, "On a question preliminary to any possible treatment of psychosis in *Écrits: A Selection* (London: Routledge, 1977).

5. J. Lacan, *Seminar XI,* op. cit.

Embarrassment, Inhibition, and Repetition

Alexandre Stevens

"Embarrassment," "inhibition," and "repetition" are three terms already put forward by Freud. They are taken up and reorganized by Lacan in his seminar on anxiety: inhibition, impediment [*empêchement*], and embarrassment. So impediment is a logical moment in the process of repetition.

To begin with, I will highlight two axes of reflection. First, these three terms appear to contrast with the Freudian triad of inhibition, symptom, and anxiety; they are not the same. Yet, with Lacan, we can show that these two series are strictly related. I will develop this point with particular attention to the clinic of obsessional neurosis. Second, the three terms inhibition, repetition, and embarrassment, seem to be opposed to the dimension of action—in other words, to what makes movement possible. For inhibition this is obvious, with its minimal definition of stopping before action. But it is also true of repetition. We only have to consider the compulsion to repeat or the function of doubt in the obsessional to see that the halting of movement, the suspension of the moment to conclude, and the barrier against the act are patent here. As for embarrassment, the term evokes well enough the suspended subject, his arms [*bras*] loaded with something that prevents him from moving or from acting. So we are going to clarify these three terms. In so doing, we will see that although each one of them is a suspension of the dimension of the act, they nonetheless take form against the background of a status of the act that differs in each case.

Inhibition, Symptom, and Anxiety

Let us begin with Freud's "Inhibitions, Symptoms and Anxiety." In chapter IV Freud distinguishes these three terms with precision in relation to Little Hans's phobia, which has to do with the incapacity of the child to go into the street for fear of the horse. Inhibition is defined as a limitation that the ego imposes on itself so as not to wake the symptom of anxiety. In Hans's case, it is his incapacity to go into the street. The symptom, which must be distinguished from anxiety (the fear of the horse), is not the phobia of the horse, but the horse insofar as it comes in the place of the father: "What made it a neurosis was one thing alone: the replacement of his father by a horse. It is this displacement, then, which has a claim to be called a symptom," writes Freud.[1] We see that the symptom—the horse—is situated in its eminently signifying character by Freud: a displacement is the minimum requirement to produce repetition. Structurally, the horse represents Little Hans for the father. The horse, as signifier of the symptom, represents the subject for another signifier. This signifying repetition does not in itself define a symptom. Above all, it is a way for the subject to fix a share of jouissance through the signifying displacement. As for anxiety, it is present in the phobic element itself—and Freud develops it in the rest of his text—insofar as the phobic element refers to castration anxiety.

It is on the basis of these three terms that Lacan constructs the following table in his seminar on anxiety:[2]

		Difficulty →
Inhibition	Impediment	Embarrassment
Emotion	Symptom	Passage to the act
Agitation	Acting out	Anguish

Movement ↓

Table inspired by Seminar X (p. 22, 93)

On this table we can read, for example, that on the axis of movement, the passage to the act is a barrier to anguish in relation to embarrassment. In the same axis with regard to the impediment, there is the symptom, before acting out, and so on.

To bring the Freudian triad together with the three terms broached earlier, we see that the impediment is outlined against the background of the symptom, and that anxiety implies that the subject is at least already embarrassed. These different modes of stopping movement are already perfectly legible in Freud's text where, in the first few pages of "Inhibitions, Symptoms and Anxiety," he examines the different modes of inhibition. He underlines the great diversity of processes employed to perturb a function. He also distinguishes different functions. Concerning the sexual function, he evokes six possibilities of inhibition (p. 88) that essentially boil down to four: pure inhibition; an impediment in the function through steps of precaution; an interruption of the function by the appearance of anxiety when it cannot be prevented from starting; and the modification of the execution of the function through its deviation toward other ends or the difficulty of execution due to particular "conditions."

First let us take impediment by security measures—in other words, through repetition. Lacan takes up this term in his seminar on anxiety in order to designate the aspect of preventing the action present in the axis of the symptom (cf. Table). The clinical forms of impediment can be specified. Some security measures are in fact characteristic of impediment as it operates in obsessional neurosis or in hysteria: the compulsion to repeat for the one, disgust for the other. The symptomatic side is manifest in both security measures, but so is the prevention, suspension of the action.

What Freud designates as interruption "by the appearance of anxiety" (p. 88) could be called embarrassment, insofar as the situation has started to develop and the subject is embarrassed by something. Lacan gives two clinical examples of embarrassment, taken from two of Freud's cases: Dora, and the young homosexual woman. When in the famous scene by the lake Herr K says to Dora that his wife is nothing to him, she is left with this bar placed over the subject. In the instant that follows, she slaps him, a passage to the act. But the moment in which she is suspended before the passage to the act is a moment of embarrassment. The other example is that of the young homosexual when her father's gaze falls upon her as she is holding arms with her lady. In this instant, too, there is embarrassment followed soon afterward by a passage to the act in which she jumps over the parapet of the railway line. In these two cases, something could not be prevented from beginning that leaves the subject embarrassed, at the limits of anguish. In each case, the suspension of movement constituted by embarrassment resolves itself through a passage to the act. I will come back to this.

As for the 'modification in the performance of a function', let's say briefly that these diverse forms take us back to the symptom as signifying displacement, with the fixation of a share of jouissance.

So we have three forms of stopping movement. These can be considered as three forms of inhibition in the broader sense of the term. Each one relates to a particular mode of the act. Impediment is to be situated on the side of acting out, embarrassment on the side of the passage to the act. Pure inhibition is to be placed in relation to the act as such. Freud presents pure inhibition as a turning away of the libido through too great an eroticization of the function. We will see that with Lacan we can write this by the inclusion of the object *a*.

Pure inhibition is a withdrawal before the eroticization of a function. Impediment is a simple form of repetition and in this respect is closely linked to the symptom. As for embarrassment, it relates to the subject as barred: the subject is here at the limits of anxiety. In this respect, the right-hand column on Lacan's table is on the side of the fascination of the subject. The different places assigned to the three modalities of the act each correspond to a different relation between the subject and the object. Acting out is the showing of the object: the object shows itself on the scene; in this respect it is a call to interpretation, to reestablish the subject in the Other, to interpret the drive object in [the dimension of] the signifier. In the passage to the act, the subject 'is barred' ['*se barre*'] leaving the scene with the irruption of the object. As for the act, which is linked to inhibition though in an inverted form, it is a relation of the subject to his disappearance insofar as the subject is not there in the act, but also that the act grounds the subject again, on condition that the subject is not without knowing the place that the object occupies for him. I will return to these points later.

Impediment and Signifying Repetition

Let us now take up the three terms in detail, beginning with the impediment [*empêchement*]. Lacan speaks of it in terms of the plight of a subject who is "prevented [*empêché*] from sticking to his desire, held back." And he adds that for the obsessional it manifests itself as a compulsion. An example is the compulsion to doubt, with what this form implies of the halting of movement and even of the halting of the movement of thought, through a form of thinking that turns round and round in repetition. But doubt already mixes symptom and impediment. It is not only a signifying repetition, a displacement in the field of the signifier, but also, and essentially, it is a mode of jouissance, for the obsessional doubt implies a jouissance, one that, in Seminar XX, Lacan calls the jouissance of thinking. So doubt is not completely suitable to define the impediment, for it already implies the jouissance of the symptom.

In order to distinguish more precisely between impediment and symptom and put them in perspective in relation to acting out, let's take the example of an obsessional compulsion described by Freud in the Rat Man. In this case study, Freud calls this compulsion an "*obsession for protecting.*"[3] Here I quote a passage from the "Original record of the case": "He went on to tell me that on the day on which his cousin left U. he found a stone lying in the roadway and had a phantasy that her carriage might hit up against it and she might come to grief. He therefore put it out of the way, but twenty minutes later it occurred to him that this was absurd and he went back in order to replace the stone in its position. So here again we have a hostile impulse against his cousin remaining alongside a protective one."[4] And in his *Case Studies,* Freud indicates that the Rat Man had himself knocked his foot against the stone while walking.[5]

We can break this brief compulsion into three times. In the first moment, the impediment: he kicks the stone and a fantasy takes hold of him. The impediment is here the stopping by the thought, the suspension of action in the return of repetition. The repetition here lies in the return of the thought of the great suffering that might befall the lady he loves—the rat torture.[6]

Second time, the symptom: he picks up the stone, a symptomatic act resolving the idea that took hold of him with regard to the lady. Immediately though, with the return of doubt, the act proposes an inversion into its contrary—the thought that this thought and the symptomatic act that accompanied it were stupid. This reversal, which entails that the act did not resolve anything, makes it a symptomatic act. It is a well-known mechanism of obsessional neurosis; it is also one that we find again in the Rat Man's great obsession, which consists in honoring a debt that, in fact, he has already repaid (which makes it particularly insoluble), but which he must resolve in order to escape the infamous rat torture. The logic of this reversal is exposed in "The great obsessive fear" and constitutes the major symptom that takes him to Freud: "At that instant, however, a 'sanction' had taken shape in his mind, namely, *that he was not to pay the money* or it would happen—(i.e., the phantasy about the rats would come true as regards his father and the lady). And immediately, in accordance with a type of procedure with which he was familiar, to combat this sanction there had arisen a command in the shape of a vow: '*You must pay back the 3.80 krönen to Lieutenant A.*' He had said these words to himself almost half aloud."[7] The same type of reversal is produced in his compulsion to protect the lady. The obsessive idea 'she could fall on the stone' was turned into its opposite. This signifying displacement belongs to the symptom. If the first moment shows "the impediment in sticking to his desire" according to Lacan's expression, the second shows, through a displacement and a reversal, a repression of the truth of the desire. The repression implies that "in its nature the symptom is jouissance" as Lacan said, for what is framed by the signifying reversal is a jouissance. The chain of reversals is fixed by the object of the drive. Here, between picking up and replacing, we have the retention and relinquishment of the anal object in the relation to the demand of the other. To pick up the stone to prevent the other from falling is a kind of gift to the other.

In this compulsion there is a third moment, this time an acting out. Twenty minutes later the Rat Man retraces his path in the opposite direction in order to replace the stone on the road. This moment is that of the manifestation [*monstration*] of the truth of his desire. The acting out is the manifestation of this unknown desire, which is hostility against the lady. It is in this sense that in the treatment he "calls for interpretation," as Lacan says in his seminar on anxiety. To propose this moment as one of acting out seems to me to be congruent with what Lacan puts forward when he locates the acting out of Freud's young homosexual woman in the act of showing addressed to her father that exposes her relationship with her lady and leaves her in the greatest embarrassment when in this "giving to be seen" she effectively encounters the gaze of her father. In the Rat Man's compulsion there is also an act of showing, a coming onto the stage addressed to the lady of his thoughts and, beyond her, to his father.

If we consider this compulsion in relation to the object, we have the moment of impediment as a moment in which the phenomenon of signifying repetition is brought to a halt without the fixation of the signifying chain by the object. In the moment of the symptom, the signifying chain is fixed by the object of the drive (anal, in its dimension of retention and letting go). And in the time of the acting out, there is a pure showing of the object, the stone destined to be set under the feet of the loved lady, a gift to the other and at the same time the presentation of this object in its relation to sadism: the point is not that she should fall, but "that rats penetrate her anus," "that it happens anyway." It is a showing for the other, but one that is at the same time a veil for the subject. It is a concealment, a veiling of jouissance, a stopping before the point at which [jouissance] would be made present. It is in this sense that acting out is a barrier against anguish. In the place of anguish, there is the conjunction of the encounter with castration and the encounter with an object in excess [*en trop*].

The impediment (which is in the strictest relation to repetition and the symptom) is thus inscribed as a moment of stopping movement in the perspective of acting out, should the movement accelerate.

Embarrassment and the Barring of the Subject

After this development on the impediment, let us turn to the second term of the series, embarrassment. Embarrassment for Lacan indicates at least the bar put on the subject. I already evoked its relation to the limits of anguish. But there is also something 'in excess' in embarrassment, as the term indicates well in French: one is embarrassed by something in excess [*en trop*], by a signifier too many [*en trop*], says Lacan. All it takes is to increase the movement by one degree, by adding a little emotion here, for the subject to be pushed to the passage to the act. In the case of the young homosexual woman, it was the reproaches that her lady voices as soon as the embarrassing gaze of the father is discovered that made her throw herself over the parapet. In Dora's case, it is the sentiment she felt for Frau K, beyond anything she felt for Herr K, that pushed her out of the embarrassment in which she had been placed the instant before with Herr K's phrase, the signifier in excess [en trop], "My wife is nothing for me." She passes to the act in what, it is true, is a more banal form: a slap.

I will give another example of the passage to the act of an obsessional subject who was annoyed by the fact that his wife was the first woman he had known. He thought that he should make up for the time lost in his youth, lost because of his mother who did not leave him enough freedom. One evening, he visited a brothel. In a hurry, perhaps too much, to realize his intention, he went upstairs with a woman and was obliged to acknowledge once she was undressed that she did not please him. He nevertheless committed the act foretold by this brief contract, but as soon as he was outside, he was embarrassed. He had something in excess [*en trop*], that something in excess that he wanted, but at the same time which wasn't at all that. He was embarrassed because something in excess mixed with the sense of disquiet produced in him by the uselessness of the potency to which he had just testified. So he decided to commit what could be called a passage to the act. He visited a second brothel and decided this time to choose his partner of an instant. He took all the time necessary to make his choice and in fact was not disappointed when she took her clothes off. She was just as he desired her to be. But this was only for him to be forced to admit that he was too tired. It was one time too many [*en trop*]. He ran off immediately, without further ado. In the previous instant, he had been in embarrassment. He had something excessive [*en trop*] in his arms, something that did not hold out any enigma, which he had searched for but which, once found, proved to be too much [*en trop*]. With the addition of emotion (arising from his relative impotence at that moment), he ran off. This flight, at the end of the sequence, is a passage to the act. It has none of the characteristics that Lacan recognized in the acting out: neither the showing of an object, nor address to another, nor presentation of an unknown desire, nor a call to interpretation. But here we certainly have a subject who bars himself in the face of what presents itself as castration anxiety. In the seminar on anxiety Lacan says of the passage to the act that it is on the side of the subject in the fantasy insofar as it is there that the subject appears as maximally effaced by the bar. It is at the moment of greatest embarrassment, with the behavioral addition of a disorder of movement, that the subject falls from the scene that is the only place where, as historicized subject, he is able to maintain himself in his status as a subject.[8] This clinical fragment lends itself very well to the little metaphor of the tap that Lacan used to distinguish between acting out, the symptom and the passage to the act. The symptom is the leaking of the tap. The acting out is simply the presence or absence of the pouring water. The passage to the act consists in opening the tap without knowing what one is doing.

This clinical fragment is not too different from one of Casanova's misadventures recalled in the *Mémoires*[9] that Lacan evokes in Seminar XI. Once again, Casanova casts his affections upon a young girl. What's more, he decides to swindle her father by promising him his help in an operation of magic to recover a chest of gold pieces buried in one of the cellars of the house. This time things turn out badly. He concocts everything with the young girl and hopes to conclude matters with her after the operation of magic. At the moment of the operation, he draws a circle on the ground, with cabalistic signs, places himself inside it, and begins his incantations. He makes it clear that he does not believe in any of it. He says to the master of the house that at the end of his incantations the whereabouts of the chest will be known. For himself, he knows that it will not be found, but he is certain that he will be able to come up with a little story to justify himself. That day, during the incantations, a storm erupts and he is seized with fear. In fact, he thinks that he caused the storm. The work in which he did not believe, these signifiers that he was in the process of uttering by calling the sky to his aid, suddenly fall into his arms; he is embarrassed. It goes beyond embarrassment because he dares not leave the circle that he traced, imagining that it is the only place that the storm would not be able to touch. He calms down and explained to the master of the house that he is having a bit of trouble, that the operation would not work and he finds himself impotent before the young girl (it is the only time that this happens in the course of all three volumes of the *Mémoires*). He then runs off. It is a passage to the act, the last line of defense before anguish.

In the same way that I situated the axis of impediment/symptom/ and acting out in relation to the object, one can situate the axis of embarrassment/passage to the act/ and anguish in relation to the subject. In embarrassment, it is the bar as such that is placed on the subject; the passage to the act is the subject leaving the scene; and anguish is the point of conjunction of the subject (as barred by the encounter with castration) with the object.

Inhibition and the Act

Let's end with the third term: inhibition. "Pure inhibition," as Freud puts it, that is, inhibition in its strict sense, designates a halting of movement. Freud writes: "The ego renounces these functions, which are within its

sphere, in order not to have to undertake fresh measures of repression—
in order to avoid a conflict with the id."[10] He adds that this "is because
the physical organs brought into play . . . have become too strongly
eroticized." In this respect, I return to an article by Serge Cottet that examines the particular case of intellectual inhibition and reformulates the
'eroticization' in terms of the inclusion of object *a:* "Is it not the inclusion of the *object a* in thought which, at the same time, renders culpable,
captivates the writer or restrains the inhibited?"[11]

So we can now discover the modes of presence of the object at the
different levels of Lacan's table: on the one hand, the object is in a relation of primary veiling to primary repression, as the object cause of
desire, as is the case in inhibition. Then, on the other hand, in a series
of secondary veilings, this object fixes the symptom and appears on
the scene in acting out. Finally, it appears as such for the subject filled
with anguish.

The holding back of too strong an eroticization identified by Freud
supplies the strict relationship between inhibition and desire. Inhibition is the place 'where desire expresses itself', but only insofar as it
is held back in a relation of a primary veiling that is structural of desire. It is for this reason that, in opposition to the two other vertical
axes of the act and thus in opposition to the two statuses of the act that
acting out and passage to the act imply, the act placed in relation to inhibition is the act as such, in its dimension contrary to inhibition, but
at the same time to be situated at the same point as anguish on the
table. There where inhibition is situated in a relation of primary veiling structural of desire, the act has a dimension of overcoming so that,
after the act, the subject is no longer the same as before. The act, in
the strong sense that Lacan gives it in his seminar on the analytic act,
does not especially require movement, and can even do without it. It is
defined through the fact that the subject 'after [the act]' is a new subject. Lacan uses the example of Caesar crossing the Rubicon for what
he calls an act 'without qualification' (as opposed to the analytic act).
To cross the Rubicon is not an 'exploit', a performance of action. It is
a pure symbolic crossing. Cesar crosses a limit such that afterward, he
no longer knows who he is. Before, he was one of the great generals of
the army; after, marching to Rome, he will either be a renegade or an
emperor. Through the act, the subject loses his previous identification,
he does not know what he will be; it is a new subject. Let us also note
that if the act is situated in opposition to inhibition, in the sense in

which it renews the subject, this is not only in an internal opposition with inhibition, but also in relation to castration, to a subject accepting that after the act he will no longer be the same as before. In this sense, if it is opposed to inhibition (and as such its referent), the act is a beyond to anguish to be inscribed at the same point on the table.

Notes

1. S. Freud, SE XX, p. 103.
2. J. Lacan, *Le Séminaire livre X: L'angoisse* (Paris: Seuil 2004).
3. 'Notes upon a case of obsessional neurosis,' SE X, p. 189.
4. SE X, pp. 306–307.
5. Ibid., pp. 189–190.
6. Ibid., p. 168.
7. Ibid.
8. J. Lacan, *Le Séminaire livre X,* op. cit. session of 23 January 1963.
9. Casanova, *Mémoires,* vol. I, Bibliothèque de la Pléiade, pp. 524–59.
10. SE XX, p. 90.
11. S. Cottet, 'Sur l'inhibition intellectuelle', *Quarto* 37/38 '*Les usage du symptôme,*' p. 22.

A Lacanian Reading of *Dora*

Véronique Voruz

> *The symptoms of the disease [of hysteria] are*
> *nothing else than the patient's sexual activity*
> (Freud: 1901, at 115, original emphasis)

This chapter will consider the articulation of love, desire, and jouissance in the neurotic structure of hysteria through a Lacanian reading of Dora, one of Freud's five substantial case studies. Clearly, the pertinence of returning to Dora a century after Freud's paper was first published is not to be assumed. Yet the case of Dora, perhaps not Freud's most successful in terms of its outcome, remains crucial in that, beneath the symptomatology of Freud's patient, the invariant traits of hysteria can be discerned. And so Lacan episodically refers to different aspects of Dora in order to expose, successively, the structure of Dora's identifications, the symbolic logic of her unconscious, and the mode of her jouissance as paradigmatic. In so doing, Lacan isolates the respective modalities of love, desire, and jouissance in hysteria in a process of logical reduction. In turn, this logical reduction will orient the direction of the analytic treatment in this particular neurotic structure.

The Case of Dora

Biographical Elements

Before presenting Lacan's numerous returns to the analytic relation between Freud and Dora—as Lacan says in his eleventh seminar, the analyst is part of the concept of the unconscious[1]—let us succinctly introduce the patient.

Dora is an eighteen-year-old girl from a well-to-do Viennese family. She is brought to Freud by her father after her parents stumble across a letter she wrote, announcing her intention to commit suicide (Freud: 1901, p. 23).[2] When Dora comes to see Freud, she is by no means suicidal, however, and merely suffers from a mild depression characterized by low spirits, lack of concentration, and little interest for the outside world.

Dora's family circle includes her two parents and a brother who is one and a half years her senior. In the patient's account, the mother remains in the background, and is described as "an uncultivated woman and above all a foolish one" (p. 20), obsessed with cleanliness and domesticity. Dora "looks down on her" (ibid.) and does not have much time for her. By contrast, her father is depicted as a bright and cultured man, in Freud's terms "the dominating figure in this circle, owing to his intelligence and his character as much as to the circumstances of his life." (p. 18)

Dora's identification with the male side of the family is immediately apparent; she herself is an intelligent and precocious young woman. First, an early, imaginary identification with her brother can be inferred from the scene of the *infans* Dora sucking her thumb while holding on to her brother's ear (p. 51).[3] In his "Intervention on transference," Lacan further points out that this scene is a clear marker of the prevalence of the oral drive in Dora (p. 221/67), a prevalence that returns in all her conversion symptoms (aphonia, cough, catarrh) and also accounts for her interest in the oral techniques to which her father resorts to satisfy his mistress despite his impotence. At this point, Lacan also adds that "the violent appeal of [Dora's] oral erotic drive" (ibid.) 'explains' her difficulty in recognizing her genital sexuality. This difficulty is the cause of Dora's extreme resistance to accepting that she could be the object of a man's sexual desire.[4] Second, her strong, symbolic identification with her father, a man of many illnesses, is attested to by her poor health and by the fact that she adopted his physical symptoms from the age of eight onward: coughing, difficult breathing, and so on.

Dora stays in analysis with Freud for three months and leaves him without notice, declaring at the beginning of her last two-hour session on 31 December 1900 that this would be the last. In the course of this brief treatment, it becomes clear to Freud that Dora is using her father's affection for her, in conjunction with her predisposition to illness ("somatic compliance," p. 40), in order to blackmail him into terminating his long-lasting affair with his mistress, Frau K. It also rapidly becomes apparent to Freud that Dora's father brings her to analysis so as not to break up this relationship, and that Dora resents her father for that reason. Indeed, Freud rapidly deduces that the suicide threat, far from being serious, was a message addressed to the father to the effect that he should terminate his relationship with Frau K. The message was perfectly understood by its addressee. Dora's father nonetheless refused to put an end to the affair, and instead brought Dora to Freud for analytic treatment. Those are the inauspicious circumstances in which Dora's analysis started.

The Love Quartet

To understand Dora's position at the beginning of her analysis with Freud, we need to familiarize ourselves with the sentimental intrigues that organized Dora's life in the years preceding the analysis. Freud's question is as follows: why should Dora, who previously used to support her father's relationship (p. 36), suddenly demand that he put an end to the affair? The simple observation of this radical change in her position leads us to question her position regarding her father's relationship. This question is itself to be articulated around the triggering event of Dora's change of position: why did she initially support the affair, and why did she suddenly demand its termination? This twofold question will guide us in our understanding of Dora's psychical organization, and so of hysteria more generally.

Dora's father is a man of poor health; most of his symptoms are related to a venereal disease he contracted before his marriage that led to his impotence (p. 47). Freud notes, in passing, that this venereal disease may be the cause for his wife's obsession with cleaning. He has also had tuberculosis, a disease that led the family to move to a thermal resort. It is in this thermal resort that Dora's family meet a couple, the Ks. Dora's father rapidly begins an affair with Frau K with Dora's support, who minds the K's children so that her father may be free to spend time with Frau K (p. 36). Herr K, on the other hand, develops a fancy to Dora, which she does not *not* reciprocate.

At the age of fourteen, Dora is kissed by Herr K and conceives an immense disgust for it. This is what Freud terms a *"reversal of affects"* (p. 28, original emphasis): excessive enjoyment is transformed into excessive displeasure. In conformity with his theory of sexuality (see the

"Three Essays"), Freud interprets Dora's disgust in relation to her own infantile masturbation and the subsequent repression of sexual desire in her childhood (p. 29). For Freud, disgust is a hysterical symptom of repression, as a result of which Dora even conceives a small phobia for men in a state of sexual arousal (p. 30).

Then, at the age of sixteen, Dora is left alone with Herr K by a lake, and the latter begins a proposal, including the words translated by Strachey as "I get nothing from my wife" [*Ich habe nichts an meiner Frau*]. At this point, Dora slaps him—or, as Freud states, gives him "a box on the ear" (p. 122)—and leaves. It is from this moment onward that she becomes adamant that all relations with the Ks should stop. We clearly have here the triggering element of Dora's present position, a position that can be summarized in the following sequence: most significantly, Dora resents her father for offering her as the price of Herr K's acceptance of his wife's infidelity (p. 36). But she also resents Herr K for treating her like a governess with whom he previously had an affair, using the exact same words of entreaty with her as he had with the governess ("saying that he got nothing from his wife, and so on," p. 106). Additionally, she resents Frau K for betraying her by mentioning Dora's intimate knowledge of sexual matters to her husband (p. 26; 62). She resents everyone, in a word, for treating her as a means to an end, an object that robs her of her subjectivity: her father, as a means to Frau K, Frau K, as a means to her father, Herr K, as an object of sexual enjoyment. Finally, she resents Freud, who is on the side of the men, and Freud himself recognizes that he made a few mistakes in the handling of the transference (cf. Postscript).

The Question of the Hysteric

What Is It to Be a Woman?

Through Lacan, we can approach Dora's position—and its disruption—structurally. So if at first sight it seems perfectly obvious that Dora's symptoms are organized around her father's love affair, a closer look will expose the structural coordinates of Dora's position. Against the background of such a structural reading, the father's affair, and Dora's interest in it, will be shown to be incidental to her real question. Lastly, to isolate these coordinates will allow us to learn about hysteria beyond the contingency of the case itself.

We can take Lacan's well-known reformulation of the hysteric structure as a question on femininity as a starting point to our commentary. In effect, Lacan's many commentaries on the case indicate that Dora's subjective position, like that of all hysterics, is an investigation in the question of femininity that allows the subject to learn about what it is to be a woman without putting herself into play in the field of sexuality. According to Lacan, the hysteric's question is whether he or she is a man or a woman (cf. *Seminar III,* chap. XII) or, more precisely, what it is to be a woman (ibid., chap. XIII). Indeed, we recall that, for Lacan, Woman does not exist, a statement that, in the present perspective, indicates that there is no knowledge in the unconscious as to what it is to be a woman. Hysterical strategies are thus to be read as an elaboration around this lack.

Object-choice and Identification in the Case of Dora

By adopting the Lacanian perspective (hysterical symptoms respond to the absence of knowledge in the unconscious as to what it is to be a woman), we can approach the case with a view to deciphering Dora's position in order to see how her identifications and object-choices structure her answer to the question of femininity. The first step is thus to understand how Dora's diverse identifications with the characters of her story relate to the question of femininity.

In *Seminar IV,* Lacan maps Dora's identifications onto his schema L. Following this schema, her position is defined through the tension supporting her identifications: Herr K and Dora are on the imaginary axis, that of the ego (in *Seminar III* Lacan will say that Herr K is Dora's imaginary other, her ego), and Frau K and Dora's father occupy the symbolic axis, that of desire.

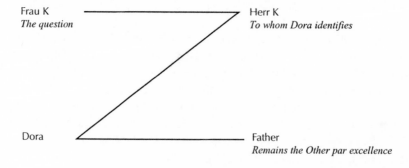

Frau K
The question
Herr K
To whom Dora identifies

Dora
Father
Remains the Other par excellence

Dora's behavior can only be understood in the light of this 'quartered' position. To find out what it is to be a woman, Dora shelters herself by means of a masculine identification with Herr K on the imaginary axis (so that she is *not* a woman), and identifies with her father's desire at the level of the symbolic (the father classically incarnates the symbolic Other for the hysteric): Frau K is the object of her father's desire, and Dora is interested in what a man *desires* in a woman.

Bearing in mind the structure of her identifications, we can now approach the pivotal point of the case, Herr K's proposal by the lake, for it is at this point that Dora's attitude undergoes a radical change, a change that points to a modification in the organization of her identifications, since the pattern mapped onto Schema L is what supported Dora's love scenario until then.

The Scene by the Lake

Cutting through the efflorescence of mundane details, Lacan's sustained engagement with the case demonstrates that Dora used these *identifications* to block the *anguish* provoked by the absence of a signifier for the woman in the unconscious. Lacan indicates that her position was largely animated by a will to secure unconditional love, love as the impossible gift, as it famously involves 'giving what one does not have' (cf. *Seminars III* and *IV*). It is also clear that Dora engaged on her quest for love under the *cover* of her identification with her father's object of desire, Frau K. It is when she is confronted with the real of a sexual demand that she is brought back to her own jouissance, which was until then comfortably channeled by the dynamics of her identifications. For when Herr K makes his ill-fated proposal, she is brutally exposed: Dora herself is now desired, not the other woman she shelters behind. The question of Dora's own femininity can no longer be deferred, and anguish ensues. Thus, the focal point of this chapter, its vanishing point, as one could say somewhat facetiously, is this moment by the lake when all Dora's constructions are revealed to be precisely that—mere constructions designed to provide a propitious background for her personal fictions—and she is threatened with her disappearance as subject.

In this chapter, I will elaborate on a possible interpretation of this scene. First, the scene by the lake has to do with anguish; second, this anguish comes about following a crucial modification for Dora concerning her identifications.

A Logical Reading of the Scene by the Lake

We can now articulate Dora's change of position in the following sequence: when Herr K declares his passionate affection, there ensues a fall of identification for Dora, which gives rise to a subsequent anguish. This anguish is 'dealt with' through a passage to the act (the slap), followed by a regression to the stage of a demand for pure love addressed to her father, *a demand no longer mediated by the metonymy of desire.*

So there are two dimensions to the question: first, why does Herr K's declaration provoke a fall of identification? And, second, why is it anguish that is produced?

The Fall of Identification

It is clear from Freud's account of the scene that Dora is very upset by Herr K's proposal, which includes the hapless *Ich habe nichts an meiner Frau.* Not only is she brutally exposed to the real of her sexuality by Herr K's proposal, she is also destabilized by the statement that on "the side of his wife, there is nothing." This sense of the German *Ich habe nichts an meiner Frau* is underlined by Lacan in his fourth seminar (p. 143) to account for the violence of Dora's reaction upon Herr K's proposal. Schematically, on the basis of Lacan's elaborations at this stage of his teaching, we may conclude that Dora could only sustain herself as subject by identifying with Frau K, who is the object of desire for both her father and Herr K, and that she thus could not bear to see this woman brought down from her untouchable position. Or, in a slightly different perspective, we could say that Frau K, at this point, no longer shields Dora from the real of sexuality and that Dora is thus awakened from her fantasmatic slumber.

This point will be further developed later. For now it is sufficient to note that Dora's position with regard to her central identification is deeply shaken.

The Regression to the Stage of Demand

This second assertion stems from a phenomenological observation of the change occurring in Dora's attitude with regard to her father's love affair with Frau K. Before the scene, she was tolerating and even enjoying it, as she could find a position for herself in their relation by deluding herself that she was essential to their love. Afterward, Dora demands that the relationship stops and that the absolute love of her father be exclusively addressed to her. On this point, we can recall the comment made by Lacan in *Seminar V* (p. 369) regarding hysterical identification: when the father is simply the addressee of the demand for love, then the hysterical subject is identified with the father. We can thus imagine that, following the scene by the lake, Dora reverts to an identification with her father, which short-circuits desire, since desire only came into the equation through the mediating function of the other woman. Dora then starts to behave as if her father had wronged her, and requires reparation: here she gives us a perfect example of the famous feminine *ressentiment* detected by Freud.

We have now postulated that the disappearance of *the* woman precipitates Dora into the troubled waters of jouissance. At this point of the argument, we need to focus on how Dora reacts to her exposure to the real of sex.

The Subsequent Anguish Resolved through the Passage to the Act

In *Seminar X,* Lacan postulates that Dora's slap is a passage to the act: in the sessions of 16 and 23 January 1963, he opposes *acting out* and *passage to the act,* relying on two Freudian cases, that of the young homosexual woman and that of Dora. Lacan defines acting out as the *monstration of an object,* and passage to the act as an attempt to restore the subject who *has been barred by the presence of an object.* Dora's passage to the act is less dramatic than the young homosexual woman's, who attempts suicide by throwing herself off a bridge, but it participates in the same mechanism, a mechanism that is elucidated in the course of the seminar.

Previously, in the first session of the same seminar, Lacan had introduced the following table in order to organize Freud's text "Inhibitions, Symptoms and Anxiety." In this table, he situates passage to the act as the last resort of the subject against anguish:

		Difficulty →
Inhibition	Impediment	Embarrassment
Emotion	Symptom	Passage to the act
Agitation	Acting out	Anguish

Movement ↓

Table inspired by Seminar X (p. 22, 93)

The link between anguish and passage to the act is clearly established by Lacan. If we are to concentrate on the event that concerns us here, it is the third column that is of interest: when *embarrassed* by the presence of an object, the subject is *barred*—Lacan remarks that em*bar*rassment resonates with bar.

In the session of 9 January 1963, Lacan provides us with another very important clue to understanding anguish: contrary to Freud's claim that anguish is without an object, he says that anguish is not without having an object, or, in French, *l'angoisse n'est pas sans objet*. This ambiguous formulation immediately indicates that anguish has to do with a drive-object, as indeed if it was any other object, Lacan would not say that anguish is *not without having* an object. It is only the specific status of object *a* that allows for such a formulation—bearing in mind that it is the fantasy that transforms a drive-object into an object of desire. Thus, if we are to combine Lacan's table and his statement as to the object of anguish, we may postulate that where there is a passage to the act, it comes as a result of an encounter with a drive-object, an encounter not filtered by desire—in other words, clothed in the imaginary scenario of the fantasy—and therefore causing anguish, the anguish of vanishing in the face of the certainty of the jouissance attributed to the Other.

On the basis of these few points we have developed our working hypothesis: Herr K's declaration produces a fall of identification in Dora, resulting in an upsurge of anguish. She resolves this anguish by slapping Herr K, the passage to the act. She then regresses to an anterior identification with her father, and subsequently demands absolute love. From this hypothesis, we can now try to work out what happened to Dora at this moment.

Demand and Desire

In chapter XX of his fifth seminar on *The Formations of the Uncon-scious,* the seminar in which Lacan constructs his graph of desire, we find a thorough elaboration of the relation between demand and desire. It is in this chapter that Lacan argues that it is insofar as Dora can *desire beyond demand* that she is content with her position in her father's af-fair, for she does not in fact identify with her father but with her father's object of desire.[5]

Let us retrace the argument. Lacan states that in neurosis the ego ideal—the identification noted I(A) on the graph—is produced after the double crossing of the line of the Other: s(A) [*signification given by the Other*]-A [*Other*]. He then moves on to situate Dora's central identifica-tion on the graph of desire, saying that such is also the case for her, but he adds that in her case, and for all hysterics, the second line ($\mathcal{S} \lozenge a$-d) represents the *desire of the father,* and that for Dora, it is after *the dou-ble crossing of those two lines* that her identification is constituted. The logical consequence of this assertion is that the ideal identification of the hysteric is precipitated *in the place of the fantasy,* a fantasy that bears the mark of the desire of the father (p. 368).

Thus, the hysteric identifies with the object of desire of the Other of love, and hence is stuck in the position of the object, a position through which she can obtain a sense of being *since it is the support of her central identification*—but at the price of a drastic alienation. Here we recall the formula of the hysterical fantasy as given in *Seminar VIII* (p. 294):

$$\frac{a \lozenge A}{-\varphi}$$

Dora places herself in the position of object of the Other's desire and be-comes resentful when she is taken for what she offers to be. This can be read as follows: *a,* the metaphoric or substitutive object, conceals her own imaginary castration (- phi), in its relation with the Other. In other words, Dora's identification with her father is not an imaginary identifi-cation but an identification with his desire. This is why we can say that Dora's object of desire is Frau K, inasmuch as she desires what is be-yond demand. But what she truly needs to be able to desire is to be the object of desire of the Other of love—classically the father—and not the object of his demand. Dora's situation is 'ideal' in a sense, for her father is impotent. She can delude herself into believing that his attachment for Frau K is sustained by a pure desire beyond demand and sexual satisfaction. And Dora shares a barred desire with him, or believes she does, thereby disavowing the presence of sexuality.

She thus identifies with this woman, object of pure desire of her father, and she does so by identifying with Herr K, not just anybody but a man who, in her mind, also desires this object of pure desire, his wife. By identifying with Herr K, at the level of the imaginary, she can also desire Frau K while also seeing herself as being desired in the same way that Frau K is by her father. When Herr K makes his hapless declaration, he annihilates the dimension of desire for Dora, who is thus returned to the status of sexual object for Herr K, assimilated to the previous object of his sexual favors, the dismissed governess—hence the importance of the number 15 for her, the notice period of the governess being a fortnight. This also implies that her father is treating her as an object of exchange, an offering of sorts to the cuckolded husband. Indeed, if Herr K does not love his wife, it means that Dora's father does not have to love her, Dora (see *Seminar IV,* p. 143). She is no longer a special, precious object of love and pure desire, but merely a woman among others, equal to others, and thus *in the field of sexuality.* Further, the woman who provides her with a ready-made solution to the enigma of femininity betrays her by exposing the fact that she read a certain explicit magazine, *Mantegazza.*

More theoretically, if she cannot sustain herself in the position of the Ideal, what does that mean? Is the Ideal for a woman equivalent to being the object of the paternal fantasy? And why is her reaction anguish, not anger or fear? On this latter point, we may venture a hypothesis: the forced reintroduction of sexuality in Dora's life undermines her fantasy, through which she enjoys on the side of privation. The irruption of something real, no longer veiled by the Ideal, shatters her fantasy, and *the fantasy is the support of desire,* as Lacan tells us in·*Seminar X* (session of 16 January 1963). If the fantasy collapses, so does desire. When desire collapses, the object becomes present, the object of the Other's demand, which indicates the certainty of jouissance. And we can start to see more clearly now that desire is a defense against jouissance, in that it introduces a significant distance between the subject and the object. Desire and anguish occupy positions of eclipse in relation to each other: when desire is present, anguish is not, and conversely. Thus, logically, the disappearance of the possibility of desire for Dora gives rise to anguish.

This is what the fall of identification renders apparent in the scene by the lake. It is then that she 'passes to the act' in order not to be *effaced* by the return of the object on her, no longer kept at bay by the fantasy.

Anguish and Desire: Approaching Jouissance

Now that we have gone through this hypothetical account of what caused Dora's anguish, let us broach the second aspect of the question: what is the mechanism of anguish? It is clear, from what has been elaborated so far, that since desire is what keeps anguish at bay, and since fantasy is the support of desire, then the fall of identification must have had a clear impact on Dora's fantasy. Her failure to incarnate the Other's object of desire shatters her fantasy, and anguish comes on the scene.

What is the function of anguish? We know that despite his somewhat fluctuating views as to the economic nature of anxiety—Strachey's translation of the German *angst*—Freud consistently saw it as a signal, indicating that some new psychical action needed to be carried out in order to restore homeostasis. Lacan did not depart from this view. We also know that Freud associated the feeling of anxiety in women with the loss of the object's love (see the last chapter of "Inhibitions, Symptoms and Anxiety"). It seems that, in Dora's case, it is losing the love obtained by means of the fantasy that allows for the return of the object that generates her anguish, the function of the object being stressed by Lacan. It is this function of the object that allows us to go beyond Freud's reading of anxiety in woman, a dual function that responds to the opposition jouissance/desire. For Lacan, indeed it is not merely the loss of love from the Ideal that generates anguish, but rather the reappearance of what the Ideal keeps at bay for the subject.

Anguish and the Object

In order to substantiate the proposition that it is the fall of identification that produces anguish, let us now turn to one of Lacan's most commented renderings of the onset of anxiety. In *Seminars IX* and *X,* Lacan develops his parable of the praying mantis to illustrate the mechanism of anguish. The parable is the following: when you see a praying mantis, and you don't know whether you are wearing a male or a female mask, anguish sets in because you *don't know* what fate is to be expected from the praying mantis. So we can understand why it is possible to say that the enigma of the desire of the Other gives rise to anguish, and we can also understand why the neurotic is constantly constructing the demand of the Other: to *eradicate the dimension of uncertainty as to the Other's* jouissance.

The initial difficulty in reconciling this first aspect of the parable, with its emphasis on the enigmatic Other, with Lacan's insistence that anguish is *not without an object,* can easily be overcome. Lacan's parable concerns the vacillation of the neurotic before the certainty of his relation to jouissance. The parable can be understood as follows: if I know for a fact that I am wearing the male mask, then anguish is at its worse because then I am *certain* that I am the *object* of the Other's jouissance. This certainty annihilates me as subject, for it does away with the dimension of desire (of the Other's desire that supports the subject's own), and it is desire that defers jouissance, that which the neurotic cannot bear. Indeed, as Lacan tells us in Seminar X, the neurotic *refuses to sacrifice his castration to the jouissance of the Other.* This refusal leads the neurotic to construct the other through his or her fantasy, itself designed to desire despite alienation in the Other (hence the correspondence between fantasy and the operation of separation). In passing, this casts some light on why the only satisfactory end of analysis should involve the exposure of the inexistence of the Other—in other words, the exposure of the fact that the jouissance one fears and one defends oneself against at great expense is attributed to an Other that is in fact tirelessly constructed by the subject. Having exposed the Other as fiction, one can then begin to address the question of the superego, that 'little bit of the real' that can no longer be displaced onto the Other. Equally, it helps us to understand why a traversal of the fantasy may be necessary to reduce the superegoic effects experienced by the subject.

Meanwhile, as long as the subject is still lured on by the charms of symptomatic truth, his or her only option is to keep his or her desire as either *impossible* or *unsatisfied,* for satisfaction would annihilate the effect of separation achieved through the fantasy. This leads me to my next section, broaching the question of desire in hysteria.

Unsatisfied Desire

Desire is thus what keeps the identification with the object of the Other's jouissance at a reasonable distance through the mediation of love achieved by means of the fantasy. The price to pay for this distance, however, is the impossibility of satisfying one's desire. For example, in analyzing the dream of the butcher's wife in his *Interpretation of Dreams,* Freud discovers that the hysteric's desire is for an unsatisfied desire, that there is thus a desire for *privation* in hysteria. One can therefore argue that the 'enjoyment' derived from privation is the substitutive mode of satisfaction of the hysteric.

How does the hysteric sustain her desire as unsatisfied? By taking an interest in the desire of the Other. The butcher's wife is interested in the enigmatic desire of her husband for her thin friend, when he usually likes voluptuous women. She is not interested in what *satisfies* him, but in what he *desires*. This clearly indicates that the hysteric is interested in the Other's lack. Why? Because her question concerns her *being* as subject, a being she obtains through the Other. This is where Lacan provides us with an answer as to what the hysteric's desire is in his "Direction of the Treatment": it is to be the *signifier of the Other's desire*—the phallus (Φ), *not the object of his satisfaction.* This explains why 'being the phallus' is a possible feminine position (see *Seminar XX,* chapter 7).

If we recall Dora's 'quartered' position on Schema L, we can understand it in the light of how she constructs and sustains her desire. First, at the level of the ego, she identifies with an *imaginary* Other, an identification that provides her with a support for her investigation of the desire of the Other (Lacan enigmatically calls Herr K the third man in *Seminar XVII,* which can be read as implying that Dora is a man as well). Second, she desires what the Other of love desires, for she can only desire through an identification with a desiring position. It allows her to explore what a woman wants. Third, at the level of being, she identifies with the object of desire of the Other, a position termed *being the phallus* by Lacan. This provides her with an answer to the question of what a man wants from a woman.

Why the phallus? Because when an object takes the place of the lack in the Other it takes on the value of the phallus. A woman may identify with man's desire, and attempt to embody it, to be the phallus, the signifier of the man's desire. By being that signifier, she acquires a way of phallicizing herself, making herself desirable in her own eyes. Why is it that the hysteric can only phallicize herself by incarnating the lack in the Other? Put simply, in hysteria the repressed returns on the body or in the Other, therefore leaving a lack in the signifying chain. The hysterical subject thus has to invent meaning from the response of the Other. This is why she is always interested in what the Other wants, and she is always challenging him to produce more sense. His answer as she interprets it is the material of her fantasy. She is not interested in drive-satisfaction, but in achieving a sense of being as subject through the movement of desire.

Passage to the Act as Resolution

When the hysteric fails to sustain herself as desirable, she can no longer desire. She is then faced with the certainty of being the object of the Other's satisfaction (in Dora's case, an object of exchange for her father, see *Seminar IV,* p. 143), a certainty that manifests itself by a kind of paralysis (here we can recall the two axes of Lacan's table: movement—difficulty). How does Dora's slap constitute a resolution of the trauma of being effaced as subject? In *Seminar X* (19 December 1963), Lacan tells us that what is at stake for the subject "is to avoid what, in anguish, is sustained by a terrible certainty," and adds that "to act is to tear certainty away from anguish." He also adds that "it may precisely be from anguish that action borrows its certainty."

These quotes illustrate how a passage to the act, insofar as it is an act, takes away the certainty that fuels anguish while transforming it into the certainty that informs the act: thus, when Dora slaps Herr K, she alleviates her anguish (this is not to say that a passage to the act is the only possible act in the face of anguish) and reconstitutes herself as subject through the certainty of action. Most passages to the act, however, as they aim at getting rid of the object with which the subject is identified, end up in more dramatic circumstances—suicide being a possible occurrence.

After this long elaboration, it is now possible to grasp the logical coordinates organizing Dora's change of attitude after the scene by the lake. We can now resituate what we have learned from Dora's particular case against the background of widespread hysterical strategies, which touch on the question of femininity. These hysterical strategies are characterized by two phenomena: first, the prevalence of privation as a mode of feminine jouissance; and, second, the tight bond attaching the hysteric's fate to that of the master, whom she constantly challenges and criticizes, but cannot do without.

Privation as Mode of Jouissance in Hysteria

The Question of Truth

In chapter VI of his seventeenth seminar, *L'envers de la psychanalyse*, Lacan returns once more to the case of Dora, this time to talk about the *truth* of the hysteric. Lacan's angle on truth touches more directly on the question of jouissance, for truth is a symptomatic production whose function is to consolidate the subject's *belief* in his symptom qua signified of the Other, and thus designed to preserve the enjoyment one derives from one's castration.

What is the truth of the hysteric, a truth that draws her always further into the entangled webs of her fantasmatic interpretations and reinterpretations of the Other's desire? From our earlier developments, it is clear that the hysteric obtains some sense of her own being by being what the Other lacks; for she strives to be at the same time the object of the Other's *desire* and the *signifier* of his lack. This is what the logic of the hysteric slipping away as object tells us, a logic noted by Lacan in his *écrit* "Subversion of the subject." She wants to be the phallus, the signifier of desire, not the object of satisfaction of this desire. It is always a close call for her to be able to incarnate the object of desire, then get out of delivering the promised satisfaction, and yet manage to retain the master's desire (being the phallus does not exhaustively define the hysteric's position, but it is a prevalent mode of being for her in relation to a certain form of knowledge, a knowledge of the sexual).

In his paper "On semblants in the relation between sexes," Miller describes 'being the phallus' as follows: "being the hole, but in relation to the Other, as if, in order to escape [her] lack of identity, one of the solutions were to displace this lack towards the Other by attacking his completeness." Beyond indicating that being the phallus amounts to incarnating what the Other lacks, more important Miller also points toward the truth of the hysteric: "We must realize that the expression *being the phallus* already implies a certain depreciation with regard to the position of *having* of the virile Other, namely a reduction of the position of *having* of the Other to the status of semblant."

And indeed, at the level of being, if the hysteric can only exist if the Other, or the master, which she confuses with the father despite all evidence pointing to the contrary,[6] is lacking, she will concentrate her efforts toward exposing the Other/master as castrated. This is her truth: *the castration of the master*.

To expose this lack in the Other, the hysteric will give up on her own jouissance; this is why it is possible to say that desire for privation is the condition of the hysteric's desire. Here we may have another angle on the scene by the lake. Herr K is for Dora someone who can bring satisfaction to her sexual desire, he is what has been called a *quart terme phallique*, a bearer of the organ. But Lacan indicates that desire for privation is what interests Dora in Herr K, thus the fact that he has the means to satisfy her sexually is important, but only insofar as another woman *deprives* her of it. Lacan derives this interpretation from Dora's first dream in Freud's case study, that of the jewel case:[7] what interests her is not the jewel, but the case. This is what she *enjoys*, says Lacan (*Seminar XVII*, p. 109). Thus, the function Frau K occupies for Dora is complicated by the fact that she is also the one who deprives her of a potential satisfaction, and Herr K's declaration exposes this belief as a construction.

Dora's second dream, the one about the death of her father,[8] is also a dream that concerns emptiness: it takes place mostly in a deserted flat, in which she finds a substitute for her father, a big book. This dream reveals another aspect of her truth: what she wants from him is the knowledge that he can produce, a knowledge on the sexual relation—Dora used to read the *Encyclopaedia* to find out about sex—and this is why she supports him against all odds.

The truth of the hysteric is thus twofold: on the one hand, the castration of the idealized father, which reveals the secret of the master, and, on the other hand, privation, that is, the acceptance by the subject of the substitutive satisfaction of being deprived.

With these elements in mind, we can now try to understand the logic behind the discourse of the hysteric, a discourse whose failure results from the fact that it is an impotent, the hysteric, questioning another impotent, the master, as to the possibility of a sexual relation only supposed to exist.

The Discourse of the Hysteric

The formula of the hysteric's discourse is well known; it illustrates that the hysteric speaks from the place of her division in order to make the master produce some knowledge about the sexual relation.

$$\frac{\cancel{S}}{a} \rightarrow \frac{S_1}{S_2}$$

Her truth is that she *enjoys* the privation involved in being the phallus as opposed to the jouissance one derives from the semblant of having or, possibly, from another form of jouissance, the Other jouissance—of which Lacan says that it does not exist in his 1974 Rome conference, "La troisième."

We know that, for Lacan, a discourse is a form of social bond. In *Seminar XVIII,* he also tells us that the discourse of the master is the discourse of the unconscious. We can understand such a statement insofar as the unconscious is structured like a language, according to the elementary signifiers of kinship. It aims at saying what *is,* or, as Lacan says in *Seminar XX, le discours du maître c'est le discours du m'être* (p. 33). It is in that sense that the S_2 is the slave signifier of the S_1 in the discourse of the master: knowledge is put to work in order to sustain the master-signifiers in their position.

$$\frac{S_1}{\cancel{S}} \rightarrow \frac{S_2}{a}$$

The discourse of the hysteric, on the other hand, interrogates the repressed or, in other words, the unconscious constituted of master-signifiers. The split subject of the unconscious interrogates the master-signifiers and reveals the castration of the master, that is, that *mastery over the body only obtains through a renunciation of* jouissance. And indeed in the discourse of the master, the surplus-enjoyment [*plus-de-jouir*] is on the side of the slave.

In *Seminar XVII,* Lacan says that the hysteric reveals the truth of the discourse of the master, namely, the impotence of man to animate his knowledge with a *plus-de-jouir.* However, the problem of the hysteric is also one of impotence: earlier, we saw that what is repressed in hysteria returns in the body or in the Other. This is why the hysteric addresses the Other to get knowledge. This is also why he or she is dissociated from knowledge and cannot invest it with jouissance, and in the discourse of the hysteric the *plus-de-jouir* is on the side of the repressed truth. This may be why her jouissance is on the side of privation.

But, as opposed to the master, the hysteric refuses to be the slave of the master-signifier. She refuses to become one through the signifier; she refuses to make herself its body, *de s'en faire le corps,* as the master does. The master acquires mastery over his body through the signifier; the hysteric refuses this one-fying power of the master-signifier.[9] This may be why she is so dependent on her identifications, for she places her being in the Other. In a sense, though, the hysteric reveals a truth that goes for all subjects: namely; that the subject only exists as masked, for the subject is not where it is represented, and conversely.

Conclusion

These elaborations on the structure of hysteria are best read in conjunction with Lacan's *Seminar XX,* a seminar in which the questions of femininity and love are prevalent and Lacan formalizes the idea of the not-all [*pas-toute*] as what of the real is irreducible to the phallic order. Femininity, the Other jouissance, are presented as that which goes beyond the dimension of the one-fying signifier. J.-A. Miller clearly signposts the necessity to think the real in connection with the question of femininity in his paper "On semblants . . . ," when he says that woman is closer to the real than man, and that it is men who are in the position of semblants. He goes on to define a semblant as that which *veils the nothing and thereby creates it as absent.* Knowing that the phallus is a semblant, this may start to make sense.

In his paper, Miller concludes his elaboration on the feminine semblants of *having* and *being* by opposing phallic jouissance—the jouissance of the owner—to the without-limit of the feminine. This seems to point in the direction of the debate surrounding the end of analysis and the pass, for where a masculine solution seems to involve an identification with the symptom—a solution favored by Lacan in his *Seminar XXIV*—and thus, in the last analysis, with a meaningless inscription of jouissance, a feminine solution seems to imply a different relation to lack, accepting the absence of unification, or *one-ification,* under the auspices of the signifier.

Are we, then, simply talking about the persistence of one's elective mode of enjoyment, in other words, is the feminine predilection for a desire that finds its source in S($\bar{A}$) simply a consequence of a jouissance on the side of privation, and is the fact that it is more difficult to desire from S($\cancel{A}$) on the masculine side of sexuation simply due to a deeper entrenchment of phallic jouissance?

Notes

1. The analyst does not interpret the analysand's unconscious from the 'outside'; on the contrary, the patient's unconscious is *produced* in the analytic relation. What the analysand produces as unconscious material is a function of the analyst's desire (the desire of the analyst supports the patient's desire), a concept developed by Lacan in his eleventh seminar. In his "Intervention on transference" (at p. 218/64), Lacan also notes that this case study is the first in which Freud acknowledges the part played by the analyst in the transference (see Freud's own "Postscript" to the case).

2. References to Freud's *Dora* will hereafter be indicated as page numbers in parentheses.

3. As indicated by Lacan in "Intervention on transference" (p. 221/67).

4. This point will become clearer in the course of this chapter. To summarize a forthcoming argument, it is because Dora, like all hysterics, refuses to subject herself to the master-signifier that her body is not one, but is fragmented, as attested to by her conversion symptoms. Not having a body-as-one, it is incredibly difficult to assume genital sexuality, in which the subject's body is the object of the other's desire.

5. This can be seen to prefigure Lacan's later concept of *père-version,* a term he coined to designate access to the feminine through paternal desire among other things.

6. Why does the hysteric identify the father with the master? Lacan argues that it is because the father, even though he may be impotent, remains father up to the end of his life. In his seventeenth seminar, Lacan compares the father to the *ancien combattants,* the French term referring to war veterans, who remain '*combattants'* to the end of their lives. He then coins the phrase "*ancien géniteur,*" ironically meaning that the father, even though he is impotent, lacking, and so on, is endowed with the power of creation until the end of his life.

7. This is the dream as narrated by Dora to Freud: "A house was on fire. My father was standing beside my bed and woke me up. I dressed quickly. Mother wanted to stop and save her jewel-case; but Father said: 'I refuse to let myself and my two children be burnt for the sake of your jewel-case.' We hurried downstairs, and as soon as I was outside I woke up" (p. 64).

8. In her second dream, Dora returns home to find that everybody is at the cemetery for her father's funeral (p. 94). Upon receiving this information from a maidservant,

she calmly goes to her father's study and proceeds to read from a big book. This dream, according to Lacan, shows that in order to access the truth of her femininity, the hysteric subject has to accept that the father knows nothing of the sexual relation. In the analytic treatment, it is often possible to identify a moment at which the hysteric 'gets rid' of her father through a formation of her unconscious in order to free access to knowledge. This moment marks the emergence of a 'wanting to know' that puts an end to some of the most elaborate hysterical strategies.

9. On this point we can see why the body of the obsessional is mortified ("am I dead or alive") whereas that of the hysteric is fragmented (as attested to by conversion symptoms).

References

Freud, Sigmund (1901), "Fragments of an Analysis of a Case of Hysteria," SE VII.

Freud, Sigmund (1905), "Three Essays on the Theory of Sexuality," SE VII.

Freud, Sigmund (1925), "Inhibitions, Symptoms and Anxiety," SE XX

Julien, Philippe (1993), in *L'apport freudien: éléments pour une encyclopédie de la psychanalyse,* Ed. Pierre Kaufmann (Paris: Editions Bordas).

Lacan, Jacques (1951), "Intervention sur le transfert," *Écrits* (Paris: Seuil, 1966); "Intervention on transference" in J. Mitchell and J. Rose, *Feminine Sexuality* (London: Macmillan, 1982, pp. 61–73).

Lacan, Jacques (1955–1956), Le Séminaire, Livre III, *Les psychoses,* Paris: Editions du Seuil (1981); or The Seminar of Jacques Lacan, Book III, *On Psychoses 1955–1956* (London: Routledge, 1993).

Lacan, Jacques (1956–1957), Le Séminaire, Livre IV, *La relation d'objet* (Paris: Seuil, 1994).

Lacan, Jacques (1957–1958), Le Séminaire, Livre V, *Les formations de l'inconscient* (Paris: Seuil, 1998).

Lacan, Jacques (1960–1961), Le Séminaire, Livre VIII, *Le transfert* (Paris: Seuil, 2001).

Lacan, Jacques (1961–1962), Le Séminaire Livre IX: *L'identification,* unpublished.

Lacan, Jacques (1962–1963), Le Séminaire Livre X: *L'angoisse* (Paris: Seuil, 2004).

Lacan, Jacques (1969–1970), Le Séminaire, Livre XVII, *L'envers de la psychanalyse* (Paris: Seuil, 1991).

Lacan, Jacques (1972–1973), Le Séminaire, Livre XX, *Encore* (Paris: Seuil, 1975); The Seminar of Jacques Lacan, Book XX, *Encore: On Feminine Sexuality, Love and Knowledge 1972–1973,* trans. Bruce Fink (New York & London: Norton, 1998).

Lacan, Jacques (1974), 'La troisième', in *Lettres de l'Ecole freudienne,* No. 16, 1975, pp. 177–203.

Lacan, Jacques (1976–1977), Le Séminaire, Livre XXIV, *L'Insu que sait de l'Une-bévue s'aile à mourre,* unpublished.

Miller, Jacques-Alain (1996) "Des semblants dans la relation entre les sexes" in *La Cause Freudienne* No. 32, or *Psychoanalytical Notebooks* 3.

Soler, Colette, "Hysteria and Obsession," *Reading Seminars I and II* (Albany: SUNY Press, 1995).

Stevens, Alexandre (1993), "Embarrassment, Inhibition, and Repetition" (in this volume).

Gaze and Representation

Richard Klein

The Lack of Desire

The object gaze, first given systematic coverage in *Seminar XI*,[1] is a most ironic object: with *a* gaze representation is brought into question. A properly functioning gaze, that is, without eyes, does not generate representations. "I only see from one point but in my existence I am looked at from everywhere." My existence is situated, evidently, in opposition to my attributes, that is, my appearance. When it does mix in with vision, the field of vision becomes agitated and desperate.

According to Lacan in this seminar, in order for an object to count as an object *a*, two properties are necessary. First, the object must be a separable organ. Second, it must have a relation to lack.[2] With these two properties the gaze is correlative to castration: "the object *a* is most evanescent in its function of symbolizing the central lack of desire, which I have always indicated in a univocal way by the algorithm -φ."[3] The gaze is the most mysterious, most hidden object, but it has enough weight to symbolize the central lack of desire.[4] Something that is evanescent, that escapes representation, but nevertheless carries some weight, can only be a superego.

It is not purely and simply lack of desire but lack of desire that promotes desire. For instance, on p. 852 in "Du 'Trieb' de Freud," the assumption of castration creates the lack that promotes desire that is desire of the Other. Castration is a lack of desire that promotes desire intertwined with the law.[5] Jacques-Alain Miller has called castration the source of libido, as the lack, presumably, that promotes desire.

Castration was the preserve of the signifier of the phallus. Now Lacan does not say that the phallus has the function of symbolizing the central lack of desire. The object *a* has this function. Consider the final footnote in "Position of the Unconscious" in which he says that he has not been able to extend the object *a* as far as the point that constitutes its crucial interest, namely, the object -φ as cause of the castration complex. It seems that this is a considerable elaboration on the lost objects of the drives that foreshadow castration in Freud's doctrine. This term "object minus little phi" does not reappear in this teaching, as far as I know. It will become the object cause of desire.

The gaze is the lack as expressed in castration.[6] How is it to be distinguished from the phallic signifier? The object *a* remains evanescent. The phallus comes into play when the subject operating with it own loss rejoins the Other, making its desire the desire of the Other. The phallus entails representation. The object *a* does not. Castration is not a representation. For the object *a* to entail representation it has to become a make-believe. In the triangle of *Encore,* the *a* in a missed encounter with the real is rejoining the Other with the emergence of the phallus. The *a* is itself heterogeneous to the Other and will be placed in it as extimate.

There is a topological orientation in chapter 9 from the symbolic to the real. The chapter is framed by the object *a,* which at the beginning of the chapter has a symbolic status: the function of symbolizing the central lack of desire. The object *a,* he says, has a symbolic relation to man.[7] Toward the end of the chapter it has a real status, but that's my supposition. Lacan does not state it explicitly in the scene described by St. Augustine. In between, there is the function of the make-believe, as Jacques-Alain Miller translates *le semblant.* It's a good translation since it implicates representation. This is the orientation that is mapped on the base of the triangle that appears in *Encore.*[8]

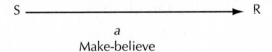

Its status as make-believe does not just implicate representation but gives the object an imaginary gloss. The object *a* has a relation to RSI at the base of the triangle.

The Gaze and the Conscious

On proposing such an object as the gaze, the issue of the conscious (the Cs) is raised. The Cs is defined as I see myself seeing myself, a double reflexive implicating the mirror stage. In the I see myself seeing myself the Cs is tied to the imaginary. Where else is one going to situate looking and being looked at but in the field of Cs? However, for Lacan the gaze is eliminated from the I see myself seeing myself. The gaze is not reflexive, let alone doubly reflexive. In its double reflexiveness the Cs is irremediably limited. In fact, it is irremediably circular and has to be for that reason excluded from the principles of psychoanalytic treatment. The gaze is the reverse side of the Cs, he says. It seems to be the least conscious object, the most lost.[9]

There can be a representation in perception and a representation in the Cs. Lacan was awoken from a nap by a knocking at the door. The representation occurs in relation to the perception. In a second moment the representation occurs in relation to the Cs when he recovers possession of the representation.[10] When the representation qualifies as the property of the subject, it is a representation in relation to the Cs. My representations, visual or otherwise, belong to me.[11] I take this notion of representations being earmarked as a form of property as Lacan's way of indicating libidinal investment. Only a libidinally invested representation can qualify as property. A representation in relation to perception is a libidinal investment in relation to the Cs. Freud combines perception and Cs in one system written Pcpt.-Cs. Lacan keeps them separate, making the dividing line libidinal investment, at least in this little development.

Lacan reconstitutes the representation around perception, which signals that he is knocked up. We would have to add that on recovering possession of it, he knocks himself up by knocking himself up. Formulated in this way does limit us to imaginary forms only. It is always the signifier that organizes the field of perception. 'Knocked up' is a signifier that represents the subject to another signifier that is unconscious. because repressed. The reflexive repetition of the one signifier indicates that the second signifier is repressed. Beyond repression is the gaze since "I am in my existence looked at from everywhere."

The Gaze in Alienation and Separation

The gaze is an operator in another version of the mirror stage in the *Écrits:* "What is operating in the triumphant assumption of the body-image in the mirror is the most vanishing object, making an appearance marginal to the exchange of looks manifest in the child's turning towards the one who is holding it."[12] The exchange is doubly reflexive embedded in a signifier in another version that would eliminate the gaze from it, and in the above version confirmed much later in *Encore* where he says that the image is held together by the remainder.[13] The remainder is not the representation, but it is holding the representation together.

According to a proposition on p. 844 of the *Écrits,* the subject is operating with its own loss with the effect of separation from the Other.[14] In the above version of the mirror stage, the subject is the gaze that has been lost in separation. In the manifest actions of this version, the subject is returning to alienation, according to another proposition on p. 844. In the exchange of looks, it is joining up again with the Other, making its desire the desire of the Other. The gaze here is the lost object.

Considered from another point of view, that of object-refinding, the gaze in this version can be said to be the cause of object-refinding. The object refound is an object connected to the nothing of the lost object as, for instance, in the schema of the veil on p. 156 of *Seminar IV.*

The Gaze and the Structure of Fetishism

The screen appears in Seminar IV in the form of the veil. At least they are the same concept insofar as an image is painted on both. The schema of the veil is supposed to represent the structure of fetishism:[15]

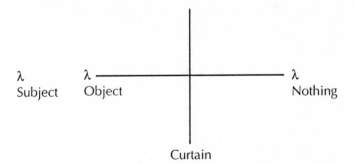

The structure of fetishism is given by Freud in the field of the visible: the shine on the nose. It is a transliteration from the English glance at the nose to the German *Glanz auf die Nase.* Freud's patient spent some of his early childhood in England. If we are in the field of the visible, then there must be something special about it since Freud tells us that this shiny nose is only perceptible to the patient. No one else sees it. We are not in a field that is essentially visual but in the field of what Lacan calls in several places in *Seminar XI* geometrical optics. The shiny nose is the object gaze. Does it have the two properties which make it count as an object *a*? Is it a separable organ and does it have a relation to lack? The shiny nose is the object connected to nothing in the previous schema. For Freud, the nothing is maternal castration, and the object is a substitute for what is missing. It is realized as image on the veil, he says in *Seminar IV*. In *Seminar XI,* the veil is the fantasy as screen that hides the traumatic real.[16] Lacan says that the phallus is the object that is symbolic.[17] A little later in his teaching, an object that has symbolic status raises it to the rank of signifier. In this case, the nose is the symbolic object, but its shine seems to fulfill the requirements of an object *a*. It is connected to a separable organ and in a relation to lack. Converging on the nose is a mixture of signifier and object *a*.

Envy

The object *a* toward the end of the chapter is operating in a clinical vignette provided by one of the church fathers. It does not conform to the proposition that the gaze escapes that form of vision that is satisfied with itself in imagining itself as consciousness. In the scene described by St. Augustine, the object gaze appears in the field of vision. There is no evident split between the eye and the gaze.[18] Nevertheless, it does not appear in the field of vision comfortably. He says that the eye has been made desperate by the gaze. A child is looking at his brother at his mother's breast. It is a bitter gaze that tears the brother to pieces and has an effect on himself of poison.[19] If the brother is an image that can be indexed on *i(a)*, the object *a* is a disintegrator of the image. The gaze here is not lost. It is jouissance. It is a will of jouissance without renunciation. It is not quite a superego yet. To function like a superego, there has to be a will of jouissance plus renunciation of said jouissance. The more it is renounced, the more intense the will. The superego has not yet been internalized.

Lacan says that envy is not jealousy. Envy, he says, is based on an object that is of no use to the subject, though it provides satisfaction to another.[20] It is distinct from jealousy in another way only implicated here. Jealousy is based on love that gives the object its use. That's not the case in the previous scene of envy. It is based on hate. The drive manifested in the scene is a pure death drive. The binary jealousy/envy seems to reflect the binary in Freud's last theory of the drive: Eros/Thanatos.

There is an incompatibility between the eye and the gaze, and it is making vision desperate. Although the scene is taking place in the field of the visible, the object gaze is not assimilable to imaginary representations. Moreover, it is outside discourse. It has nothing of the signifier about it. It is real based on the death drive.

Appearance and Being

Appearance and being are a traditional metaphysical binary that crops up a few times in the chapters on the object gaze. According to Aristotle, to say that something exists does not describe it. A thing's appearance is the effect of description. The subject passes from existence to the function of the first attribute.[21] If in my existence I am looked at from everywhere, then the function of first attribute is a defense against the object gaze. That has to be an ideal signifier from where I see myself as the Other sees me. It is the signifier that represents the subject to the other signifier. Appearance implies representation. Existence, then, does not necessarily fall under representation. The subject must be given the chance one day to exist at the level of drive that ex-sists, says Lacan.[22] The drive is on the side of being and not on the side of appearance. There is already an orientation here from appearance to ex-sistence or from representation to ex-sistence.

Anamorphosis is an artifice based on a disconnection of being from attribute or of being from appearance. Lacan calls it an existential divorce, with the result that the body disappears into space, reevoking the substance that was lost, reevoking an initial extraction of jouissance.[23]

Although the animal, too, breaks up into being and semblant in the natural world of mimicry, it doesn't seem that natural mating behavior is in question here. The semblant in the natural world is the paper tiger shown to the other. The subject is playing with the function of the screen that could be the mask. Appearance is based on the mask. The masculine and feminine are conjoined in the mask. According to Riviere on the masquerade, the mask has feminizing effects. Lacan adds the masculine to the mask. The masculine and feminine ideal are represented in the psyche in the term "masquerade."[24] As semblant, the mask is a paper tiger. Mao used it because a paper tiger is not the essence of the tiger. Appearance is not essence. Representation of femininity and masculinity does not imply the essence of masculinity and femininity. These gender terms are a paper tiger.[25]

It is not just a matter of gender distinction through the mask. Through the mediation of the mask the masculine and feminine meet in the most acute, most intense way. One supposes that this is the sexual encounter. Gender always implies the sexual relation. If it is mediated through the mask, then it, too, is a paper tiger. But what is this gaze beyond the mask or screen on which the sexual encounter is taking place?[26] Is it the lost object?

Light, the Screen, and the Painting

The screen is the locus of mediation between the man and the woman insofar as Lacan seems to be using the notions of mask and screen interchangeably.[27] The fantasy is the screen that conceals something else, namely, the drive as lack of representation.[28] The fantasy, then, is the locus of mediation between the man and the woman. The sexual encounter takes place on the screen mediated by the mask, slightly different aspects of notions that are sometimes taken as synonymous. In *Seminar IV,* the masculine pole of the encounter is constructed on the veil. On choosing the screen for the encounter the effect is fetishistic love. He says that the veil is the best way to imagine the fundamental situation of love. What is loved in the object is something beyond which is nothing. The nothing is there symbolically.[28] Whatever is projected on the screen is material for the symbolic. He calls the phallus a symbolic object at this time. Something rather flimsy is promoting the symbol so that the symbol itself needs support. Love is a way of shoring up the symbol. The subject plays with the screen,[29] that is, he fantasizes, is concerned strictly with his fetish. He does not confront his own castration beyond the screen. Beyond the screen castration becomes the gaze.[30] Castration looks and does not generate representations.

In a mutual attraction between the screen and light, the cinema is a marker of modernity in that it has become a prosthetic device for the sexual relation that does not exist. It seems that, on the contrary, what emerges here is an antagonism between the screen and light in the case where light is the gaze. That which is gaze is always a play of light and opacity. Light looks at me.[31] The screen and the light that look at me are mutually antagonistic. If there is supposed to be an image on the screen, when the gaze emerges, the light retreats from the screen, which allows the object to emerge.[32] The light I enter through the gaze is the light that retreats from the screen.[33] This gaze incarnates light and prevents me from being a screen.[34] The image on the screen can be indexed on $i(a)$, and, when the light retreats, the a emerges. My supposition is that the retreat of light is equivalent to the crossing of the fantasy. The withdrawal of light from the screen undermines the sexual encounter insofar as the subject enters the sexual relation by way of fantasy.

The story of the sardine can is supposed to reveal the subject's relation to light.[35] Lacan escaped from his student life in Paris and went to sea with Breton fishermen. At sea, Petit-Jean spotted a sardine can floating in the water, glittering in the sun. He said to Lacan: "You see that can? Do you see it? Well, it doesn't see you." Petit-Jean eliminated the imaginary from his utterance. There is no mutuality between Lacan and the can. It enabled Lacan to experience the can looking at him. The can is an object a that has fallen, being the waste material of the fishing industry. In this 'looking at him,' Lacan, it seems, experienced an identification with the can that was not comfortable. What sort of representation would such an identification have generated? The can has separated from the Other of the canning industry that is the destiny of every can. Is it the vicissitude of every analyst to become a used sardine can? The can is to be situated at the point of light in the little triangle.[36] If it has separated from the Other, there is no place to inscribe the Other in the schema of triangles. The schema of triangles is based on the barred Other.

The can is placed at the point of light in the little triangle on p. 91.[37] This is the point at which everything that looks at me is situated.[38] The can embodies light, and Lacan enters light through the gaze. He cannot be a screen in this light. In other words, no image forms. Light and screen are antagonistic. The most he can expect is to be inscribed in the painting as stain.

A painting is not a representation.[39] There is an absence in it, a hole and reality are marginal in it. However, I think that a painting has to be a representation in order to say that there is a hole in it, that something is absent in it. Lacan also raises this question: "what is a hole if nothing surrounds it?"[40] There is a gaze in the picture.[41] A representation that provides a space for the gaze has a hole in it. The artist imposes himself on the spectator as gaze.[42] In other words, the artist is lost in the painting, and it is this being lost that holds the image together. Take especially the self-portrait. Involved with the gaze, the artist more than anyone is a subject operating with its own loss.

Are not the two ambassadors of *The Ambassadors* representations and surrounded by representations of the arts and sciences? Lacan says it in his way: the two splendidly dressed figures belong to appearence,[43] and are a part of the *vanitas* of this painting, the paper tiger. We cannot register the two ambassadors on the schema of triangles because they are representations, and the painting is not a representation. The flying phallic object in the foreground can be registered. Why shouldn't it be a representation? Representations become the subject's property. If something raises a question like What is it?, it is not something so familiar as property. The object is on the side of being. This is the anamorphosis of the painting where a hidden image is installed. It is otherwise a skull or the annihilated subject or the minus little phi of castration.[44] It's the point of existential divorce in this painting, the disconnection of being from appearence.[45] It is the point at which the body fades into space.

The Gaze and the Names-of-the-Father

Chapter 9 starts out on the question of what a picture is. It is answered in the last paragraph of the chapter: the function of the picture is to tame and to civilize.[46] He also calls it a pacifying function.[47] If we introduced such a picture into the scene that St. Augustine describes, would it bring peace to the subject? I doubt it. What will bring peace is to let the gaze drop. Letting the gaze drop is the renunciation of jouissance. Satisfaction in renunciation is encouraged by the painting, he says,[48] if the spectator is susceptible, if the spectator is civilizable. In the scene of envy, a will of jouissance is operating, but the brother has not yet renounced this form of jouissance.

This is one of the places in *Seminar XI* that the abandoned seminar on the Names-of-the-Father makes its appearance anyway in reference to the icon. The icon holds us under its gaze.[49] The icon is an object *a*. It has the opposite effect to the earlier scene of envy by inviting us to lay down our gaze. The icon is one of the Names-of-the-Father, still written with capital letters. Here God is made present through the gaze, as an object connected to renunciation. The gaze is a will of jouissance and also as a Name-of-the-Father it brings renunciation of said jouissance. The signifier of the Name-of-the-Father has now become an object *a*, and this will not be the end of the decline in the function of the father in Lacan's teaching.

This chapter was part of a seminar held at the New York Freud Lacan Study Group on 17 December 2000.

Notes

1. J. Lacan, *Seminar XI: The Four Fundamental Concepts of Psychoanalysis* (London: Penguin, 1977).

2. Ibid., p.103.

3. Ibid., p.105.

4. Ibid., p.17.

5. J. Lacan, "Du 'Trieb' de Freud et du désir du psychanalyste," in *Écrits* (Paris: Seuil, 1966) p. 852; also in *Reading Seminars I and II* (Albany: SUNY Press, 1996).

6. J. Lacan, *Seminar XI,* op. cit., p. 77.

7. Ibid., p.105.

8. J. Lacan, *Seminar XX: Encore,* trans. B. Fink (New York & London: Norton, 1998), p. 90.

9. Ibid., pp. 80–83.

10. Ibid., pp. 56–57.

11. Ibid., p. 81.

12. J. Lacan, "De nos antécédents," in *Écrits,* op. cit., p. 70.

13. J. Lacan, *Seminar XX,* op. cit., p.6.

14. J. Lacan, "Position de l'inconscient," in *Écrits,* op. cit., p. 844; also in *Reading Seminar XI* (Albany: SUNY Press, 1995).

15. J. Lacan, *Le Séminaire IV: La relation d'objet* (Paris: Seuil, 1994), p. 156.

16. J. Lacan, *Seminar XI,* op. cit., p. 60.

17. J. Lacan, *Le Séminaire IV,* op. cit., p. 152.

18. J. Lacan, *Seminar XI,* op. cit., pp. 73–74.

19. Ibid., p. 116.

20. Ibid.

21. J. Lacan, "Remarque sur le rapport de Daniel Lagache" in *Écrits,* op.cit.

22. Ibid., p. 662.

23. Ibid., p. 681.

24. J. Lacan, *Seminar XI,* op. cit., p. 193.

25. Ibid., p. 107.

26. Ibid.

27. Ibid.

28. Ibid., p. 60.

29. J. Lacan, *Le Séminaire IV,* op. cit., p. 155.

30. J. Lacan, *Seminar XI,* op. cit., p. 107.

31. Ibid., p. 77.

32. Ibid., p. 96.

33. Ibid., p. 108.

34. Ibid., p. 106.

35. Ibid., p. 96.

36. Ibid., pp. 95–96.

37. Ibid., p. 91.

38. Ibid., p. 91.

39. Ibid., p. 95.

40. Ibid., pp. 108, 110.

41. J. Lacan, *Le Séminaire XXIII* (Paris: Seuil, 2005), session of 18 February 1975.

42. Ibid., p. 101.

43. Ibid., p. 100.

44. Ibid., p. 88.

45. Ibid., pp. 88–89.

46. *Écrits,* p. 681.

47. Op.cit., p. 116; Ibid., p. 101.

48. Ibid., p. 111.

49. Ibid., p. 113.

The Perception and Politics
of Discourse

Bogdan Wolf

Lacan's notion of discourse has always struck me as belonging strictly to the Freudian field. Before devoting a whole seminar to the structure of discourse, Lacan acknowledged this by plowing the fertile land of one of Freud's works.

Let's just say that Freud left for us in this work, *Entwurf* by name, a sesame of signifiers that logically condense, posthumously and in a strange kind of way, his entire corpus. His testimony, legacy, intuition, and science of psychoanalysis are already there in the *Project*. It would be even justified to speak about an alliance between this work of Freud and Lacan's teaching of the seventies. Where exactly can we find this alliance?

Here, I would like to return to some of Lacan's elaborations that enabled him to take a step toward a construction of discourse in *Seminar XVII*. This step, taken by Lacan a decade earlier in *The Ethics of Psychoanalysis,* leads him to the open sesame. And he does this with the words I have always found intriguing and seductive—"the perception of discourse." The full sentence reads: "That which emerges in *Bewusstsein* is *Wahrnehmung,* the perception of this discourse, and nothing else."[1]

Beyond Freud

Several things emerge from this phrase. 'Perception of discourse' is at the same time subversive and innovative. It breaks the deadlock of psychology and reaches beyond ontological and phenomenological accounts of the psyche from Plato to Heidegger, although it is precisely the 'beyond', the topology of beyond, that Lacan brings under scrutiny.

If Lacan made a step beyond Freudian psychology—this is it. It is the beyond that will form the principle of an alliance between the *Project* and Lacan's late teaching.

Most important, in the *Entwurf,* Freud lays the foundations for approaching the question of the ethics and politics of psychoanalysis, and he does this by means of three elements: quantity (jouissance), representation (*Vorstellung*), and the subject (*das Ich*).

But the most amazing thing of all—and this is what truly distinguishes Freud's conception from any other—is that this apparatus in question, this psychical engine of Freud, this most complex and yet simple piece of machinery is designed to show that it does not work! What gapes open in the heart of the apparatus is a failure or a fault, and the machine of Freud is there to cover up this fault, to make up for the loss, and to produce a representation *in lieu* of this failure.

Anything written on the subject before Freud is merely a model.

Accordingly, Lacan stresses that Freud's *Vorstellung* is detached from the philosophical tradition, and that it has a status of an empty, uninhabited abode. It is a dwelling place without dwellers, although it is only through libidinal investment—appropriately called by Freud *Besetzung,* which also means "to occupy"—that this dwelling place can also be exchanged as residence. What we can say with Lacan is that the Freudian *Vorstellung* is without meaning.

'Perception of discourse' opens a dimension that escapes psychology in that it separates discourse from speech.

What Lacan introduces us to is the "dominance of a signifier in a subject's unconscious chain."[2] We will have to see what this dominance implies for Lacan, and how it promotes the signifier to the rank of the master.

First, an external, raw quantity enters the outer layer of the apparatus, called φ, which stands for the nerve endings, muscles, reflex action. Then, there is a very complex network, system ψ, of ramifying tracks through which a quantum $Q\acute{\eta}$, transformed from the raw Q, passes in such a way that the aim is discharge with a certain level of $Q\acute{\eta}$, necessarily, to remain. A given level of quantity cannot reach zero, as the apparatus would come to a halt.

The *Bahnungen* led Strachey to introduce a term that raised Lacan's objection, namely, "facilitation." Not only do the *Bahnungen* fail to facilitate passages but also, Lacan adds, the term implies something opposite to facilitation. How are we to take this opposition here? What is involved in the movement of speech, *Bewegung,* in the passage from one signifier to another—during which some quantum is discharged, some transformed and some remains—is a difficulty, here overcome by way of clearing a path. The metaphor of railway or rail track is clear enough, although we also need to include in this the process, and effort, of laying down the track. The difficulty would therefore rule out a translation of *Bahnung* as "conduit" or "conduction," which is a grist for the mill of neurosciences and does not take us anywhere.

Quite simply, *Bahnung* is a track or a pathway. But the pathway—the term *Wege* is used by Freud in the *Project* a number of times and is already manifest in *Bewegung*—only becomes a pathway when it is trodden, passed through more than once, through repetition then. In short, *Bahnung* is an articulation of saying the same thing over and over, which is what Lacan said he always did. And what he extracts from Freud's articulation is that as far as the signifying structure ψ is concerned, a quantity is replaced by a quantity plus *Bahnung*. This seems crucial to me if we are to grasp the repetitive character of these passages. A libidinal investment in the subject's identification thus produces a pathway—and Freud speaks, even shows us diagrams, of the width and passability of a pathway, which makes clear that *Bahnung* has nothing to do with the mechanics of conduction—while also producing an irreducible sediment.

In the heart of the ψ system, which is the unconscious, there is *das Ich,* the subject. What is striking is that Freud accounts for it solely on the basis of quantity and distribution. He isolates *das Ich* as a cluster of neurons, although it is obvious by now that one is enough, as we are dealing with a metaphor and have to speak about the representations by which the subject is constituted. The cluster of *Vorstellungen,* caught in the signifying chain, is characterized by the uniform distribution of libido. The subject has an unconscious function, and what Lacan highlights is that there is no difference between *das Ich* and ψ. The subject is unconscious.

The unconscious, ψ, the only system exclusively responsible for reproducing and remembering, represents for Freud a storeroom. As he writes in Letter 73 to Fliess, the unconscious appears as a larder, *Vorratskammer,* of the Other, or a knowledge of the Other, from which, as he shows us, he can draw at will, subject to the pleasure principle that guides him through associations. But the discovery of the unconscious by the father of psychoanalysis is inaugurated by none of the systems I have mentioned so far.

So far nothing has been said about quality.

The Question of Quality

If the sesame is a term I use here to designate the treasure of knowledge, the question remains as to what open sesame ushers us in. Its opening, as Lacan demonstrates to us in 1959, is a matter for signifiers or, more precisely, for a perception of signifiers. According to Lacan, the entry to the unconscious is made with "the perception of discourse, and nothing else." What opens the way to the unconscious, no longer to a reservoir but to structure, is an intervention of reality through the third system, namely *Wahrnehmung,* perception.

The signifier is without quality. This is what Lacan insists on. He insists not only on the primacy of the signifier but, above all, on its dominance. The signifier is without quality, yet it undergoes a qualification. At this moment, Freud tries to combine the essence of science with the ethics of subjectivity. Quality, which touches on the unconscious, gives meaning. Signification is an immediate effect of what Freud calls the experience of satisfaction. At the origin of ethics there is an intervention of reality. The emergence of the Other becomes for the subject the first response, the first intervention to the cry of helplessness. At the origin of discourse, the Other gives meaning to the cry of helplessness. Lacan marked this primary gift as $s(A)$, the signified of the Other in the structure of the subject. He thus linked signification with the perception of discourse.

The primary signifier, responsible for the formation and reproduction of *memoria,* does not belong to the semantic order of quality. What does the signifier without quality indicate to us if not a disjunction? It is the disjunction between the signifier and the signified, which indicates that there is a disparity between the signifier and the signified sediment left over from the *Bewegung* of representations.

What Lacan alerts us to is that no matter how radical this disjunction, it does not account for everything involved in this relation. Jacques-Alain Miller highlighted this by pointing out that in the structure of the signifier not everything is signifier. If the signifier does not belong to the order of meaning, if it does not suffice to account for the signifier in terms of quality it is because there is in the structure of the signifier something of the order of the unqualifiable.

Not only is there a fault in the apparatus, but also there is a failure of reduction, of liquidation of what the intervention of reality isolates in the subject as the subject's permanent and irreducible kernel. On the one hand, as I have mentioned, for Freud of the *Entwurf* there is no difference between the subject and the mnemic representation. On the other hand, the complex of perception, where the qualification is fixed, circumscribes the unqualifiable Thing.

The reduction of libido to zero may well be a failure, but it is a strange kind of failure indeed if it bears the marks of life. Life is both a refusal of this failure and its negation. It is therefore not a success either, given that in analysis a promise can only act as a deception on the side of the subject. How could we ever make a promise that analysis be successful?

Whither Oedipus?

As both a refusal of failure and negation, life remains ambiguous. Its ambiguity can be traced to different definitions Lacan gives of it. For example, in the seminar *RSI* he situates it in the real. In his reading of Freud's *Entwurf* in 1959, the principle of life is symbolic because it is linked to the pleasure principle in the signifying chain. But Lacan also shows us in the schema of double intersection in *The Ethics* that life spills over between the pleasure and reality principles. Life intervenes in the principle of life. This relation seems to me as correlative to the distinction between life and the living being Jacques-Alain Miller discussed.[3]

And he says that life is coupled not with truth but with knowledge. But how? Life cannot stand knowledge. This is how the story of Oedipus ends. Although life that cannot stand knowledge is blind and mute, and perpetuates itself without any why or when or whither, a knowledge of life is caught in the body of the Other. The subject's knowledge of life can thus become an admission of the refusal to know. This refusal has to do with the fact that knowledge of life, being caught in the signifying chain, solicits the question of the knowledge of death. The refusal to know, which is on the side of repression, is thus twofold. Life refuses to know and life is refused. Both concern the subject's desire of the Other. In the last hours of Oedipus's life, there is an appeal to life that is refused—namely, to life as real, life as life. Here we have a nostalgia of life.

At the very end of *Oedipus at Colonus* we encounter the last moments of Oedipus's passage. He bids farewell to his beloved daughters, then walks away alone as if life was already over for him, and as if this life that is over offered no place of rest for him but was already a hollow, an empty place that drives him toward life. This is Oedipus's nostalgia. It is difficult not to notice that these words were written by Sophocles when he was about ninety-five—the age when the sense of castration eclipses perhaps the dignity of its analytical use. According to Lacan's logic of the refinding of the object, life can only be refound when it is lost. Such is the sense of castration.

Finally, when all alone, the gods call him: "You, you there, Oedipus—what are we waiting for? You hold us back too long! We must move on, move on!"[4] This is the end of Oedipus, the whither of Oedipus, although the translation embroiders on the dramatic effect more than the original. Is life on the side of the real? At least we can say that Lacan placed the gods on the side of the real. And Sophocles gives us an illustration of the real that moves on and on without why or when or whither. Will Oedipus catch up with it or does Sophocles, at the age of ninety-five, play a joke on us of the Achilles and tortoise kind?

Life as real remains in the shackles of the double refusal because 'no man alive can say' how Oedipus died. All this is narrated to us through the messenger who eloquently shuffles the words of the gods, the facts of Oedipus's enigmatic departure, and the impossible to tell. It is perhaps the most dramatic monologue in the play. From the time of solving the riddle of Sphinx to the time of his blindness and beyond, Oedipus only comes to realize that there is knowledge he does not know, what Lacan calls an unknown knowledge of the body of the Other that is refused in favor of nostalgia for life. If the gods are on the side of the real, then this is what intervenes in reality. What is passed on in this call of urgency, perhaps impatience of the real beyond law, has to do with the Other. Oedipus's departure is tied to this call of the gods, to the last intervention of the Other. He identifies with the object and vanishes, according to the messenger, beyond Oedipus. He has now become a riddle.

Hither *Nebenmensch*

The conclusive moments of the Oedipus story show us that there is life that is refused. Jacques-Alain Miller called it the subject's refusal of the body of the Other. He then elaborates this refusal in terms of the relation between the ego and sexual drives. We already find the signs of this refusal in Freud's introduction of the *Nebenmensch*. Lacan calls it the intervention of reality. How does reality intervene for the subject?

There is life in the intervention of reality that is refused and that remains unqualifiable. This intervention of reality as unqualifiable is elaborated by Freud under the *Nebenmensch* complex. The complexity implies here two elements and their simultaneous occurrence, which is why Freud situates them in the subject. These two elements are only distinguished at the level of judgment—that is, at the level of signification. And it is through this distinction, so strikingly discussed by him in "Negation" in 1925, that he introduces what in the subject's experience of quality becomes isolated as the mysterious *das Ding*. An experience of attribute is how the subject enters what Freud called the experience of satisfaction, *Befriedegungserlebnis*, which takes place *in vivo* and *in medio*. And it is *in medio* of the experience of the *Nebenmensch* that an alien and hostile object becomes absorbed into the subject. No English term seems to have done justice to the *Nebenmensch*, as "neighbor" is, quite simply, too weak. It is rather the most intimate—Lacan will say extimate—partner of the subject, its mOther.

Let's note in passing that Freud designates *das Ding*, the permanent and self-identical part of the complex, with the letter *a*. The intervention of the Other thus introduces the relation of neighborhood, at the same time difference and identity, togetherness and disjunction. The step that Lacan takes to mathematize this relation between the primary signifier and the unqualifiable thing consists in designating a place to be occupied by the master signifier at one time, and by the object *a,* at another.

At the beginning there is a hallucination, which accounts for identity or sameness between the wish for an object and the signifier of perceived object. It is one of the relations between the real and the symbolic. And it is with respect to the perceived signifier of the object that Freud reserves for it the name of the 'signs of perception', *Wahrnehmungszeichen*. Quality is solely on the side of how the perception of discourse comes into contact with the unconscious representation of the object. The appearance of quality touches on transference, and transference as the supposition of the unconscious knowledge leads to the sexual reality of the drive. I will not elaborate it here.

Toward Discourse

This brings me back to the question of what opens the unconscious. But the unconscious is no longer the reservoir, the *Vorratskammer* from the letter to Fliess. The unconscious is only entered through a discourse. What opens the unconscious is 'a perception of discourse, and nothing else'.

Lacan's efforts in *The Ethics of Psychoanalysis* well anticipate what ten years later, in *L'Envers de la psychanalyse,* he will elaborate as a structure of discourse. The ethics of the unconscious serves as the cornerstone of discourse.

What is the ethics of the analyst? According to this moment in Lacan's teaching, the ethics of the analyst involves the qualification of *das Ding in medio* of discourse. How is *das Ding* qualified for the subject? In short, what qualifies the analyst? These are the questions Lacan tries to address in this seminar in view of the most radical treatment of the real. He returns to them, inevitably, in *Seminar XI.* What concerns him in *Seminar VII* is the qualification of the analyst, the question he will raise again more directly in the "Proposition of 1967."

The Freudian thing is doubtless at the center of Lacan's return to the *Entwurf.* But where exactly does Lacan position it? What are its coordinates? *Das Ding* is a constituent of the perception complex. It belongs to the indeterminate part, and remains constant, permanent, and unchangeable. But it is not *das Ding* that forms a relation with words, *Wort.* Lacan focuses here on Freud's article "The Unconscious." The unconscious as structure, or as system ψ, is only affected when the unconscious as perceived discourse succeeds in affecting it, Lacan says, retroactively. One of the differences between structure and perception is achieved through the temporal effects of retroaction.[5] What is perceived retroactively occurs at the level of *Wortvorstellungen.*

The unconscious as a retroactive perception of discourse, as *Vorstellung,* forms a couple but not with *das Ding.* And he adds, *das Ding* is elsewhere. Where? *Wort* forms a couple with *Sache,* whereas *das Ding* is found elsewhere. And then follows this beautiful metaphor through which Lacan illustrates the relation between *Sache* and *Wort,* thing and word: "the straw of words only appears as straw insofar as we have separated it from the grain of things, and it was first the straw which bore that grain."[6]

Whether conscious or preconscious—the difference is superseded by the retroactive effect that is our only evidence of the multilayered apparatus Freud constructs in Letter 52—the discourse imposes itself as *de libero* articulation of thoughts, doubts, shames, justifications, explanations—in short, as a discursive reality that is addressed to the Other.

And that is what distinguishes speech from discourse. Contrary to what some linguists believe, they are not the same.

The actions of the unconscious like parapraxes or dreams appear to us as instances of speech. In dreams the unconscious speaks, in a hallucinatory kind of way, because a wish for an object is fulfilled. A dream is a little hallucination, but it also preserves sleep. The unconscious does not cease to speak in dreams, in slips of the tongue, and in jokes. The unconscious is, perhaps, a perfectly infatiguable speaker. It knows no exhaustion or intervals and does not cease to speak. But what does the unconscious want to say in the speaking that does not cease?

The question reveals to us another level at which the addressee is involved. Discourse addresses another. That is why, Lacan says, discourse is a form of social bond. In other words, discourse testifies to identification, to the fact that there is no subject other than the identifying one. There is no other subject in the discourse than that of identification because, as Jacques-Alain Miller remarked,[7] there is no unconscious for nonidentifying subjects. It is, precisely, the identifying subject that allows us to speak—beyond Freud—about, to use Jacques-Alain Miller's expression, "the subject's absorption into S_1." This is well known in the schema of separation. The subject's identifications are constitutive of the subject represented by a master signifier.

To the extent that the subject identifies, or even further that it comes into existence *in medio* of identification, it, the subject, is already in the discourse, in the master discourse to begin with

Master's discourse	$\underline{S_1} \rightarrow \underline{S_2}$	agent	Other
	$\underline{\$}$ (a)	truth	production (loss)

This is Lacan's starting point—the master's discourse, also called the discourse of the unconscious. What does it mean to say that the master signifier signifies the primary identification? From the perspective of Lacan's elaboration of the *Entwurf,* the primary identification corresponds to the subject's entry into the symbolic, into language. It is an identification with the Name-of-the-Father. One could think here of those initial moments in analysis when the first address is made to the Other. The analysand tries to explain and justify his complaint, which is not yet a demand for analysis. Not that something imposes itself on the analysand, this too, but this imposition takes him in a particular direction, so he makes choices, tries to fight off those that appear as external to him, that are stronger than him. This is Freudian ethics—that he must go to be where the cause was. There is an orientation in this pursuit of the cause. In this orientation, the Other is always right, always commands and imposes a direction. In short, there is a must of the signifier to which the choice, the selection of signifiers coming *from* the Other testifies.

But what does Lacan mean when he calls the discourse of the unconscious the discourse of the master? After all, the master signifier does not vanish from the discourses, which are supposed to be unmasterly. Here, it is important to distinguish the elements constituting a discourse from the places they occupy. In this respect, Lacan of *L'Envers* says that in the master discourse the master signifier, S_1, is not in the position of the master. The term to consider here is "dominant."

Where Is the Master?

It is a term Lacan uses in this seminar in order to distinguish the discourses.[8] It is a term by which he can, as he says, 'finally designate' each of the discourse structures, of which there are four. What is the significance of this final designation called "dominant"?

Lacan says that dominant does not signify dominance. We can find this surprising, given his choice of references on the subject of courtly love in *The Ethics of Psychoanalysis*. Here the emphasis is put on dominance when he speaks about courtly love. The dominance is linked with the position of the Lady as a love object.[9] The Lady—*La Dame* in French or *La Donna* in Italian, which also means the woman—occupies the position of love object with the proviso that this object dominates. Hence, *Domna,* the woman who *domnei,* dominates. In short, courtly love is the name of discourse Lacan gives to those forms of sublimation that dominated sexual relations in the poetry of the Middle Ages. As forms of sublimation, they concerned *das Ding* raised to the dignity of a feminine object. What dominates in those relations to the object is the presence of *das Ding* as absent.

In discourse constructed as a social bond of identifications, the final designation falls, Lacan says, not on domination but on the dominant. He introduces us here, without saying so, to a strictly musical term. In the *Encyclopaedia Britannica,* "dominant" is defined as "the fifth tone of the diatonic scale, e.g. G in the scale of C." It therefore designates a place. What is the significance of Lacan's use of "dominance of the signifier" in *The Ethics* and of "dominant" in *L'Envers*? It is by means of *dominanta* that he "finally" designates "the diverse positions of these radical terms," namely, S, S_1, S_2, a. But why "finally"? Lacan's introduction of *dominanta* as the last, fifth term in the constitution of discourse is decisive in two ways.

First, it accentuates the way in which the elements of discourse turn and move through places. Starting with the master's discourse, in which the master signifier occupies the place of the agent, we can now begin to count: one, two, three, four, and five. Once we go to five, the S_1 moves. As if by magic touch, on counting five, the master signifier shifted by one place. The master signifier did not disappear but, as if guided by the rhythm of *das Ding*—Freud says "rhythm of the drive"—moved. But why did it move if not because the accent of *dominanta* altered its status and value? The significance of the fifth is therefore crucial for Lacan, as it is through a change of the status and value of the four terms that it seals them and the four positions they fall into. It is on the fifth that the terms take on motion and shift. How does Lacan call this movement of the unconscious? He calls it hysterization.

Second, the dominant designates a place that is occupied by S_2. This designation, although Lacan calls it final, is also inaugural, as it determines the place of the master, and of what he calls all-knowledge, in the discourse of the master. In short, this allows us to understand what keeps the master signifier in its place.

With the master signifier we move to the place of the master, which, according to Lacan, is to be found in the place of the Other. Why? Because in the master discourse the Other is always right, always commands and dominates. Thus, the position of knowledge, as supposed by the subject, becomes crucial. At the very least, the position of knowledge allows me to address why Lacan called the discourse of the unconscious the discourse of the master. On this point he makes a striking remark: "the desire for knowledge has no relationship with knowledge."[10] The desire to know, contrary to Aristotle's belief in a generalized drive to knowledge, has nothing to do with knowledge. And Lacan adds: "the desire to know is not what leads to knowledge." After all, to want to know implies for the subject to suppose a knowledge of the Other's desire.

Why do the last moments of Oedipus touch us? It is not because we are confronted with the death of the living Oedipus the King. Nor because he leaves behind him his children. Nor even because we take pity on the self-blinded and self-tormented man. Oedipus, without a doubt, was a master. But his mysterious death is not a death of the master. The death of Oedipus has rather to do with a disappearance of the one supposed to know about death.

When in the *Ethics* Lacan speaks about the death of God, this is only the first step in which he allows us to grasp the sense of the inexistence of the Other. The second step consists in the fact that God does not know about it, for he has always already been dead. And in this Lacan makes a link between the subject supposed to know and the inexistence of the Other.

Oedipus has always already been dead, and his enigmatic disappearance to join the movement of the gods is a dramatic example of erasure of knowledge of death. When it comes to the question of death the Other does not know. The whole enigma of the disappearance of Oedipus has to do with a little comedy the messenger plays for us when everyone supposes that he knows something. And to this effect he speaks well.

But the subject does not know either. To the extent that the subject confides in the representations he draws from the perception of discourse, that he makes choices and selects reality to its own taste—namely, for its own good, Lacan says—it is precisely this that the subject does not know. The subject does not know it because of its happiness, which is also its ignorance. To the extent that the subject is supposed by S_1, the subject's desire is not for knowledge but for making it work. But let's not confuse the subject's happiness with *dolce far niente*. It is not laziness that makes him ignorant, but his belief that the master is happy, too. And this was no doubt the case with Robinson Crusoe. He was not exactly master of the ship, which is where the term "master"—the guardian of the mast—seems to originate. But when he discovers on the famous island that he is not alone, he becomes nothing else than a master of culture, a messenger of the civilized order with the mission to restore, recreate, reproduce an image of what? That what works in one place works anywhere else.

The Hysteric and Science

What leads to knowledge is not a repetition of desire to work. What leads to knowledge, Lacan says, is the hysteric's discourse. The interesting thing about the hysteric's discourse is that it is one of two discourses in which the place of the agent—that which acts *in medio* of representation—is not occupied by a representation. Instead, we find here the divided subject acting as an agent. The Lacanian subject, clearly, is not a representation. The subject is a gap between identifications, between signifiers in the chain. The subject arrives in the place of this gap, precisely, where identity is supposed.

$$\text{Hysteric's discourse} \qquad \frac{\text{\$} \to [S_1]}{a \;//\; S_2}$$

In other words, the Lacanian subject is the unbearable of the division, which in the hysteric discourse acts as an agent. We could, for example, present the subject as the unbearable of the simultaneous yes and no. That is, a repression is present at the moment of the statement, so that a no in the statement could couple with the yes in an enunciation. Freud's early work with hysterics allowed him to think in this way. Let's take an example of science. The scientific research into a possibility of cloning humans places the scientist, whether he or she knows it or not, in the position of the divided subject. On the one hand, there is a yes to a blind pursuit for the knowledge of the real—I would even say of the real as such to the extent that the function of the imaginary, and therefore of fantasy is marginalized. In science the imaginary does not support the symbolization of the real, as Lacan remarks somewhere, but is a means of realization of the symbolic. Hence, the question of truth is altogether sidetracked in favor of production of knowledge. There is a big, but silent, yes to the so-called progress of human knowledge—and Freud found himself on the crossroads of the scientific progress—but this yes is not without a no of unhappiness of the neighbor from a good Christian to a bad journalist. This yes of science is therefore not without a secret—a secret island, as in the case of the geneticist Antinori, the beyond of any public witness or without a *Nebenmensch*—where cloning could proceed unperturbed. There is a yes to the master knowledge and there is a no to what comes from the place of the Other.

On the other hand, we have the master signifier in the place of the Other. To the subject's demand for knowledge, the Other does not respond because the response is already inscribed in the demand. The position of the master signifier subsequently places the subject in relation to two masters. How to serve two masters at the same time, how to serve the yes and the no simultaneously? How to obey the silent master, the S_1, that does not complement the subject because it is the very condition of identification? And how to refute the master that is always right and dominant as the supposed author of the law?

We can see that in the hysteric's discourse an alliance exists between the hysteric and the scientist. Both have a relation to the master knowledge, which is at the same time extolled to the place of the ideal, and then overthrown, abolished as inadequate and insufficient. In this discourse, the subject seeks from the Other a knowledge as complement but in response remains barred. In this sense the hysteric supports the scientific knowledge because the latter claims access to the real. But this alliance is only above the bar. Below the bar, this alliance ceases to exist because the truth of jouissance is not articulated in the scientist's work.

If it is knowledge that is produced in this discourse, it is not produced by the Other but as a subject's loss. And this is what Lacan achieved in his school. In the Lacanian School we have encounters, *journées,* study-days where knowledge is produced. The production of knowledge in these encounters articulates the subject's experience of truth. In other words, the experience of truth as wrongfooting the good of the subject is correlative to the production of knowledge as always already lost. The loss implies a lack. What comes to the fore is the subject's division and the lack of a complement from the Other. The subject appears as a gap between representations to the extent that the gap is also a break in the chain, an intrusion of the little real. The effect Lacan seems to have achieved in the school is that of plurality, of analysts speaking there one by one and not without a grain of dissatisfaction.

Ecco Analiticus

I will conclude with the analyst's discourse because it was for Lacan the basis for the analyst's political position.

In the analyst's discourse, the question of an author is subverted. The question of the paternal law without the father is raised by Lacan to the level of the real outside law—beyond Oedipus then. Let's notice that the search of the author of the law proves valid for the feminists. There are two sides to this search for an author. On one side, one can hear an echo of the master's search for another master, namely, the Self. In his early teaching, Lacan refers to the mother as master. There is plenty of room for mastery in the child/mother relation because the triangle they form with the phallus is imaginary. Hence, the question, posed also from the perspective of *L'Envers de la psychanalyse,* where is the father?

On the other side, we have a question of authorization. Lacan takes a creationist's perspective, and it is the father of creation that he evokes in the "Proposition of 9 October 1967 on the Psychoanalyst of the School." He does this, more precisely, in the famous statement about the analyst's self-authorization—"the psychoanalyst derives his authorization only from himself."[11] It is perhaps one of the most misunderstood ones in Lacan's entire teaching. The politics of the analyst has as an axis what is at stake in this self-authorization. Where would we be if the question of 'self-authorization' raised by Lacan could be reduced to the kind of 'all-knowing' that we found in the place of the Other in the master discourse? And we remember the ancient formula with which Oedipus set forth not so much in search for the truth but in search for knowledge that would explain the truth of which he was already a bearer. That is why Oedipus's formula, γνωθι σεοιτόν, *know yourself,* is not a formula of psychoanalysis.

To begin with, Lacan's proposition was understood as a rebellious challenge to the IPA where it is the father, just like in the Church, who authorizes. But Lacan does not approach the analyst's self-authorization from the perspective of knowledge of psychoanalysis. He rather approaches it from the perspective of the analyst's discourse. And it is in this sense that he makes a distinction between the analyst's discourse and the psychoanalyzing discourse. No wonder he anticipated at the time the future of the academic discourse according to which the discourse of the analyst is supposed as 'morally' supreme.

Lacan's proposition "the analyst derives his authorization only from himself," although stated two years before his actual formalization of discourses, finds its basis in the analyst's discourse. We do not find in it a representation in the place of the agent. In the place of the agent, which is the place of desire, there is no less, but perhaps more, than the unrepresentable object, the little real. What does Lacan indicate to us in the logic of the analyst's discourse? We must recall here his remarks from 1967 concerning psychoanalysis.

The unrepresentable object in the position of desire gives us an indication of where transference is generated. And he says that to claim to know what psychoanalysis is tantamount to speaking from the position of the subject supposed to know. The object in the position of the agent indicates that being the mainspring of transference, it is not the analyst who carries the function of the supposed subject of knowledge. If the analyst supports transference, it is because the analysand speaks as a master, namely, through the chain of representations—the position we find both in master and university discourses. He supposes to know how the object should return to the subject.

Jacques-Alain Miller showed that the shift of the object and master signifier occurring in the analyst's discourse in relation to the master's discourse—which is not without retroactive effect—is not only a question of these two elements swapping places. What comes to the focus here is also their change in status and value. The shift implies separation and refers to disidentification of the subject, namely, its destitution. In separation, the subject's absorption into S_1 creates a void.

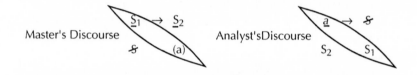

It is in this sense that I want to take up Miller's remark that "Lacan's entire effort is to construct the hallucination as a phenomenon of communication."[12] Where could hallucination become part of the relation with another, part of the relation with the *Nebenmensch,* and part of the social bond? What is that *in medio* of which the hallucinatory comes into circulation as uncommunicable?

If in the analyst's discourse we find the unrepresentable object *a* in the place of desire, it is because Lacan grafts into the analyst's position an element of hallucination. And, by doing so, he presents the real on a par with the symbolic. In hallucination, the real and the symbolic are on a par. This allows Lacan to speak in *L'Envers* of knowledge as truth. The question he poses there is: "How can we know without knowing?" In other words, how can we speak of Oedipus beyond Oedipus?

What is decisive in the change of value of knowledge is the beyond we have found in the *Nebenmensch* of Freud, in the *Oedipus* of Sophocles, and now, with Lacan, in the analyst. To these two enigmas we add the third, an enigma of the analyst. This enigma, of course, has to do with the desire of the analyst who, like the Sphinx, is supposed to know the answer. Which is why the self-authorization in question brings to the fore interpretation as enigma. For Lacan, the analyst's interpretation—which arises from the analyst's discourse—is where his desire is. His desire, Lacan says, is his enunciation. This is the link with the object *a* through the drive. In this sense, the interpretation not only fixes signification. It not only qualifies jouissance as that which lies in the place of truth in the analysand's master discourse. Interpretation also puts the real and the symbolic on a par as a knot, that is, allows, through the cut and where the real and the symbolic are knotted, to isolate S_1. To isolate it means to produce it.

The question of the analyst as self-authorized demonstrates an effect of this production. It points to an integration of the phenomenon of hallucination into the analyst's discourse. What do we find as dominant in the place of the master? We find there a division, the beyond of Oedipus as inscribed in the subject. The topological value of the barred subject is the same as that of the barred Other, $\mathcal{S} \equiv \mathcal{A}$. What remains in question is the Other as desire. "What is the creature that. . .?" the Sphinx asks. And Oedipus answers: "It is man," it is I. And he trots off to his misfortunes. The beyond of Oedipus opens the dimension of politics as desire that while serving the Lacanian School testifies to the little real.

If the analyst draws his authorization from himself, it is because there is no Other to qualify him. Lacan's proposition is therefore a negative one. The analyst's qualification derives from the inexistence of the Other where knowledge is supposed as the life of *das Ding,* which Lacan designated as $\mathcal{A}$. In this sense, Lacan said of his teaching that it is 'unrivaled' because no teaching speaks about what psychoanalysis is.[13]

Notes

1. J. Lacan, *Seminar VII: The Ethics of Psychoanalysis,* trans. D. Porter (London: Routledge, 1992), p. 62.

2. Ibid., p. 37.

3. J. -A. Miller, "The Symptom and the Body Event," trans. B. P. Fulks, in *lacanian ink* No. 19, New York, 2001, p. 15.

4. Sophocles, *Oedipus at Colonus,* trans. R. Fagles (London: Pelican, 1986), p. 380.

5. J. Lacan, *Seminar VII,* op. cit., p. 49.

6. Ibid., p. 45.

7. J.-A. Miller, "Quand les semblants vacillent . . ." in *La Cause freudienne* No. 47, Paris, March 2001, p. 12.

8. J. Lacan, *Le Séminaire XVII: L'Envers de la psychanalyse* (Paris: Seuil, 1991), p. 47.

9. J. Lacan, *Seminar VII,* op. cit., p. 150.

10. J. Lacan, *Le Séminaire XVII,* op. cit., p. 23.

11. J. Lacan, "Proposition of 9 October 1967 on the Psychoanalyst of the School," trans. R. Grigg, *Analysis* No. 6, Melbourne, 1995, p. 1.

12. J.-A. Miller, "The Symptom and the Body Event," op. cit., p. 31.

13. J. Lacan, "Proposition," op. cit., p. 3.

PART V

Sexuation

Love and Sex Beyond Identifications

Alexandre Stevens

"Sexuation" is a Lacanian term. It is a new concept. Sexuation is not sexuality. Nor is sexuation equivalent to the Anglo-Saxon concept of *gender identity*. It is also not equivalent to the Freudian distribution into boys or girls under phallic primacy: it is, rather, a complex reformulation of this distribution. It is a term that is well suited to the era of globalization.

Gender Identity

There was a big debate in the Anglo-Saxon world in the seventies and eighties on the subject of sex and gender. On the one hand, there is biological sex, which is determined by the presence or absence of secondary sexual features, among which one finds the penile organ on the male side. Biological sex is scientifically deduced from the presence of chromosomes XX or XY. It is a factual matter, in the field of the visible—be it under the microscope. On the other hand, there is the person's sentiment, the 'gender', that is, the gender that the subject feels it belongs to at the level of its preconscious, of its imaginary identification as man or as woman. A disjunction is therefore possible between the feeling of the ego and the biological sex that presents itself to the subject as its own.

Important studies were carried out in the seventies and eighties on this question, and in particular those of the American IPA analyst Robert Stoller that focused on a large number of cases of transsexualism. He made many interesting remarks, recently reinterpreted by Eric Laurent.[1] Very logically, one encounters two types of cases in transsexualism: a man who wants to be changed into a woman, because he feels like a woman, and a woman who wants to be changed into a man.

Stoller points out that it is not at all the same thing in both cases. For women who want to be transformed into men, we must distinguish different hypotheses. These range from hysterical desire to psychotic demand, and include a whole series of possible forms, some concerning very disturbed women, and some concerning women who are not that disturbed. On the contrary, men who want to be changed into women always demonstrate a very strong and very fundamental subjective disturbance. In other words, as interpreted by Eric Laurent, in the case of men this is always psychotic—the men who feel like women, in the sense of the transsexualism of the seventies and eighties, are always on the psychotic side. Here we can catch a glimpse of Schreber's transformation into a woman through the will of God. But in the transsexual form of this delusion, the Other is Nature, whose mistake can be corrected by science and surgery.

Schreber makes a very interesting point on the subject of transsexuals, a point that in all these cases allows us to speak about psychosis. As children, these subjects did not generally have the immediate feeling of belonging to the other sex, but they had, very early on, the idea that they were not of their sex. It is the little boy who thinks to himself: "I am not a boy like the others, I am not a boy," and, in general, that is as far as it goes. It is a supplementary, delusional construction that leads him to say 'so I am a girl', and, later on, certainty attaches itself to this construction. But the first phenomenon to manifest itself is the subject's impossibility of legitimately appropriating its own sex. This was a debate of great clinical subtlety.

Yet today, the debate is over in the ranks of the IPA. There is no longer any debate on transsexualism, in the sense of diagnosis and its causalities, going on in the pages of the *International Journal of Psychoanalysis*. In its place one finds protocols, a questionnaire at the end of which, if the subject falls within its criteria, he can be operated on. That is a big change. The protocol in question means that the question of rectification of the biological sex is posed solely in terms of surgical conditions. It is not the enigma of the disjunction between discourse and body that counts, but the identification chosen by the patient.

In any case, the more recent debate no longer bears on the question "Are you a man or a woman?," but focuses instead on the number of sexes there are. There are not only two—there are many. This is what biologists argue according to a number of different criteria. There is a continuum between men and women. On the man/woman axis, some are situated here, and others there, and others still are situated more or less on the man's side or more or less on the woman's side. These biological theories include the intermediary and very rare situation of the true hermaphrodite.

The Community-making Identification

The question that is fundamental for us is situated in the subjective perspective. If we think in terms of the biological continuum, we could deduce that on the subjective plane, on the axis of identifications between men and women, there are numerous possibilities: a woman or a man, naturally, then also gays, transsexuals, and so on. The question then becomes that of the choice of a collectivizing identity:[2] gays, transsexual movements, and even, as in the United States, a group whose members claim to be neither men nor women. This leads to the constitution of communities that function as lobbies, as pressure groups in the same way as Puerto Ricans, blacks, Jews, steelworkers unions, and so on—that is, that they constitute a communitarian demand.

This communitarian demand appears to settle harmoniously what Lacan called the fatal destiny of love.[3] The main idea behind this theory is that the problem of sex is presented in terms of the choice of identification, and that the subject is happy if his identification allows him to be part of a community. It is no longer the IPA theory of ego psychology, which used to say "Let's adapt the subject to reality." In this community theory, on the contrary, what matters is that everyone is able to find a community with which he will identify, and that will constitute the reality to which he has to adapt. This thesis remains a fundamentally adaptive one, except that now one can choose one's Other before adapting oneself to it.

These communitarian identifications, founded on certain biological theories, constitute a problem that is consistent with contemporary civilization. It is a question of rights: everyone has the right to choose—therefore, why not the right to choose one's sex, and also to change it? As Eric Laurent pointed out, the problem is very up to date because we encounter it at all levels of society. It is also what television produces: "You are a star—why am I not one, too?," and thus people enroll for *Big Brother*, for reality shows. Why should every spectator not think that he or she could very well be a star, too? This is a demand everywhere on the increase: "why not me?"

The Phallus

Lacan's response on sexuation is completely different from these responses through identification, yet it allows us to interpret our modernity. You know Freud's response, which, though it was very well formulated, does not allow us to respond accurately to the question of sex today. Freud's response to the question of the choice of sex is situated in relation to the male organ, the penis: there are those who have it or those who do not. The feminist movement, which is also of the order of communitarian identification, pointed to the obsolescence of this position: that's not the way we think today. Still, we must insist that Freud's theory is a little bit more subtle than that.

In Plutarch's text on the myth of Isis and Osiris, Isis is a woman who is particularly loyal, since after her husband was cut into pieces, and these pieces were scattered in the Nile, she spends her time looking for them in order to reconstitute his body. But there is a piece she cannot find—the penis. Thus, in all the places where she fails to find it, she erects, according to Plutarch, a statue to the phallus. The Greek words are very precise:[4] where she does not find the organ (τό αἰδοῖον), she erects an image (μίμημα) of the phallus (τον φαλλόν). The male organ, its imaginary representation, and the phallus are not the same thing. In the same way, Freud presents the fetish as a substitute for the penis, but it tends to be the substitute for what the mother lacks. Freud specifies that it is therefore a substitute for the phallus.[5] The primacy of the phallus is therefore essentially the primacy of a lack. It lacks, which means that the expressions "I have it" or "I do not have it" are merely the two possible answers of girls and boys.

The Paradoxes of Satisfaction in Freud

For Freud, the question of sexual satisfaction is not limited to the question of identification. Its paradoxes anticipate the concept of jouissance formulated during Lacan's late teaching. From his earliest texts, Freud associated symptoms with the existence of a trauma. The subject experienced a trauma that reactivates an earlier trauma and gives rise to symptoms. This is the principle of symptomatic causality in Freud at the beginning of the invention of psychoanalysis.

However, he underlines the difference between hysteria and obsessional neurosis.[6] In hysteria, the satisfaction that is initially perceived is marked by displeasure. It is a negative satisfaction because it is experienced passively. In obsessional neurosis, on the other hand, the primal trauma is experienced with a positive satisfaction, an excess of pleasure that is associated with an active position. In relation to what one imagines constitutes pleasure, Freud therefore underlines that this satisfaction always fails: it is always either too much or too little. It is this paradox of satisfaction that is traumatic, and that is at the origin of the Freudian symptom. The shift from the theory of trauma to the theory of fantasy does not change anything in this respect.

The case of Emma[7] is an example of a satisfaction that bears a negative imprint. Her symptom is specific: she can no longer go into a grocery store alone. It is an everyday discomfort. The triggering trauma does not objectively appear as a massive trauma. Walking past two laughing men bears no common measure to, for example, the tragedies of pedophilia. On the contrary, the case concerns a trauma that is objectively very limited. It is only subjectively that it takes on a traumatic function because this scene replays another scene that was repressed. At the age of eight, she went into a shop to buy sweets, and the shop assistant caressed her genitals through her skirt, laughing profusely. We have here a series of signifiers—skirt, laughter, grocer, shop assistant—that link the two scenes. She returned to the shop a second time, with a feeling that was rather pleasant, but at the same time something had bothered her. She encountered a passively experienced satisfaction, associated with a negative feeling. To us, this trauma appears to be objectively traumatic; yet, for her, it did not seem to be subjectively traumatic at the time. It only assumed its value as traumatic retroactively.

There is, at this point, something that she does not succeed in expressing in speech: the incomprehensibility of sexual satisfaction. As Jacques-Alain Miller emphasized, the real trauma is language in all cases. It is the mystery of what is not transformable into words, of what remains on the edge of language when the subject begins to speak. It is the encounter with the enigma of jouissance when there is no speech, or when speech fails to formulate it.

This paradox of satisfaction is a first anticipation of what Lacan will call the real of jouissance. Later, Freud will give a new formulation of it with the death drive, which brings this paradox of satisfaction to a second degree.

Sexuation

With sexuation, Lacan responds very well to the question of collectiviz-ing identifications. His response is threefold. First, sexuation is an iden-tification, a signifying positioning assumed by the subject. This does not mean that the subject has to collectivize its identifications, but that it assumes its feminine or masculine position as a choice. Second, the question of sexuation is not solely posed in terms of identification, but also in terms of a position of jouissance, a way of enjoyment, namely, a way of life. Third, it is not enough for the subject to recognize itself as a man or a woman through identification, or to assume one's mode of en-joyment—it is still necessary to recognize the Other sex.[8]

The Choice of Identification

Lacan presents identification in the tables of the formulas of sexuation in a logical form that differs from the variety of biological choices. There is choice as man and choice as woman. They are, as Lacan says, two choices. One does not put oneself there because one's biological body is more or less man or woman, but because of choice. What Lacan writes with his logical formulas of sexual identification are the two pos-sible responses to Russell's paradox.[9] We are no longer dealing with questions of biological continuum, but with the order of discourse.

Either one chooses to recognize the exception, which allows one to take place in the set of men, those who are under the phallic law. Lacan writes its logical formula: $\exists x\, \overline{\Phi x}$ therefore $\forall x\, \Phi x$. On condi-tion that the paternal exception is recognized, all men can be placed under castration—namely, under the legitimate assumption of their sex. This is the masculine side, which includes the exception. It is also the position of enunciation, the position of the subject who invents, and it opens to the possibility of the series of identifications—which can be collectivizing.

The other response to the paradox does not recognize the exception, and it is therefore not possible to limit the set, which remains open. It is the structure of limitless infinitization of the feminine. This is what Lacan writes as: $\overline{\exists x}\, \overline{\Phi x}$, therefore $\overline{\forall x}\, \overline{\Phi x}$. On this side, the subject cannot end up in the position of exception, but it also cannot end up being serialized, as is the case on the masculine side. It is both not-all and limitless.

This not-all, which Lacan ascribes to women, is different from the Freudian not-all.[10] In Freud, the not-all in women is situated in relation to the organ. On the one side, there is the set of men, those who have the organ, and, on the other side, there is the set of women, those who do not have everything, that is, those who have a little less. In Lacan, on the contrary, the not-all of the feminine side signifies that there is a little more. There is more because there is no limit. We therefore have two modes of identification: the orderly side—the masculine side—and the 'slightly mad' side—the feminine side—because women are clearly less identified. This implies two modes of jouissance. This is the response we can construct with Lacan to collectivizing identifications.

The Choice of Jouissance

Lacan writes the positions of jouissance in the lower part of the tables of sexuation in *Seminar XX*. Phallic jouissance is experienced through the fantasy, where man does not seek a reunion with the other partner, but with the sexual object that allows him to find his sexual jouissance. "To make love, as the very expression indicates, is poetry," but the act of love is something else. "The act of love is the male's polymorphous perversion."[11] It is the autistic side of male jouissance, without a partner other than the object *a,* more or less imaginarized on the feminine side and ranking among what counts as man's sexual objects.

On the woman side, where ~~The~~ woman does not exist, the reference to the Φ persists. But the limitless implies that she has access to an Other jouissance, what Lacan calls feminine jouissance, and which he wrote on his table as $S(\bar{A})$.

What is this feminine jouissance? There is an extremely enlightening text by Jacques-Alain Miller on the subject.[12] On the woman's side, jouissance is possible—first through access to phallic jouissance, as it is for men, and second through access to the Other, supplementary jouissance that has to be considered in its two dimensions. The first side concerns the body. Where, on the masculine side, physical jouissance is essentially localized in the organ, women attest to a jouissance that is sometimes less localized in the body—what Lacan calls a jouissance taken in its contiguity with itself, namely, not limited to the organ. This is what Freud tried to approach clumsily under the term of vaginal jouissance. Freud had the idea that in order to become a woman, the little girl had to move from clitoral jouissance, masculine by nature, to vaginal jouissance, which implies the idea of a displacement outside the limits of the organ. But Freud did not draw the consequences of this as clearly as Lacan did. This Other jouissance has a second side, which is not corporeal but discursive. It is a jouissance of speech, for it is a jouissance that includes love. Lacan does not situate love in the same place on the masculine and feminine sides. On the feminine side, love is part of jouissance.

The initial operation of Lacan's late teaching is very visible here. The Other of the signifier is not considered in the first instance. There is first of all jouissance as autistic process—in other words, without the Other. And it is through the Other sex, through the woman side, that jouissance becomes civilized, through love, that is, through the inclusion of the Other in jouissance. The Other side is thus the feminine side. It is she who introduces the dimension of the Other with love.

The Other Sex and the Necessity of Love

The third point is that whatever side one chooses, the Other sex must be recognized. For instance, when commenting on the case of Dora,[13] Lacan can say that a woman has to be able to consent to being the object of a man's desire. It is a recognition of the Other sex. And on the man's side, he has to be able to recognize the necessity of love.

In the last pages of *Seminar XX*, Lacan tries to circumscribe the function of love between sexes. There is no sexual relation, that is, there is no relation of jouissance between the sexes, because it is not about the same thing, because it can only fail. But when one encounters love, in the contingency of the encounter, namely, in the state of being in love, an illusion is produced that the sexual relation exists through love. Love comes as an illusion to the place of the sexual relation that does not exist. But love has to pass from contingency to necessity. Love as necessary, as decision, can then produce a substitute—which is not the same thing as an illusion—for what lacks of the sexual relation. It is no longer simply an illusion, for one shifts from the imaginary to the symptom—the new love, as Lacan called it by reference to one of Rimbaud's poems.

A Delusion of Courtly Love

So what comes from love in the place of the symptom as a metaphorization of the real (the sexual nonrelation) can be declined in several ways.

From *The Man Who Loved Women*[14] to the most extreme forms of erotomania, this necessity takes numerous forms. Let us take, for example, the case of a young adult I have met in an institution, and whom I diagnosed as suffering from a delusional outburst of courtly love.

Major psychotic phenomena begin at thirteen. He feels disorientated, lost in his school establishment, and is hospitalized. We do not have any detail on the circumstances that provoked the triggering, but the phenomena that follow are hebephrenic in type: a great disorientation with a withdrawal of libido from the external world. He stays alone, spends hours on end in his room. He will be hospitalized twice again during the three following years, each time with a recurrence of the same signs.

He constructs two responses to this subjective deliquescence, each of which attempts to reestablish a libido turned outward, but outside of the body [*hors corps*]. The first—shortly after the first hospitalization, when he is still with his family—seeks to cling to a communitarian identification. The second—three years later, at the Courtil Clinic—unfolds on a mode close to erotomania.

At fourteen, in the course of his stay in a psychiatric hospital, he converts to Islam. Born in a Catholic family, he had previously thought of becoming a priest. But his father claims to be an atheist, and in his area he feels threatened by North African youths. His apostasy gives him the feeling of being readmitted to a community and allows him to better integrate with groups of young people in his neighborhood. Since his arrival to the Courtil Clinic, he attends the local mosque, whose keys he has been allowed to keep. It seems to be a rather modest place of prayer. His conversion is thus helping him to reconstitute a social bond. However, a certain mode of the relation with jouissance is being unsettled. He recently explained to me that his personal link with the land of Islam is Spain, which used to be one of the high places of this culture, and where he spends his summer holidays with his parents. But at present the young people of his area push him to go training in Pakistan, where he will find true Islam. This is the limit, which could become devastating [*ravageante*], of the communitarian identification he found in his first response.

For some time now, he has started to construct a second response. A female participant in the Courtil Clinic occupies almost all his thoughts. When speaking of her, he smiles and becomes lively. Why her? It remains a mystery for him. It is not a simple friendship, in the sense of λφα, or a love that expects to be requited. It is the core of his thoughts and his new form of libido outside the body [*hors corps*]. He only wants her to feel good, without bothering her in the least. He worries when he does not see her, but withdraws when he sees her in order not to embarrass her. He gave her a bottle of Chanel perfume. She accepted it reluctantly, because it was not possible to refuse, and told him that this should remain an exception. "In fact," he told me, "she was right, it is exceptional to give such a perfume to a lady." Equivocation serves him well here. He wants to get her another present—for Mother's Day, he tells me. He then specifies: "For Mother's Day, but not as if she was my mother, rather because I love her as my daughter, as my mother used to love me." He puts himself in the place of his mother in order to love himself like a daughter, as she loved him when he was a baby. It is a touch of feminization.

He wants to protect her and raises her to the level of the feminine ideal. This is not really an erotomania, but rather a delusional outburst of courtly love. He turns it into a way of life in order to refind some life in himself. What could be feared concerning the erotomaniac touch of transference in this situation is less worrying than the possible ravage of the communitarian identification.

Notes

1. In the early 1980s, at his DEA Seminar in Paris.
2. M. Bassols and G. Brodsky developed this point during the International Encounter of the Freudian Field in Paris, in July 2002.
3. J. Lacan, *Seminar XX: Encore* (New York/London: Norton, 1998), p. 131.
4. Plutarch, "Isis and Osiris," *Oeuvres Morales* (Paris: Les Belles Lettres, 1988).
5. S. Freud, "On Fetishism," 1927, SE XXI.
6. S. Freud, "The Aetiology of Hysteria" (1896), and "New Remarks on Psychoneuroses of Defence" (1896), SE I.
7. S. Freud, *The Project for a Scientific Psychology* (1895), SE I; *The Birth of Psychoanalysis* (1956).
8. G. Brodsky developed this point during her conference in Brussels in January 2002; cf. "Le choix du sexe" in *Quarto 77*, July 2002, pp. 36–39.
9. As developed by J.-A. Miller in one of his seminars.
10. I owe this precision to J.-A. Miller, "Of distribution between the sexes," *Psychoanalytical Notebooks*, pp. 9–27.
11. J. Lacan, *Seminar XX*, op. cit., p. 68, for both quotes.

12. Published under the title "Of distribution between the sexes," op. cit.

13. J. Lacan, "Intervention sur le transfert" in *Écrits* (Paris: Seuil, 1966), p. 222; "Intervention on transference" in J. Mitchell and J. Rose, *Feminine Sexuality* (London: Macmillan, 1982), p. 67.

14. Truffaut's film.

Feminine Positions of Being

Eric Laurent

Freud and the Clinic of Perversions

"A Child is Being Beaten"[1] is a landmark in the psychoanalytic clinic of perversions since it is the article in which Freud demonstrates for the first time that perversions are not deducible from the functioning of the drive but are organized by the oedipal structure. Until then, including in the 1915 additions to "The Three Essays on the Theory of Sexuality" (SE VII), Freud had followed the great classifiers of the clinic of perversions—and primarily Krafft-Ebing who, in the ten years between 1890 and 1900/1902, had classified perversions in a nosography that still makes sense today and that inspired Freud when writing his "Three Essays." The notions of voyeurism, exhibitionism, sadism, masochism are collected and organized by Krafft-Ebing, who completes his nosographical project within the space of time in which the clinic of psychoses is developed. The person who held a similar chair in Vienna to the one that Kraepelin held in Munich applied himself to construct this exhaustive description. His thesis was that the pervert is a subject who cannot master his drives, who is dominated by his drives, who very quickly deviates from the right direction—which is originally what "perversion" means. There is a correct direction, and then there are inversions, when one chooses the opposite object, and perversions, when the drive goes astray. So the sexual instinct is classified: we have the asthenics, who no longer have a sexual instinct, they are lost to science, as it were, there is nothing left to get out of them; we have the genital types, too sthenic, they have to be calmed down, which gives rise to all the projects that have in any case always animated psychiatric teaching, and are projects of castration (see all the research on chemical and surgical castration, etc. in order to calm perverse criminals down). All this classifying effort based on the idea of the sexual drive, the sexual instinct, culminates in Krafft-Ebing's grand project, his grand classification.

In his own way, Freud follows the psychiatric trend in at first deriving perversions from different partial drives. When I say that he follows the psychiatric trend, it is in his own way because, for him, there never was a unified sexual instinct—the famous term highlighted by Lacan in "The Three Essays on the Theory of Sexuality," where Freud insists that the particularity of man, in the sense of human subject, means that there is no representation of a unified sexual tendency in him or her— *"die ganze Sexualstrebung"*; *ganze,* that is, unique. The sexual tendency has no unique representation; it is always represented as fragmented. It is on this point that Freud is in opposition to the entire psychiatric trend of his time. Whereas in the unifying project of Krafft-Ebing, who is the most systematic exponent of it, we have one sexual instinct and then deviations in relation to the instinct that allow for a regrouping, a definition of a complete nosographic system, for Freud we have at least four instincts, at least four fragments of the sexual instinct that are impossible to unify. We have the oral and anal, and though Freud adds neither the scopic nor the voice, he does add voyeurism and exhibitionism, masochism and sadism. It will fall to Lacan to unify these four fragments of the sexual instinct under the single rubric of object; a particular object, since the gaze had to be recognized as having the status of drive-object. We also had to complete the Freudian doctrine on this point by recognizing the particularity of the function of the object-voice in perversion (whether sadistic or masochistic) in the crucial function of the command. The sadistic command opposes itself to the masochistic contract, which is what is left over from the voice when speech is removed from it and when the voice is sedimented in a system of letters.

Genesis of Perversions and the Oedipus Complex

So in the very moment in which Krafft-Ebing is constructing his classificatory work, Freud is subverting its order by presenting the impossibility of a unique instinct. Nevertheless, he maintains until 1915 that these drive stages, this infantile drive organization, are not elaborated around a constructed object-choice and therefore not articulated within the Oedipus complex as he established it as the dramatization of the structure of object-choice. It will be the analysis of the Wolf Man that will convince Freud of the existence of infantile stages of drive organization, when he is surprised that the Wolf Man's disorders of appetite are linked to an oral stage of sexual organization.

Freud adds something to it. He is not satisfied to say that everything comes back to the oral stage. What is a novelty for him is that this stage, this oral drive, concerns the father; the little boy does not think about the father with his penis, he thinks about the father with the oral drive. Until then in the Oedipus complex, one thinks about the father because one wants to use his prick/tail [*queue*], like the little lizard. Here, in the case of the Wolf Man, one thinks about the father by using the act of devouring. For Freud one thinks with the oral drive, like Lacan said: one thinks with one's soul, an Aristotelian term. What's new for Freud is the discovery that the oral organization concerns the father through the devouring and that the cannibalistic meal is there at the outset. This is what will lead Freud, in his text on identification, to pose a primordial, cannibalistic identification with the father. Here we are on the road where, in the analysis of the Wolf Man, in his preoccupations, Freud discovers the emergence of infantile stages in the sexual organization. So, in 1919, one year after the publication of his text on the Wolf Man, Freud emphasized the novelty of his thought as follows:

A perversion in childhood, as is well known, may become the basis for the construction of a perversion having a similar sense and persisting throughout life, one which consumes the subject's whole sexual life. On the other hand the perversion may be broken off and remain in the background of a normal sexual development, from which, however, it continues to withdraw a certain amount of energy. ("A Child is Being Beaten," p. 192)

It is the perverse trait that is preserved. A little further on Freud adds: "It would naturally be important to know whether the origin of infantile perversions from the Oedipus complex can be asserted as a general principle" (ibid.).

Freud does not think that it is established; he thinks that it has to be demonstrated: "If, however, the derivation of perversions from the Oedipus complex can be generally established, our estimate of its importance will have gained added strength" (p. 193).

In short, Freud considers that the universality, let us say the clinical span of the Oedipus, would thereby be confirmed once again. Toward the fifth part of "A Child is Being Beaten," one begins to understand why Freud begins his text in such an understated manner, outlining proposals that resemble those of an astounded empirical researcher:

It is surprising how often people who seek analytic treatment for hysteria or an obsessional neurosis confess to having indulged in the phantasy: "A child is being beaten." Very probably there are still more frequent instances of it among the far greater number of persons who have not been obliged to come to analysis by manifest illness. (p. 179)

One may wonder why Freud only noticed this in 1919. He could have noticed it a lot earlier. This is really the artistry of Freud, who takes the reader by the hand, puts him to sleep a little at the beginning of his articles with empirical considerations such as "It happens that . . . ," "One frequently says . . . ," and then demonstrates the universality of the Oedipus in any perversion! This is what he has just discovered, and he wants to consider it as the fundamental change of thesis that he is in the process of effecting. In this respect, it is starting with the nucleus of Freud's demonstration that one will approach the reading he makes of the whipping fantasy, of the fantasy of being whipped. This fantasy is very nineteenth century: it is in the nineteenth century that the theme of happiness in evil appeared in literature, a truly post-romantic theme. In this category a worldly author, Sacher-Masoch, had a great success for his considerations on flagellation.

A Child is Being Beaten—A Story of Disorientation

Freud underlined that in analysis he realized that any quest for the trauma was useless and that a point is reached at which it is lost. The origin of the fantasy, the whipping fantasy, is lost without a date, in a zone where it is precisely impossible to mark a discontinuity, which is what the trauma marks. This fantasy is presented with the mythical flavor of having always been there. Freud shows 'the child entangled in the excitations of its parental complex', and so not in a traumatic story, but in one of disorientation, of entanglement in a structure. For this reason, he can describe three extremely logical phases, three phases of permutation, a thousand miles removed from any anecdotal description. Freud, from a distance, constructs a permutation:

The first phase of beating-phantasies among girls, then, must belong to a very early period of childhood. Some features remain curiously indefinite, as though they were a

matter of indifference. The scanty information given by the patients in their first statement, "a child is being beaten," seems to be justified in respect to this phase. (p. 184)

In other words, in the first phase one has "a child is being beaten" and
what remains, the agent, remains undetermined. On the other hand, the
object, one is sure that it is not the one who is speaking, the subject.

I would like to draw your attention to a detail of the Freudian method,
his attention to what is not there, his method of considering as a positive, remarkable fact something that remains impossible to determine,
of not considering that it is a fault, an incapacity to determine, but that
this impossibility to be determined is in itself a fact. And this is a central
question of method in Freud's so delicate clinical examination of all the
modes of negation. Freud is a clinician of negation as there have been
few in history. He is an Aristotle of negation.

But another of their features can be established with certainty, and to the same effect in
each case. The child being beaten is never the one producing the phantasy, but is invariably another child. . . . The phantasy, then, is certainly not masochistic. It would be
tempting to call it sadistic, but one cannot neglect the fact that the child producing the
phantasy is never doing the beating herself. The actual identity of the person who does
the beating remains obscure at first. . . . later on this indeterminate grown-up person becomes recognizable clearly and unambiguously as the (girl's) *father.* (pp. 184–185, original emphasis)

What Has Never Existed Does Not Cease to Be Written

Then comes the second phase: "the person beating remains the same . . . ;
but the child who is being beaten has been changed into another one and
is now invariably the child producing the phantasy" (p. 185).

So the agent is the same, but there has been a change of object, which
this time is the subject. The phrase is formulated as follows:

I am being beaten by my father. It is of an unmistakably masochistic character. This second phase is the most important and the most momentous of all. But we may say of it in
a certain sense that it has never had a real existence. It is never remembered, it has never
succeeded in becoming conscious. It is a construction of analysis, but it is no less a necessity on that account. (ibid., original emphasis)

What does Freud mean when he says that it is the most momentous of all and that it has never had any existence? It is this phenomenal contrast which is that whatever has never been realized does not cease to be realized. In fact, he will say that in the psychoanalytical clinic there are violent fathers. There is even a clinic of beaten children, of abandoned children, that has grown up in the last ten years, since it is a social scourge. But what is effectively happening is of another order than what Freud describes. The catastrophes provoked by the maltreatment of children are something other than what Freud designated with this fantasy associated with a high degree of pleasure, and where the formulation is "I am being beaten by my father," which has never existed and which nevertheless is what does not cease to be written.

The third phase, says Freud, rediscovers a certain resemblance with the first one:

The person beating is never the father, but is either left undetermined just as in the first phase, or turns in a characteristic way into a representative of the father, such as a teacher. The figure of the child who is producing the beating-phantasy no longer itself appears in it. In reply to pressing enquiries the patients only declare: "I am probably looking on." Instead of the one child that is being beaten, there are now a number of children present as a rule. (pp. 185–186)

	Agent	Object
A child is being beaten	Agent?	Subject
1. My father is beating a child	My father	Subject
2. I am being beaten by my father	My father	The subject
3. Children are being beaten by a substitute father	Father	Subject

What is identical with the first phase is what links: it is not the father and it is not the subject. This is a fantasy in which it is not him and it is not her either. It is structured like the story of Alphonse Allais "The masked ball where the Canoe and the Mask have to meet, and it was not him, nor her." This is the deployment of the fantasy; the story of Alphonse Allais is the writing of a fantasy that has this type of fantasmatic logic that gives it its charm. It is not the subject, and we have a crowd;

we have that explosion which, in the Freudian logic, is characteristic of a narcissistic mechanism: wherever the crowd is, there are fragments of the subject's ego. It is rather like Irma's injection, for instance. There is Irma who enters the room; Freud goes up to her and examines her throat; then there is the crowd that fills up the room and Freud analyzes that this entry—what Lacan calls the entry of the clowns—this entry of all the vacillating identifications of various grandees who are populating that room are fragments of his own ego that has dispersed itself, like light through a Newtonian prism, through Irma's throat. And here it is really the entry of the clowns, for in little girls' fantasies there are always boys, says Freud, there are lots of boys. In the great majority of cases in the fantasies of girls, it is boys who are beaten without being known individually.

The Mysteries of the Second Phase of the Fantasy

So Freud guides us through a perfectly common fantasy, nevertheless connected to a perversion, but which, as fantasy, cuts across hysterical and obsessional neuroses, is transstructural, as it were. It is not necessarily realized as a perversion, and precisely little girls also have a right to the use of fantasy, which is Freud's way of disabusing his readers from the idea that only boys have access to masochism. There is a little surprise for us in this text, which is to explain how between the first and this second phase there are formidable mysteries because in the second phase, which doesn't exist, the pleasure is intense. There where the pleasure is intense, there is no representation, if one closely follows the consequences, because this phase must be reconstructed, the phase of intense pleasure, and then in the third this pleasure disappears.

The phantasy of the period of incestuous love has said: "He (my father) loves only me, and not the other child, for he is beating it." The sense of guilt can discover no punishment more severe than the reversal of this triumph: "No, he does not love you, for he is beating you." In this way the phantasy of the second phase, that of being beaten by her father, is a direct expression of the girl's sense of guilt. (p. 189)

This is what makes Freud back off from the idea that one could find this phase of the fantasy. This phase would be the pure voice of the conscience of guilt, and one would then have to put one's finger on the genealogy of morality. At last! There would be a direct expression of the universal foundation of morality, which is what Nietzsche was looking for through all the philosophical representations of that morality; a pure voice that would arise: "My father is beating me, and I am enjoying it," which would be the scandalous foundation of morality. These are the points that Nietzsche tried to approach, or Kafka with his punishment machine: the machine wrote the sentence on the skin of the condemned man, when at the last moment of the sentence the condemned man dies; an inspired invention in that atrocious conjunction of the text, the law and the mortal action of the law. Freud, on the other hand, says that the second phase does not exist insofar as the conscience of guilt is always disguised; it is seen only through its effects. Freud does not suppose any direct expression. For that reason he backs off, saying that the second time:

... is a direct expression ... so the phantasy has become masochistic. So far as I know, this is always so; a sense of guilt is invariably the factor that transforms sadism into masochism. But this is certainly not the whole content of masochism. The sense of guilt cannot have won the field alone; a share must also fall to the love-impulse. (p. 189)

This is the structural import. Beyond clinical arguments of the type: "we can find subjects who recall very well being beaten by their father and experiencing pleasure," and one comes across them—the point that is never found is the pure expression of the conscience of guilt and its link with the death drive, when there is this part between Eros, love of the father and its link with the other dimension that is the conscience of guilt.

The Perverse Metaphor

By means of which the following transformation is obtained: in the place where normally prohibition dominates jouissance, it is the perverse metaphor that consists in supporting jouissance through prohibition:

$$\frac{\text{prohibition}}{\text{jouissance}} \qquad \frac{\text{jouissance}}{\text{prohibition}}$$

There where prohibition should be resistance to enjoyment; on the contrary, the perverse maneuver consists in restoring jouissance where there was prohibition. This is why the pervert, according to Lacan, is a crusader, a soldier, who has a mission. The mission of the pervert is that he has to do with a desolate world, *a wasteland,* to use the title of T. S. Eliot's poem. He takes up the theme of the deserted land as developed in the myth of Parsifal or of *Matière de Bretagne* reorganized by Chrétien de Troyes, the myth of the Fisher King, where the land is desolate; it has to be regenerated, and if the land is a dead desert, it is because of a king's sin. But if the pervert is a crusader, a soldier, his mission is, in the face of a land rendered desolate by prohibition, to make everyone enjoy, hence the relentless, proselyte nature of the perverse subject who wants to convince everyone that one does not enjoy enough on this earth, that one has to enjoy more. To enjoy more does not mean more pleasure; one very quickly leaves the terrain of pleasure to enter into more horrible spaces, but which are part of the relentlessness of his mission. He is a soldier working for that metaphor [jouissance over prohibition], and it is what makes Lacan call him a soldier working for an obscure god to whom he sacrifices all his interests in order to return to the world the surplus jouissance it lacks. When Freud calls this restitution "the essence of masochism" and speaks of it in terms of regression (p. 189), we can use our minimal bit of writing to see the structure that is in play, and which is reestablished. But what is very odd is that Freud, in this text which is truly a surprising one, says:

This second phase—the child's phantasy of being itself beaten by its father—remains unconscious as a rule, probably in consequence of the intensity of the repression. I cannot explain why nevertheless in one of my six cases, that of a male, it was consciously remembered. This man, now grown up, had preserved the fact clearly in his memory that he used to employ the idea of being beaten by his mother for the purpose of masturbation. (p. 189)

The compliant reader thought that everything turned around the father. But there he says: "being beaten by the mother." Does Freud mean by that there is a symmetry between little girls, "being beaten by the father," and little boys, "being beaten by the mother"? That is basically what seems to emerge. In this respect, one sees that Freud has not yet established what he will do in two phases, in 1923 and 1932: the total dissymmetry between the boy and the girl. He has not yet established the changes of objects, a single change for the girl: first the mother, then the famous passage to the father, so difficult. Freud is not yet walking along this route with any certainty. He introduces, as if it were normal, as if it went without saying, this symmetry between the sexes: "I found the phase of the fantasy 'being beaten by the mother'." At this point we may feel like telling him that he would have found it in more than one case. It occurs in lots of neuroses. Everything depends on what one calls the pleasure that is experienced as a result of the beating fantasy, but, in any case, I can state that in a series of cases, several dozen, I have found the expression "having been beaten by the mother" for a little boy, who used it consciously as a masturbatory fantasy—it is extremely common. And Freud highlights it as exceptional by saying "curiously." It seems to me that this also goes with the difficulty that one had, in Freud's time, with the question of whether the relations between the sexes should be thought, with respect to jouissance and to these metaphors of the relations between prohibition and jouissance, in a symmetrical or dissymmetrical way.

The Extension of the Fantasy to the Subject's Entire Life

Freud notes very quickly that there is, however, a substitution:

In two of my four female cases an elaborate superstructure of day-dreams, which was of great significance for the life of the person concerned, had grown up over the masochistic beating-phantasy. The function of this superstructure was to make possible a feeling of satisfied excitation, even though the masturbatory act was abstained from. In one of these cases the content—being beaten by the father—was allowed to venture again into consciousness, so long as the subject's own ego was made unrecognizable by a thin disguise. The hero of these stories was invariably beaten (or later only punished, humiliated, etc.) by his father. (p. 190)

It is on this point that the story begins to touch on the extension of the fantasy to the subject's life. He describes two women who not only had such fantasies supposed to have been acknowledged—unconscious fantasies—in the analysis, but also had what Freud calls an "elaborate superstructure," an extension of the fantasy to the entire life by means of constant daydreaming. This constant daydreaming is the way in which the subject secures sexual satisfaction, "make[s] possible [the term is very delicate in Freud], make[s] possible a feeling of satisfied excitation."

What does it mean? We understand better when Freud says: "In one of these cases the content—being beaten by the father—was allowed to venture again into consciousness, so long as the subject's own ego was made unrecognizable by a thin disguise. The hero of these stories was invariably beaten (or later only punished, humiliated, etc.) by his father" (p. 190).

So for the women—two out of four—this is going to be the essential turning point of what masochism will be for Freud; the obvious or manifest forms of feminine masochism is that it is possible for girls to experience consciously, in daydreams, the satisfaction of being beaten by the father on condition that there is a disguise. The gender of the persons used in the fantasy is constant. In this third phase, the one that is manifest, "a child is being beaten" is always "a boy is being beaten," and Freud notes:

This characteristic is naturally not to be explained by any rivalry between the sexes, as otherwise of course in the phantasies of boys it would be girls who would be being beaten; and it has nothing to do with the sex of the child who was hated in the first phase [that is, nothing to do with whether it was a brother or a sister]. But it points to a complication in the case of girls. When they turn away from their incestuous love for their father, with its genital significance, they easily abandon their feminine role. They spur their 'masculinity complex' . . . into activity, and from that time forward only want to be boys. (p. 191)

This paragraph is crucial for the rest of the piece, where the notion of feminine masochism appears. It is the first time that Freud presents this alternative: all girls have to do is to give up expecting a child from the father in order to turn into boys:

For that reason the whipping-boys who represent them are boys too. In both the cases of day-dreaming—one of which almost rose to the level of a work of art—the heroes were always young men; indeed women used not to come into these creations at all, and only made their first appearance after many years, and then in minor parts. (p. 191)

This is a magnificent description of these daydreams that span adolescence, in which the subject, unbeknownst to all, lives her life in these dreams for many years; an all-the-more-beautiful description since very probably the person of whom Freud is speaking is his daughter. In the biography of Anna Freud, written by E. Young-Bruehl, there is an entire passage on the analysis of Anna Freud.

Elisabeth Young-Bruehl stressed that the fifth patient whom Freud is speaking about, who "had come to be analyzed merely on account of indecisiveness in life, would not have been classified at all by coarse clinical diagnosis, or would have been dismissed as 'psychasthenic'" (at 183) was probably Anna Freud herself. In her article on "Beating fantasies and daydreams,"[2] Anna Freud refers to the psychasthenic patient whom she takes into analysis and distinguishes her own case:

Anna Freud presents a little girl who adored her father, and whose incestuous relation was transformed according to a regressive process into an anal-sadistic scene which was realized as a conscious masturbatory fantasy of punishment. These fantasies appeared before the little girl returned to school, between the fifth and sixth year, then to be replaced by more agreeable stories, in English, 'nice stories'. These agreeable stories had apparently no more relation to the punishment stories, although she admits, admits to her analyst as well, that the punishment fantasies suddenly break off these nice stories, and that she was punishing herself by refusing to take refuge in these nice stories for a certain time. The analyst notes for the patient that her punishment fantasies and the nice stories have a very similar structure. The nice stories always open up with a weak young man who was doing something stupid and found himself at the mercy of an older man. And in scenes of increasing tension the young man is threatened with punishment until he is finally pardoned in a scene of harmony and reconciliation. The patient understood the similar structure between the two and ended by recognizing that these stories were interchangeable.

In difficult periods, that is when the patient had to face up to difficult external demands, or felt himself reduced in his capacities, the nice stories were no longer fulfilling their function, and he came to a conclusion at the height of his fantasies when pleasure was replaced by the old situation of punishment which emerged and which alone led to the effective discharge of excitation. But these incidents were quickly forgotten. . . . In the meantime, for several years the patient of whom Anna Freud is speaking moved from these dreams to writing short stories, novellas. They didn't have the same structure, they were not constructed around episodes as isolated as punishment and reconciliation, probably it was an attempt to sharpen up a strong poetic production, to sharpen up a novel.

We have to note that we have a letter from Anna Freud to her father a little while after he finished editing 'a child is being beaten', a letter from Anna Freud to her father in which she says that she is in the course of writing the grand history of childhood.

In this grand history of childhood, it's about history which is modeled on the story of a medieval knight. . . .

We are at the beginning of the twentieth century and there are symbolist stories—all this must be roughly contemporary with Pelléas and Mélisande. Medieval history fascinates Anna Freud, and she throws herself in these stories; we know they were about a knight, a boy. This converges with the girl of whom Freud speaks, who turns away from her feminine role to be a boy, and also with the case of the woman in which the phenomenon of feminine masochism is elaborated. It is his daughter, and concerns her transformation of the paternal bond. What surprises him is the ease with which she renounces her position of daughter in order to become that wise virgin who will characterize Anna Freud. What is also astonishing is that the end of analysis is the moment in which Anna Freud is going to speak in public.

The person whom Freud shows us in his daughter Anna happens to be in a fantasy of being punished before being able to enter into competition with others. Elisabeth Young-Bruehl recounts in an entertaining way that Freud had the idea of making Anna befriend Lou Andreas-Salomé so that she would learn about life, so that they might have women conversations, that she relax a little and surmount her inhibitions—a sort of treatment that is presented rather summarily. Freud invites Lou Andreas-Salomé to spend her holidays with the family in saying: "It will do Anna a lot of good." That is not wrong. It certainly helps her. You know that when Freud wrote "The Economic Problem of Masochism"[3] he was suffering horribly from his jaw and kept the whole house awake because he did not sleep at night. He had to have someone to try to overcome his pain. He worked a little in the morning, wrote a little in the afternoon, and at night demanded that Anna look after him. She herself is exhausted from the care she has to give her father and writes to Lou Andreas-Salomé:

I am currently very busy, but the annoying thing is that last week my nice stories resurfaced and invaded my days in a way that they had not for a long time. They have quietened down a little now, but I was impressed by their force and the unchanged character of this day-dream, although they have been analysed, torn apart, published, mistreated in all sorts of ways. I know that it is really shameful, especially when I give myself up to them between my patients, but it was in any case very pleasant and it gave me a lot of pleasure.

So we see that, at the moment when effectively demands are weighing down on Anna again—she had a lot to do, especially to busy herself with her ill father—and, faced with her father's death, the fantasy recovered its full strength and she set out again in her daydreams, which were at the heart of her life.

The Question of Feminine Masochism

Between 1919 and 1924, Freud radicalizes his point of view, since he presents masochism not only as one fantasy among others, but also as the privileged access to a real that is the death drive. He notes:

> . . . we must perceive that the *Nirvana* principle, belonging as it does to the death instinct, has undergone a modification in living organisms through which it has become the pleasure principle . . . we obtain a small but interesting set of connections. The *Nirvana* principle expresses the trend of the death instinct; the *pleasure* principle represents the demands of the libido; and the modification of the latter principle, the *reality* principle, represents the influence of the external world. None of these three principles is actually put out of action by another. . . . The conclusion to be drawn from these considerations is that the description of the pleasure principle as the watchman over our life cannot be rejected. ("The Economic Problem of Masochism," pp. 160–161, original emphasis)

Just as the watchman over our sleep does not stop our awakening in anxiety dreams, the watchman over our life does not stop masochism from coming to light insofar as it is the privileged relation to the tendency toward the *Nirvana* principle. In this sense masochism is the component drive par excellence since it is the one that reveals that every drive has a dimension, an aspect of the death drive.

How should we situate feminine masochism once the death drive is introduced?

> If one has an opportunity of studying cases in which the masochistic phantasies have been especially richly elaborated, one quickly discovers that they place the subject in a characteristically female situation; they signify, that is, being castrated, or copulated with, or giving birth to a baby. For this reason I have called this form of masochism, *a potiori* as it were . . . the feminine form, although so many of its features point to infantile life. (ibid., p. 162)

Freud calls feminine masochism what goes back to childhood and which is not necessarily feminine. It is called feminine because it has a signification: "being castrated, or copulated with, or giving birth to a baby." He adds: "feminine masochism is entirely based on the primary, erotogenic masochism, on pleasure in pain" (ibid.).

This precision, added in 1924, is also a way of answering the question raised for him by his daughter, that is: where does the force of these daydreams, of these fantasies, come from, since they were analyzed? In fact, it is their directly erogenous side that accounts, for Freud, for the difficulty of ridding girls of their relations to their fantasies.

Here we find the writing of the position of feminine sexuality that Lacan gives: the subject's division between, on the one hand, the relation to the drive, on the feminine side, a direct relation to the drive, and, on the other hand, a direct relation with what in the Other is a privileged signifier. At first Lacan called this signifier the Name-of-the-Father: as long as he had to do with a consistent Other, the guarantee of the Other was in the Other; it was this particular name in the name of which everything signified. Then, Lacan emptied the Name-of-the-Father of its function of guaranteeing the signifying order to isolate, with the Name-of-the-Father, the place of the signifier that lacks in the Other—a signifier that is written S (Ⱥ), the signifier of lack, distinct from what is in the Other, which is written outside and in which there is for Lacan the writing of an entire series of logical paradoxes that are germinal in the idea of writing a signifier outside the Other. ·

This is what Freud added between 1919 and 1924. In "A Child is Being Beaten" (1919) everything turns around the place that Lacan will call the Name-of-the-Father. From 1924, the place of the death drive will be developed. And this is also how Freud explains to himself why, despite the analysis of her fantasies, the analysis of the place of the father—in these diurnal fantasies, this veil that descended over Anna's life—there is a remainder that means that she never completely separated from this position and from her use of daydreams.

In 1969, in the course of *Seminar XVII, L'Envers de la psychanalyse*,[4] Lacan picks up the commentary of "A Child is Being Beaten" and he notes that the central moment, the second moment of the father, is that the one who is doing the beating is not named, and that the statement of the fantasy, the "you are beating me," has to be distinguished from its referent.

Lacan says this: "the *you are beating me* is that half of the subject whose formula makes his link to jouissance. No doubt, he receives his own message in an inverted form—here it means his own jouissance in the form of the jouissance of the Other" (p. 74).

This is one of the clearest reformulations of Lacan reading of sense as 'enjoy-meant' [*jouis-sens*]. What he called, in the semantic years, the meaning that the subject received from the Other—he received his own message in an inverted form—in the 'jouissance' years he notes that the structure functions, but what the phrase "you are beating me" means is that I enjoy, I am receiving my jouissance from you who are beating me. And it is necessary that the father is supposed to be enjoying this, that he is the guarantor of it, and that he occupies the function, the place of jouissance.

At this point, the strange function of the father appears, who is both, since he is the place of jouissance, ravaging, as it were, since he is the one who beats, but at the same time, for the second operation, who is the guarantee that there is a share of jouissance reserved for the subject. The father, especially in the fantasy in question, "a child is being beaten" in its feminine version, guarantees the just distribution of jouissance in the one that he carries out. In so doing, he protects the subject from an unprotected relation that would be even more deleterious with the death drive, one that would not be marked by a seal, by a signifier, by a name. In short, "a child is being beaten" protects the subject from an erogenous masochism. So this is why, concerning feminine sexuality, the stake of the Seminar *Encore*[5] is to separate S($\cancel{A}$) and *a,* these two algebraic letters in their functioning on the feminine side.

The Being of the Woman

One has to resituate Lacan's critique of the Freudian conception of this masochism. What Lacan disagrees with is probably the affirmation that this masochism would be "the expression of the woman's being." It is around the notion of the being of the woman that the essential of the debate revolves. It is not about the phenomenology of these fantasies; they are not deniable and even rather common. It is not the particular relation of [. . . pleasure . . .] and pain that Lacan is going to criticize, but that permanent assignment of pain in the pace of pleasure to the being of the woman. And this will be the force of the concept of privation, when Lacan introduces it: to be able to account for the particular jouissance a woman may experience in divesting herself of the register of having, without it having to do with masochism in the least.

Lacan introduced the concept of privation at the end of the fifties, first to distract the analysts who were stuck in the Anglo-Saxon conception, having bet everything on frustration. In the Anglo-Saxon world especially, the presuppositions of the subject conceived by John Locke mean that the Lockean subject watches over its interests. This subject of liberalism is a subject that watches over its 'having', and every time it cannot have something, it suffers, is frustrated. This is around this idea that the Anglo-Saxon concept turned, not around what is refused by language, *Versagung*—in Freud, the concept *Versagung* corresponds to the translation given as "frustration"—but around what is avoided in the telling [*dire*], *Sagung*. Lacan tried to translate it as "what is refused": language's refusal to tell, highlighting relations to demand; there is something in demand that cannot be said. What is fundamentally frustrating, to use the English term, is that one cannot succeed in saying one's desire in the demand. Whatever the sexual games are in which a person tries to lead his or her partner to tell him or her what makes that person *jouir*—and there is a whole range of erotic games that precisely consists in using words that should not be used, forbidden words, in twisting language, in succeeding in making the other say what makes him or her *jouir*—in whichever way, that escapes us, because it is always between the lines and it will always be the point that will escape being formulated. In this sense, what is really frustrating is this point.

The Concept of Privation: From Having to Being

The idea of privation was made to get psychoanalysts to think in another register than that of having and of what can be demanded. There is a register in which one does not demand, which is that of being. Through a long trajectory, the question of being in Lacan is complicated. Lacan's advances attracted the attention of psychoanalysts in the fifties to the fact that boys and girls both lack being, and that because they lack being, for instance, they lack being a boy or a girl in a total identity, they desire, and this desire is not to have. There are phrases to which we must give their full weight: "desire is the metonymy of the want-to-be/lack-of-being." Those of you who have read Lacan fifty times know this phrase by heart, but still it has to be looked at anew because one could say, if one were a psychoanalyst obsessed by frustration, that desire is a metonymy of the want-to-have: all you need is to have what is frustrating you and then you will be delighted. One obtains satisfaction by getting hold of the forbidden object, and so on.

The whole problem is as follows: what causes the relation to this object, to having, to be transformed or not in the register of being? And on the basis of the introduction of the theme of being, Lacan challenges the idea of a feminine masochism that would explain that women derive their being from that point, by consenting to pain. In the end, they are also deprived but, on the other hand, boys and girls are distinct in their relation to being.

Confront Castration or Getting Rid of Having

Boys manufacture being on being threatened to lose what they have: masculine castration, more precisely, castration involving the masculine genitals, creates a threat. They make their being out of confrontation with the castration threat, but they never confront it totally; it is a kind of Hegelian struggle between master and slave. In Freud, in the genesis of being on the boy's side, it is a battle in which the boy must confront castration—and the boy will only have being through his confrontation with castration. He will not have being in trying to obtain from a more or less cuddly mama the thing he needs not to be frustrated. This is a pathway that, especially among men, creates a profound weakness: to try and obtain from women the little extra thing they need. The path that Freud proposes for the boy is to confront castration. That does not mean to behave like a psychopath knocking everyone about as sole objective in existence; it does not mean having no God or master; it means: to choose those for whom one reserves an affect of admiration and that this admiration does not preclude that what is at stake is to confront the threat of castration in a certain kind of battle. And women adore pushing men into this: as soon as two men admire each other, a little game starts up: "Oh, oh, you're not a man, it's always you that gives in." It's a push to crime.

On the other hand, there is the feminine being. Here, Lacan takes up or makes use of what Freud had established: castration cannot be a threat since it has already happened. Therefore, the woman fears nothing, and, if she creates her being, it is by unloading herself of her having. A very decided subject, a feminine subject, who has difficulties in her relation to having, recovered a memory in which she recalled perfectly well that in kindergarten, before primary school, so before she was six, there was at the back of her school a courtyard and a vertical drop, a kind of little ditch, and that she spent her time—which gave her an enormous satisfaction—throwing over the fence into the ditch everything she was given to take to school with her. From her pencil case she used to throw away the rubber that she loved, the pencil that she also loved, she threw them away and never understood why. She only noticed one thing: she acquired a lot of prestige among her little schoolmates doing what she did. This is a subject who, in her life, had followed this path, suffered from love, and this is exactly the point that was established: she enjoyed being deprived of having and of whatever she might love, her objects. She manufactured being for herself, and her little schoolmates recognized very well that she was manufacturing some prestige, some being, in that kind of potlatch, to take over the term that Native Americans use to designate those ceremonies of struggle for recognition in which everyone sacrifices more than the next: instead of offering gifts to the other because it is vulgar, one simply burns them. In honor of the other one destroys things, and each one destroys more than the other. Well, this little girl very early on got the idea that by sacrificing that to one does not know what obscure God, she made some being for herself.

The jouissance of privation, that's what it is, it is to manufacture a plus for oneself on the basis of a subtraction in having because she herself is not threatened by castration. From then on, Lacan can say that women—who before him were situated in the register of masochism, like those mystical persons who withstand so much pain—in stripping themselves of everything they had, their worldly goods, make a being appear that, through this strange dialectic, takes on all the more value in being, exists all the more in being, that there is this loss in having. And it is on this point that the notion of ek-sistence takes on its meaning in being written the way it is. This being is a being on the outside, it is not a being in the register of having, it cannot be 'in', it cannot be possessed. This is really the intuition that Lacan had, no doubt through the Catholic readings of his intellectual formation, no doubt through debates with his brother, although he did everything, as he says, to keep him from joining an order. In any case, he remained sensitive to the fact that mysticism and all the relations of women to God could not be treated by scientific denial or primary anticlericalism. He is indeed receptive, he said so, to the joy of the mystics, to the fact that there are no doubt women who cannot have a relation to the man except in this way, by way of the Names-of-the-Father, as allowed by mysticism.

Feminine Madness and Masculine Fetishism: Two Styles of Love

Lacan made privation the instrument for rethinking the being of women as it had been left by the heritage of masochism. Retrospectively, he denounced the masochistic illusion as a biological illusion. If the links with this biological condition are broken, which means that women have on occasion consented to the man's fantasy in subjective positions in which pain and humiliation are linked, it is because they are sheltered from the threat of castration. For that reason, they can go further than men along the paths of devotion to love, and this is the reason why Lacan prefers the term "ravage" that a man can on occasion inflict on a woman to the term "masochism." It is not the case that women are masochistic; it is because as there is no limit, no barrier placed by the threat of castration, they can be much more decided in giving themselves and their body to reach the point at which the jouissance of the Other is secured, at which they ensure that the "you are beating me" returns to them in an inverted form. And the examples carefully collated by psychoanalysts of the generation of Joan Riviere, Helen Deutsch, and Anna Freud must be considered again on the basis of the feminine decision, of the 'unstoppable' feminine, of the fact that it is always a surprise for the man when having thought he had to do with the most reasonable of women, he now has to take into account that the most reasonable has become the most unreasonable of them all. What is this jouissance, which alone can guarantee the feminine position of the subject? This is what Lacan formulated in the register of 'feminine madness', of what in women is the erotomaniac style of love, and not fetishistic; in men there is a limit that is obviously the fetish. Basically, men are easily pleased, it is well known, in contrast to the feminine pole that does not have that limit.

For your consideration I will conclude by underlining the effectiveness of the concept of privation, which spans all the facts known under the name of feminine masochism and allows one to place them in an entirely different perspective, a perspective that nonetheless preserves the phenomena.

Notes

1. S. Freud, "A Child is Being Beaten" (1919), trans. J. Strachey, SE XVII.
2. A. Freud, "Beating Fantasies and Daydreams," in *Int. J. Psychoanal.* 4:89 (1922)
3. S. Freud, "The Economic Problem of Masochism" (1924), trans. J. Strachey, SE XIX.
4. J. Lacan, *Le Séminaire XVII: L'Envers de la psychanalyse,* 1969–70 (Paris: Seuil, 1991).
5. J. Lacan, *Seminar XX: Encore,* 1972–73, trans. B. Fink (London & New York: Norton, 1998).

Women and the Symptom: The Case of the Post-Freudians

Pierre-Gilles Guéguen

Many post-Freudian female analysts have been sensitive to the two sides of the symptom: production of meaning—in other words, production emanating from the symbolic, but also production of jouissance through the implication of the real in the symbolic. It is in light of this distinction, elaborated by Lacan in the last years of his teaching, that we will examine the treatment of the symptom by some women who greatly contributed to psychoanalytic theory.

It is often their own analysis that led these analysts to interrogate the modes of feminine jouissance, and they return these interrogations to us through cases that are sometimes their own, and can still teach us today. They also attempted to account for the desire of the analyst in its effectuation in practice (often in articles said to be of psychoanalytic technique).

So they were confronted, perhaps more than men, with the question of the operativity of the concept of the phallus and its usage as *semblant* in the analytic clinic, but also with the horizon on which the signification of the phallus stumbles, with this zone beyond the Oedipus where feminine jouissance only responds to the phallus on the basis of the 'Other which does not exist'.[1] They proposed subtle formulations on the nature of the symptom, on its sense and its jouissance, commensurate with the point that each of them had reached in their analytic trajectory.

On several occasions, and this is not the least of their merit, these analysts provided Lacan with a stepping-stone for his own advances on the nature of the symptom in his teaching. There is indeed a Lacanian treatment of the Freudian concept of the symptom that has been able to strengthen and differentiate itself on the basis of the clinic of these women and in opposition to the clinic of object-relation analysts.[2]

First, we will examine some contributions that account for the nature of the symptom and the conditions of its analysis in the practice of the treatment. On this point, Ella Sharpe and Lucia Tower have, among others, contributed some useful elements, different aspects of which Lacan has emphasized at different times of his teaching.

Then we will see how the question of the symptom is dealt with by female analysts concerning the very crucial point of the supposed female masochism and the feminine condition in general. The path that was thereby opened has largely been followed by the sociopolitical developments of feminism; and Lacan did not hesitate to orient us in the same direction, and so to orient the current developments of psychoanalysis on the contemporary symptom according to his thesis of the non-existence of the sexual relation. This dimension has been explored by Helen Deutsch and Joan Riviere in particular, but also by Anna Freud.

The Hidden Face of the Symptom

Because of the attention that she brings to the signifying substitutions in the analytic treatment, Ella Sharpe would seem to prefigure Lacan's developments on the metaphorical value of the symptom and in particular those of "The Agency of the Letter in the Unconscious." This cultured, erudite analyst, who is attentive to the virtues of the symbolic, develops with great finesse, in a central chapter of her book on dream analysis, the diverse significations that a mild coughing symptom can have for a patient. Lacan, in his rereading of the case, stresses two of its aspects that show how his conception of the symptom, inspired by structuralism and borrowing from Jakobson and Saussure, is more complex than that of Ella Sharpe and produces different consequences in the treatment.

Ella Sharpe[3] leaves it at a simple articulation between symptom and fantasy. She does not distinguish them clearly and rather situates them in continuity with each other. This leads her to consider that in the case of the patient under consideration, the point is to develop his repressed aggressivity and permit him to express his unconscious rivalry toward his father. So despite her confidence in the symbolic, she ends up interpreting in the patient's reality, and this unfailingly provokes an acting out that she does not pick up on.

In opposition to this thesis, Lacan draws the precise consequences from his schema L, where the imaginary axis intersects with the symbolic axis, by insisting on the point of intersection of the two axes and transcribing it onto the graph of desire.[4] This leads him to underline that the symptom is not simply the blocked message that so pleases Ella Sharpe, but that it also brings to light a point of negativity, a point that does not respond to the dialectic of the signifier. Lacan stresses this on the basis of a notation that Ella Sharpe had made without drawing the consequences from it.[5] The English analyst realizes indeed that her patient's fantasy, like those of neurotics, implies a not being there where he is called to manifest himself in a sexual conjunction and, by displacement, each time where he has to display a virile behavior. It is, however, very different to consider that it is a question here, for the subject, of a dream of omnipotence or to show that there is a jouissance there for the subject that he wants to preserve. And, indeed, Lacan proceeds to show that the symptom is truly an unconscious message of the patient, the trace of his relationship to the dead father and the young sister with whom he is identified, but also that there is something else in play: *no doubt, the symptom is a metaphor for the phallus, insofar as it evokes sexual desire, but it is also its metonymy, the simple sign of its presence insofar as it relates not only to the subject's want-to-be/lack-of-being but also to the fixity of his* jouissance. So, here, Lacan introduces a distinction within the phallic clinic between the phallus as signifier of the ego ideal and the phallus as index of jouissance (this distinction will find its notation in "Subversion of the Subject and Dialectic of Desire"[6]).

From then on, the symptom and the fantasy are no longer homogenous; they are articulated around an object of jouissance or rather, as Lacan puts it at the time, 'of the signifier of jouissance' at play in the transference, and which will have to be extracted in the treatment. And Lacan indicates very precisely the maneuver to be operated in the treatment of this obsessional: whereas Ella Sharpe does her best to leave empty the place that her patient wants to retain as such in his fantasy of not being there, Lacan's point of view consists, on the contrary, in pointing out that the analyst must not maintain herself as the stake of the treatment in this way, but should rather make herself recognized as an object that the analysand can lose.

With Lucia Tower, Lacan aims to highlight a different point.[7] Indeed, he searches for the trace of the real in the symptom, that which, like anxiety [*l'angoisse*], does not lie. And his 1962–1963 reading of the cases of the female analysts who believe in countertransference could be reinterpreted today in light of a later Lacan as attempting to circumscribe the

nature of the links between symptom and *semblant,* in order to elucidate the way in which the symptom makes the symbolic enter the real.
In Lucia Tower's example, there are two cases of men in analysis, two
cases that the author diagnoses as anxiety neuroses. The analyst correctly points out the sadistic dimension present beneath the symptoms
of a failed love life and the subservience of these men to their respective wives, and so the signifying dimension of the symptom that free
association yields. But what interests her is that she succeeds with one,
but not the other, in obtaining a softening of his position toward women
in general and in the analysis in particular, and this in a way that she initially, but erroneously, attributed to herself. She dreamt one day that
this patient's wife was on her side, that she was no longer the adversary
determined to sabotage her husband's treatment. She can then modify
her position with respect to this patient's desire and thereby leave the
place of the dead where he was keeping her immobile. From then on, a
'sadistic' negative transference triggers on the side of the patient,
which she manages to support and that allows the patient to explore his
fantasmatic position.

Lacan underlines something here that has to do with the very nature of the symptom such that Lucia Tower can, without really formulating it, conceive of it: by occupying the place of the object for this
patient, she was able to uncover this object and, in particular, to generate the address to a feminine Other by operating with her own lack,
thereby allowing the patient an access to his castration. So of course
the question is raised—and Lacan responds in the negative—as to
whether this was not a masochistic response on her part to the sadistic fantasies of the patient.

This case illustrates and reexamines in several respects the difference between a neutral position of the analyst and the putting into play
of the *semblant* in the form of object *a* (including a certain type of im-
mobility) in the analysis of the symptom. Here Lacan stresses the fact
that there is a kernel of jouissance at the heart of the symptom that is
not to be interpreted, but that is, however, treated by transference love.
The problematic that will be developed in *Seminar XI* is already in
place, and it is not the problematic of an interpretation of the symptom
to the point of its reduction, but that of the extraction of the object.
Lucia Tower did not have very clear views on this point, but she knew
at least not to be blinkered by the 'technical' norms regarding the correct position of the analyst.

Is Femininity a Symptom?

Helen Deutsch and Joan Rivière tackle another dimension. Just as the analysts previously mentioned could be considered to have dealt with the question of the symptom through a 'technical' bias, with Helen Deutsch it is femininity itself that becomes the problem to resolve. The conflict is no longer envisaged as the dissatisfaction emanating from a blocked and repressed libido that would cause displeasure, but as a question that bears on being and truth. This is why the themes of the failure to reach the feminine position and of the 'as if' (tomboys and child-women) are so pregnant in her work. She treats the subject's division and her own as the sole question, the essential question, of psychoanalysis.

It has been said that her loyalty to Freud, which made her a target for feminists, is certainly an homage, but one that conceals a very personal interpretation of what a woman is.[8] This may well be the case, but it remains necessary to identify the way in which she errs. On the one hand, she considers that the symptom is but a pathological exaggeration of a normal problem that each woman encounters on the way to sexed realization.[9] On the other hand, she organizes her idea of development on biological foundations that, she believes, explain the passage from clitoral sexuality to vaginal sexuality. From these dubious premises, she nevertheless produces a conclusion that will give rise to a great deal of discussion and that corresponds in inadequate terms to a clinical experience that will have to wait for Lacan to find its logical formulation.

In effect, she postulates that the girl always passes through a masochistic drive polarity from the moment that she detaches herself from the mother in order to await the child of the phallic promise from the father. Furthermore, she considers that this phase is necessary and characteristic of the feminine position. Femininity would become permanently fixed here because of the disarray in which the girl finds herself from having to face her own castration and, having exited the phallic clitoral phase, from no longer being able to tie her libido to an organ. This would entail a veritable anal and oral regression and a new jouissance of a masochistic order, which would find its conclusion in the pain and jouissance of childbirth.

Not without logic, Helen Deutsch deduces a whole clinic of 'the excesses'[10] of masochism from this thesis, whether they be due to the mother's unconscious and 'pre-oedipal' hatred or to the virility complex

in the woman. No doubt, this thesis has its value, but one should understand that it is built on the basis of an equivalence hastily constituted
from Freud.[11] In point of fact, as Eric Laurent shows: "She establishes
an equivalence between masochism and passivity, between sadism and
activity, in order to deconstruct man-woman relationships. . . . There
where Freud says that the girl expects a child from the father, Helen
Deutsch considers that this expectation is equivalent to a passivity, and
that in fact it is equivalent to saying: expecting a child from the father
and occupying a masochistic position."[12] This is to confuse the play of
the drive in the fantasy with the symbolic value of the call to the father
for the realization of the phallic promise. In so doing, and all the while
believing herself to be completely loyal to Freud, Helen Deutsch aims to
correct him by making the expectation of a child from the father equivalent to the girl's identification with the father (this was her immovable
position in life). In the last analysis, the essential confusion in Helen
Deutsch's thesis has to do with her reduction of any feminine division to
the register of the male norm, to the empire of the All. For his part,
Lacan will situate this division in the register of the not-all and from the
"Guiding Remarks for a Congress on Feminine Sexuality" onward, he
gives a radical critique of, on one hand, the confusion between 'feminine masochism' and perverse masochism (which aims at the other's
anguish), and, on the other hand, the anchoring of the psychoanalytic
thought of his time in a biological conception that the concept of feminine masochism draws on. What is a symptom for Helen Deutsch, who
is nonetheless well aware that the real of the symptom is always situated
in relation to the other sex, is that she fails to realize that feminine sexuality is not a matter of identification, but of jouissance, of a jouissance
that makes the woman other from having to receive the phallus from the
other, the man, but at the same time from not having to receive a limit to
the jouissance thereby acquired from this phallic Other. This is why,
even though she was a mother, she remained a girl for both Freud and all
the men that she knew throughout her life.

On this question of feminine masochism, the complement to Helen
Deutsch is supplied by Anna Freud. If Helen Deutsch presented masochism as a necessary element of woman's access to sexual satisfaction,
Anna Freud shows the fantasmatic flipside of masochism and its translation in symptoms of inhibition and consolatory daydreaming, but that
ties the feminine subject to the masculinity complex. This is the focus
of her article "Beating Fantasies and Daydreams."

And it is indeed after discovering the fantasy "a child is being beaten," whose key was in all likelihood handed to him by Anna, that Freud develops the concept of the death drive, thereby designating a jouissance included in the analytic symptom, but that does not for all that respond to interpretation. The 'negative therapeutic reaction' is related to this same observation: the symptom does not or no longer lets itself be totally absorbed by the symbolic, by the process of *significantization*. So Freud had to accept to leave Anna at a point in her treatment where the homosexual components—the virility complex—could not be undone. What is in question here is no longer 'feminine masochism', but rather the fixation of a primordial jouissance included in the symptom insofar as the symptom itself is a response to the real.

These are the problems that also interested Joan Rivière, and in particular that of 'femininity as defense,'[13] to take up the title of one of the chapters from her collected articles. She is best known for having proposed the term 'feminine masquerade' to oppose the pathways of the quest for feminine satisfaction and the position of rivalry with men. This problem, as well as what she called her negative therapeutic reaction, and which no doubt refers to her treatment with Jones, who was her first analyst, were at the origin of her request for an analysis with Freud.

The very term of masquerade is picked up by Lacan, who thereby extracts it (at the same time as frigidity—but this is addressed more to Helen Deutsch[14]) from the register of neurotic symptoms to which Joan Rivière had confined it in order to raise it to the level of a structural trait of women's jouissance.[15]

Notes

1. E. Laurent and J.-A. Miller, *L'Autre qui n'existe pas et ses comités d'ethique* (1996–1997), unpublished, with the exception of the lesson of 20 November 1996, in *La Cause freudienne* No. 35, Navarin/Seuil, Paris, 1997, pp. 3–20.

2. J.-A. Miller, "The Seminar of Barcelona on *Die Wege der Symptombildung*" in *Psychoanalytical Notebooks* No. 1 (London, 1998), pp. 10–65.

3. E. Sharpe, *Dream Analysis* (London: Hogarth Press, 1937).

4. See the relevant sessions of J.-A. Miller's course *Donc* (1993–1994), unpublished.

5. E. Laurent, *Séminaire de la Section clinique de Paris, 1985–1986*, unpublished.

6. J. Lacan, "Subversion of the Subject and Dialectic of Desire in the Freudian Unconscious" in *Écrits* (London: Routledge, 1977).

7. L. Tower, *Counter-transference,* 1955, and J. Lacan, *Le séminaire* X: *L'angoisse,* 1962–63 (Paris: Seuil, 2004).

8. N. Kress Rozen and H. Deutsch, *Une théorie de la femme* in *Ornicar?* No. 15 (Paris: Lyse, été 1978).

9. H. Deutsch, preface, *The Psychology of Women* (1945).

10. M.-Ch. Hamon, *Pourquoi les femmes aiment-elles les hommes? Et pas plutôt leur mère* (Paris: Seuil, 1992). This excellent work details this clinic and its subtleties, as well as its pitfalls and impasses.

11. H. Deutsch, *The Psychoanalysis of Neurotics.* In the preface to this work, Helen Deutsch indicates that since the thirties, when the principal texts of this work were written, she has converted to ego psychology. In a 1930 article entitled "The Part of the Actual Conflict in the Formation of Neurosis," she defines neurosis as an unconscious conflict reactualized in reality. When the ego cannot resolve this conflict, the subject regresses. Following this, the famous false 'technical' window was established, which would prove useful to object-relation psychoanalysts with its ternary 'aggression, frustration, regression', and lead the treatments into the impasse of the analysis of resistances.

12. E. Laurent, "Feminine Positions of Being," 1992–93, Séminaire de la Section clinique de Paris, unpublished, except for the chapter in this volume.

13. J. Rivière, *The Inner World and Joan Rivière, Collected Papers: 1920–1958,* edited with a biographical chapter by A. Hughes, prefaced by H. Segal (London-New York: Karnac Books, 1991).

14. On these points, the reader is referred to the book of psychoanalytic studies collected by Marie-Christine Hamon, *Féminité mascarade* (Paris: Seuil, 1994).

15. J. Lacan, "Guiding Remarks for a Congress on Feminine Sexuality" in *Feminine Sexuality,* trans. by J. Rose in J. Mitchell and J. Rose (Basingstoke & London: Macmillan, 1982), pp. 93–94.

Sexual Position and the End of Analysis

Marie-Hélène Brousse

I would like to defend the following thesis in this intervention: the definition of the passage to the analyst, and so of the end of analysis, is correlative to the advances of the theory of sexuation in psychoanalysis. My claim is that any definition of the analyst, and consequently of the analytical work that is required of the analyst for his or her production, corresponds to a conception of sexuation. This thesis implies the development of several points.

First, why link sexuality and the formation of the analyst? Let us recall that the field of psychoanalysis is the field of the sexual, that psychoanalysis has no other pertinence than as the clinic of sexuality. It is there that we treat the effects of jouissance on a subject of the unconscious determined by its capture in language. Consequently, the knotting of jouissance to the unconscious is the very object of an analysis.

On the other hand, psychoanalysis implies a definition of sexuality as sexuation. The point is not so much to stress the dimension of chronological development of this process as to take note of a disparity between the biological real of sex—defined in the human species by the difference between male and female, and so by a duality—and its symbolic determinations, namely, the different solutions imposed on the subject by the structure of language and the defiles of the signifier. Sexuation is a process of complex identifications and so analysis, which is a movement of the fall of identifications, has for objective to reach the point of separation between the jouissance that sustains the subject and the identifications with which the subject covers it.

Lastly, my thesis implies that the knotting of sexual jouissance to the unconscious is, to some extent at least, open to formalization and thus transmissible. There is no clinic without epistemology; this is one of the aspects of the ethics of psychoanalysis. The Freudian cause is the cause of the formalization of knowledge against the bloc of the ineffable, unspeakable. It could be shown, although I will not do so here, that all the analysts who have contributed to the elaboration of analytical knowledge have been led, often implicitly, to formulate a theory of sexuation, and that it turns out that their conception of the conclusion of the treatment depended on their theory of sexuation. The formalization of the real, in psychoanalysis as in other fields, modifies the frameworks of the real. I will only envisage this articulation with respect to Lacan's teaching, since it is on the basis of his teaching that this point could emerge explicitly. But I will do so within the limits of this intervention, not in a systematic and erudite way, as would doubtless be appropriate, but starting from the pressing actuality of my current work on a question that the pass unveiled for me.

The Freudian approach to sexuation took the form of a myth, that of Oedipus. This epic form allowed Freud to approach structure as the dynamic of sexuation and to grasp in an imaginarized form the knotting of the sexual, traumatic jouissance of the body to the unconscious as ordered set of signifiers. We know that Lacan reinterpreted this Freudian sexuation with the paternal metaphor. And, thus, a conception of the end of the treatment is deployed correlative to this formalization of Oedipus through the writing of the paternal metaphor, that is, through the link between the function of the Name-of-the-Father and the Desire-of-the-Mother. In a seminar of January 1991 in which he problematized the chronology of Lacan's teaching regarding the formation of the analysts and the transmission of psychoanalysis, J.-A. Miller studied the modifications of the conception of the concept of the phallus in the theorization of the end of analysis. We also know that the phallus is the key signifier in the definition of the masculine and feminine sexual positions. In 1958, and at the beginning of the sixties, that is, notably in "The Signification of the Phallus" and in "Remarque sur le Rapport de Daniel Lagache," the phallic function organizes the minimal combinatory that, based on a unique signifier, the phallus, allows the production of the two formulas of masculine and feminine desire: $\Phi\,(a)$ and $\bar{A}\,(\varphi)$. As a consequence, it is also on the basis of the phallic function that analysis is thought. The phallus is the mark of desire as such, so much so that the end of analysis is envisaged from the perspective of the uncovering and revelation of this mark. At that time, the sense given by Lacan to the term "mark" is different from what it will be in, for example, the "Note italienne." At the time of "The Significa-tion of the Phallus," it refers to a signifying mark, an indelible mark that language effects on the subject. The end of analysis takes account of the indelible, unsurpassable aspect of the phallic mark of desire. This epiphany is strictly correlated to the Name-of-the-Father; some-thing unnamable of the maternal desire is symbolized by the phallus as lack, consequence of the function of the symbolic law. The phallus is the signifier of the feeling of life as it results from signifying mortifica-tion. The two formulas that I have just quoted come to replace the Freudian solution of castration anxiety and penis envy. Therefore, the analysis ends on the phallic master signifier, unveiled as the spring of desire operating in the shadow of the paternal function. From this per-spective, the end of the text "The direction of the treatment" traces the portrait of the analyst, in the event Freud, as 'man of desire', the one who unveils the 'uncoupled signifier' that speaks [*dit*] the unique sense of life, namely, that desire is carried toward death by the very fact of signifying mortification.

As early as the end of the *Écrits* another definition of the phallus emerges that, by insisting on its correlation with the castration of the Other, situates it in the perspective of phobia and, above all, the fetish, as an element that allows the subject to maintain himself in the posi-tion of "I don't want to know anything about it." Phobia and fetish are two possible responses to maternal castration for the neurotic subject and, by the same token, to the difference between the sexes. And at the end of "Science and Truth," Lacan envisages two possible issues for the end of the treatment, phobic and fetishist, on the basis of the phal-lus defined in this way. The phallus is no longer envisaged as sym-bolic, a bar on the subject testifying to its relation with language, but as 'index' of a point of lack that it contributes to veiling. Jacques-Alain Miller stressed that the phallic mark of desire then revealed the central point of repression, and that the reduction of the phallus to its function of fetish allowed for a movement toward a dephallicization of the subject at the time of the end of analysis. But, correlatively, this dephallicization opened another perspective as to sexuation. Until then, the latter remained open to formulation on the basis of the signi-fier 'phallus', and therefore strictly reliant on the universal of the pa-ternal function, the metaphor of the Name-of-the-Father allowing the writing of a relation between father and mother. The definition of the phallus as fetish, and so as veil of the castration of the Other, opens a way beyond the Oedipus and toward that which, of the sexual relation, cannot be written.

The movement of the dephallicization of desire takes place in the critique of the two Freudian myths, that of Oedipus in the seminar *L'envers de la psychanalyse,* and that of Eros in the seminar *Le savoir du psychanalyste.* The thread followed by Lacan remains Freud's desire, and it is from Freud's stumbling blocks that Lacan brings to light a different position of the analyst.

Elsewhere, by taking up certain passages of the seminar *L'envers de la psychanalyse,* I have developed the fact that Lacan used the notion of the paternal metaphor to show that it was his interpretation of the Freudian myths of the father, but that, besides this reinterpretation, their structural analysis also allowed for a formulation of the quilting point of the desire of Freud, of the analyst; it is a desire to equate desire with law, or again the function of the dead father with the condition of jouissance: for Freud, there is no salvation outside the phallus. This analysis allows Lacan to displace the end of analysis, as well as sexuation, toward a horizon not limited by the father and the universality of the phallic function. I will not take it up again here. Let us, however, stress two points. First, castration is no longer defined on the basis of the register of the symbolic but from that of the real: castration is not a fantasy, "it is the real operation introduced through the effect of the signifier, and it may be any signifier, in the relation to sex." We can see that the status of sexuation is modified by the fact that Lacan insists on the register of the real to envisage sexuality rather than keeping it in the register of the symbolic, that is, to envisage castration only in the perspective of the Other of the signifier.

Second, "there is a cause of desire only as product of this operation" and "the fantasy dominates the whole reality of desire, that is to say, the law." It is the operation of 'real castration', as we have just defined it, that produces the object, the object that fantasy—an heterogeneous construction—will put in relation with the subject of the signifier. The object *a,* at the level of its production, is therefore not of the same cloth as the signifier 'phallus' that comes to veil it.

Sexuation is no longer to be taken as the result of the structure of the paternal metaphor alone; it requires that a real that is foreign to the signifying combinatory be integrated into it. Sexuation is defined by Lacan in "Remarque sur le rapport de Daniel Lagache": while it introduced this major simplification of the phallus as signifier, this definition still went under the Freudian banner of the phallic phase and implied a symmetry between the two sexes on the basis of the axis of the phallus. And the stress put on the real of sexuality requires a supplementary construction.

Just as in 1969–1970, Lacan tangled with the myths of the father in Freud and thus introduced an orientation of sexuation grounded on the object beyond the father and a dephallicization of the end of treatment, in the following year 1970–1971, in the Seminar *Le savoir du psychan-alyste,* it is through the critique of the myth of Eros that Lacan will introduce a new conception of the 'One' that will allow him to think the real of sex in the symbolic order.

On the side of biology, that is, of the real, there are two sexes: "The fact that we may know with certainty that sex can be found there, in two little cells which do not look alike . . . in the name of this the psychoanalyst believes that there is a sexual relation." On side of the real therefore there is 'something of the two,' but no relation.

On the side of the signifier, it is from the phallic signifier and the paternal exception that the sexual position is formulated. But no other relation than that of the paternal metaphor inscribes can be formulated: the father cannot be assimilated to the man and the woman is always contaminated by the mother.

And yet the Freudian myth of Eros is designed precisely to be able to think that two can make one; in other words, Eros is there to state the possibility of a relation. "To find, in Freud's work, the idea that Eros is founded/merges [*se fonde*]—notice the equivocation—by making One out of the two, is a strange idea from which proceeds this outrageous idea, which Freud nevertheless repudiated with all his being, of universal love. Life's founding force would entirely be in this Eros, the principle of union."

Lacan's concern, in his critique of the unifying myth of Eros, is to be able to think the One without introducing the idea of union, of the relation between the sexes. For all that, he does not define this One on the basis of the unicity of the phallus for the two sexes, since we have seen that the position of the primacy of the phallus in sexuation becomes untenable from the moment when all in sexuality is not phallic, namely, when the not-all signifier is introduced beyond the dead father. The stake is to produce that which can be said of the One to fight this crude mythology, for, I quote, "nothing is more dangerous than the confusions arising as to what is the One." Why dangerous? Because the idea of the

One obtained from the fusion of two is precisely introduced through the power of speech, and because all the clinic of love yet shows that in no way, and for both sexes, is there a question of becoming One in love.

Thus, to the One of Eros Lacan opposes the One of the set: the set consists of different elements, all distinct, but without any support of either imagination or the order in which they are enumerated. In fact, every element is of the same value [*se vaut*] and is repeated: Lacan speaks of the *sameness* [*mêmeté*] *of absolute difference*. It is on the basis of this difference between the One of the set and the One of elements that are repeated that Lacan moves on to think the position of jouissance of a subject. It is possible to situate this mark of jouissance through its effects, and to go from the One that is repeated to the One-all-alone that makes the difference, non-enumerable, non-countable. In this sense, an analyst is in the position of a traumatic parent, as Lacan says in the same seminar, since he must return to the point of junction at which in a particular speech a unique signifier marked a body, thereby constituting a mark of jouissance that is repeated. It is therefore no longer the at-least-one of the father or the One of the phallic signifier that gives its orientation to the analysis, for the latter also requires that this trace of the anchoring point of S_I on the body be isolated through its repetitions and, in the process, dissociated from object *a*.

From this critique of the two Freudian myths Lacan produces the following advance.

The step beyond [*pas au-delà*] the father through his reduction to the exception that sustains the universality of symbolic castration and the quest for a definition of the One in psychoanalysis, resting on a mathematical model that allows it to elude the fusional relation, come to their conclusion with the formulation of the set of the four formulas of sexuation that constitute a set without which, as Lacan says in the Seminar *Le savoir du psychanalyste,* "it is impossible to orient oneself correctly in what is at stake in analytical practice insofar as it deals with this something which is commonly defined as being man, on the one hand, and, on the other, this correspondent, similarly called woman, who leaves him alone."

The link between sexuation and the definition of the end of analysis is therefore established. It seems important to stress the following elements.

There is a Lacanian orientation of the end of the treatment because Lacan made a decisive step as to sexuation. It is a double step: on the one hand, there is a dephallicization of desire that goes together with a taking account of the real of the object-cause of desire; on the other hand, there is a desymmetricization of sexual positions, one being the universal masculine one, that is, including all subjects, the other feminine, not entirely governed by the universal and therefore, to this extent, of the order of inconsistency. Any analysis is therefore conducted on the basis of the set of the four formulas of sexuation that sustain the statement of that which is the compass of the analyst, the axiom: "There is no sexual relation that could be written," a statement that comes in opposition to that which founds the order of speech.

At the end of an analysis, therefore, a new dialectic of love and desire is produced. This novelty is introduced, on the one hand, by a modification of desire that is no longer defined solely as the repression of castration but on the basis of the object that crystallized the subject's jouissance and, on the other hand, by an inversion of the movement of love: love goes from the traumatic encounter with the real toward phallic necessity, namely, from a contingency defined as a 'ceasing not to be written' toward a 'does not cease to be written'. In analysis, the movement goes from the phallic necessity 'which does not cease to be written' toward the refound contingency of the encounter with the real: what has been traumatic for a subject.

But to say that analysis is oriented through the set of the formulas of sexuation, and that it thereby requires that the feminine position be glimpsed at [*entrevue*], does not authorize us to say that the analyst is in a feminine position. In this case, what is it that differentiates the feminine position from that of the analyst? I propose the following idea: the common point between the feminine position and that of the analyst lies in contingency, a contingency that, let me remind you, is characterized by the encounter with a real that can finally be written and is defined in the formula: $\overline{\forall x} \ \Phi x$, which is the formula of the not-all. That which distinguishes the position of the analyst from the feminine one is not, either, the fact that the formula of the not-all can only be sustained there as supplementary to the two masculine formulas of the universal, since it is also the case of any feminine position. What differentiates the position of the analyst from a feminine position lies in the formula of the impossible, written by Lacan $\overline{\exists x} \ \overline{\Phi x}$, that is, at the junction point with the real, this point that is of the order of the undecidable. It is thus on the basis of the contingency of desire, on the one hand, and of love as determined by the nonrelation, on the other, that I suggest we can grasp the analyst's position. It is unprecedented in the sense that it is differentiated from a desiring position organized by the empire of the phallus and from a feminine position that remains organized by the object.

This text was originally delivered at the VIIIth International Encounter of the Freudian Field in Paris (10-13 July 1994).

References

J. Lacan, "Note italienne" in *Ornicar?* No. 25, 1973 (Paris: Lyse, 1982), pp. 7-10; also in *Autres écrits* (Paris: Seuil, 2001), pp. 307-311.

J. Lacan, "Lettre du 26 janvier 1981" in *Actes du Forum* (Paris: Pub. De l'ECF, 1981) p. 1.

J. Lacan, "Remarque sur le rapport de Daniel Lagache: Psychanalyse et structure de la personnalité" in *Écrits* (Paris: Seuil, 1966), p. 683.

J. Lacan, "The Direction of the treatment and principles of its power" in *Écrits: A Selection* (London: Routledge, 1977), p. 276.

J. Lacan, "La science et la vérité" in *Écrits*, op. cit., p. 877, "Science and Truth" in *Newsletter of the Freudian Field*, No. 3 (1989), pp. 4-29.

J. Lacan, *Le Séminaire XVII, L'envers de la psychanalyse* (Paris: Seuil, 1991), p. 149.

J. Lacan, *Le Séminaire, Le savoir du psychanalyste,* 1971-72 (4 May 1972), unpublished.

J. Lacan, *Seminar XX, Encore* (London & New York: Norton, 1998), p. 78.

Afterword

The Response of Psychoanalysis to Cognitive-Behavioral Therapy

Jacques-Alain Miller

In Paris, I used the term "struggle"; I spoke in terms of struggle. That is because in France, CBT (Cognitive-Behavioral Therapy) is not yet a dominant model, far from that. In our milieu, it is something that we have only just discovered and that is not prevalent in hospitals or care institutions. It has only come to our attention through the recent Accoyer amendment and the INSERM study,[1] which emerged from the outside as something new and surprising. We did not see CBT surface from clinical practice. Perhaps we were inattentive because there certainly was some kind of literature written on it in the last ten years. But it was not present in everyday practice. As soon as we realized it was something new, we began to be interested in it. And I believe it is because we discovered it in this surprising way in France, that you are meeting today at this Forum in London, to discuss the rise of CBT.

I do not think that you would have held such a meeting before, here in England, or in the Freudian Field. I believe that our surprise, or ignorance, our indignation and the ethical uprising in France, had some consequences for you. It made you question what is much more commonplace here. For this reason, I do not believe that the struggle we have initiated in France can be transposed here. We are not synchronized. You are faced with it here where, I feel, although I may be mistaken, CBT is already the dominant model of talk therapy. A new field called talk therapy has been created, and in this talk therapy field the dominant model is CBT rather than psychoanalysis. Does that describe the phenomena?

In France, and I think it is the same here, CBT is a development led by bureaucracy; it is led by state bureaucracy and by insurance bureaucracy, and the 'psys' [*practitioners in the entire field of psychotherapy and counseling*] feel the pressure of all these bureaucracies. It is a new aspect of the last, let's say, ten years: the fact that 'psys' have become a political and an economical factor. Twenty years ago we spoke as private practitioners who may also have a role in the institution. But the core practice was private and motivated by individual patients asking for treatment. Whereas now we are in a completely new world. 'Psys' are an important economical factor of the whole health system, which further-more is driving up the financial deficit in all modern democracies.

That means that we have a new Other in the field, one we did not have before, who is asking for treatments that are more speedy, less costly, en-tirely predictable, and whose end-point and duration can be anticipated. With this, we are facing a new kind of demand. Before, we had an individ-ual asking us for treatment. Now we have a collective, generalized Other who makes demands. How should we treat that? How to treat the financial Other, or the bureaucratic Other, who is demanding and commanding, and who does not give up but gives us orders? I would say it is a new kind of patient! How should we treat this new patient? From this point of view, the word "struggle" is not the best way to engage with this patient. "Strug-gle" could be counterproductive and perhaps we should not call it a strug-gle. It may be that we have to accept the basis of the demand in order to do some judo with it; to demonstrate, perhaps, that CBT is not so effective or speedy or less costly as it seems. That is my suggestion.

And it depends on how far you have got to here in Britain. In France, for the time being, this Other is still small. It does not have a very pow-erful voice at the moment. But this can change in two or three years. In a way, I am here to understand what our future could look like because you may turn out to be our future. For a long time we have hoped that France would be your future in psychoanalysis. Instead, now it seems possible that we are going to discover your kind of problem in France.

I am not sure that the United States is more 'advanced' than Britain in this respect. Three years ago, an article in the *Washington Post* said that CBT is more popular in Britain than in the United States, and that in Britain it is the "first line of treatment." What may be more developed in the United States is the pressure the individualistic judicial interest groups exert—"we have rights, respect our rights"—to them, psycho-analysis appears to be disrespectful of judicial rights.

My opinion with regard to evaluation is that it is a lost cause. I mean, it is so costly and not possible to implement. The data that you get through evaluation cannot be processed; it just accumulates and at the end cannot be used. Underlying it is an attempt to get a transparent subject supposed to know. A total subject supposed to know, for me, is a very strange phenomenon. How is it possible, after all that has gone before? How can you have a total subject supposed to know at the same time as 'God is dead', and general relativism, which the new pope deplored? As a matter of fact, we see in our society a new ideal of total knowledge; a new ideal of a general quantification of everything human. It is rather like God reborn, an intellectual God reborn, or born again, if I may say so, and I believe it is going to fail by its own logic. Although it may take some years to fail, and I do not know if the time to fail is going to be the same in the United States and in Europe. Apparently twenty percent of all the cost of health is in evaluation. Someone gave this figure recently in the *New York Times*. It is difficult to believe it is going to go on like that forever. But for the time being, it is a world conception, a new *Weltanschauung* that is very contradictory to our way.

Why did psychoanalysis develop outside state regulation, and why did it want to develop like that? It could be that for a long time it was not a mass concern; it was not a mass practice, but a niche practice. It was able to develop in this way because psychoanalysis's desire is to question all beliefs, all ends, all notions of benefit, and even the very notion of reality. This means that the psychoanalytic session takes place in a different space; be it in an imaginary space or a symbolic space, that is not important, but it is not the common space of ordinary communication. So, it was essential to the analytic practice not to be regulated from the outside. It was even a question how it could be regulated from the inside, mainly for those psychoanalysts who thought they could not share their values, their methods, and their results with other practitioners.

Thus, it is for structural reasons that there is this savage, unruly aspect of psychoanalysis. While Freud tried to civilize it in his time, Lacan critiqued it and tried to develop it into something outside of common values, outside the 'common wealth', outside the things 'you know' and all those structures of universality that are so anonymous. And we have to accept that at this moment this kind of anomalous growth is considered intolerable. It is insufferable for the level of state control that you have in the United States and that is now operating not only in every European nation but in Europe as such.

For us in France, who are used to state control for many centuries, England was a country where you had much more leeway, where you were not subjected to the same kind of state control as on the continent; this was because of your aristocratic heritage that you had so far maintained. This, I was told, is disappearing every day here. I was saddened when I learned that there is now a question of a national identity card in England. Although it may not be implemented immediately, as I was informed today at lunch, it shows that state control now also comes to the English, at least much more than before.

Being confronted with CBT, we are faced with new phenomena. Is CBT just the use of suggestion that we know from long ago, which we had in the nineteenth and at the beginning of the twentieth century, only in a new edition? I fear it is not a new edition of suggestion, because it is a kind of horrible side product of psychoanalysis itself. That's the new thing. It is in some way post-analytical, post-Freudian.

When you read the recent interviews with A. B. in the *New York Times* and the *Washington Post,* you find that he is, or was, a psychoanalyst and he got bored. He could not listen to people saying the same thing over and over anymore. And that for fifty minutes, I suppose. He became bored with the analytic practice and found work with patients exhausting because the goal seemed so unclear. That's the way Mr. B. remembers his practice. The idea is that if you sit back and listen and say "hm, hm," somehow, eventually a secret would come out. But you would also get exhausted by the helplessness of it all. That is his description as an analyst of how he got dissatisfied. And not only did he get worse, or ill, but for him his patients got worse, too. As he says, "The more I let my patients free associate during the session, the worse they feel." Well, it is a well-known fact of the practice that you have the crystallization of symptoms.

If we are to understand this phenomenon, we have to understand CBT not only from the point of view of psychoanalysis, but as a by-product of psychoanalysis and, I would say, as a by-product of American psychoanalysis. Because when you read about CBT, you can see that it is made up of commonsensical statements, which shows that it is referring itself to the extreme standardization of the analytic practice in America. There is this idea of some kind of pure neutrality of the analyst, and this 'purity' is what, through CBT, they have tried to correct in some way, in order to rehumanize the analytic process. Therefore, if we are to continue this study, we have to study it as a type of by-product of psychoanalysis, not of Freudian psychoanalysis but of the American or English kind of psychoanalysis, which in France we saw appear as something coming from the outside. We do not feel that it is born from our practice. That is the first point.

The second point is this: The basis for the CBT point of view is their idea of language. They do not theorize what language is for them, but I consider it to be a theory of language, namely, a theory of description. They believe fundamentally that language is unambiguous, or at least that language may easily be used in an unequivocal fashion and that it can be explicit. That is why they believe it is possible to have a prior agreement, between patient and therapist, on what the trouble is and how to cure it. It is thought, in CBT, that you can agree on a therapy and that the patient can agree on a prior description of the trauma. This way they agree on the result, which is, consequently, the suppression of the previously described problem. They assume that if you take a black box and get inside it—the black box being the treatment, the process of the treatment—you can get inside the described trouble and then have an outcome, that you can perceive the described trouble and agree that it has disappeared. In this logic, the treatment itself has no influence on the description of the trouble, which remains a constant that is not dependent on the process. They built a process that has no influence on the description of the trouble and the description of the trouble itself is a creation, as Thomas Svolos has shown earlier.

But the description of the trouble *is* a creation. The trouble, as it is described, is, I would say, a 'phobiazation'. Phobia is here the general model of mental problems, a fear of all mental life. We have here the idea that what is insufferable translates into fear and into distance. A general trouble is always turned into avoidance, so that the mental problem *is* avoidance. We could say that the universal model of CBT is avoidance; it corresponds to the idea that something triggers consequences, that you can act on the triggering mechanism and that it can be modified. This is just an outline. Perhaps we could show, in practice, why this model is not justified. I think it can be conclusively shown. The starting point of the evidence-based hypothesis is the idea that what was before is the same as what is after, so you can show something has disappeared. It is an idea of language as enabling one to give an unambiguous description of something, which is already a nullification of treatment, as we saw. Whereas we consider that the very concept of reality for each subject/patient is modified by the treatment. Ours is therefore a self-contained theory, something that unifies the essential point of the treatment.

The attitude we adopt toward this Other and whether we refer to it as struggle or criticism, or whatever, will depend on the attitude of our civilization at this moment. Will people accept this level of state control and regulation? Will people desire to be considered like machines? Or are they going to reject it, a factor we cannot guarantee. In principle, we cannot have much effect. It is a question, as Thomas Svolos said, of an ethical response. For me, the model of language of CBT is exactly the same as the user manual for an apparatus; when you buy an appliance you have an unequivocal instruction of how to switch it on and off. That is the model or concept of language used in CBT. Maybe people are going to consider that a machine is a superior state of humanity. And if this happens, I do not think we can do much.

What is the most surprising fact for me is that the religious establishments, the churches in the modern democracy, have gone along with this assessment! It seems to me that, before, there was a humanistic rejection of mechanism by what was referred to as the house of souls. We had allies then. Even though Freud was considered demonic, it was still obvious, for Lacan, that there was an alliance between religion and psychoanalysis against mechanism and science. You could feel that very clearly in the fifties. While what is equally noticeable now is that you do not have that. Nowadays religion does not compete with science. They leave the earth to science and quantification, without hesitation. They just add one thing: that the essential idea is the defense of life; the defense of life and the other world. Simultaneously, they accept quantification to an extreme degree, and this is the big change. It produced a change in the relation of forces, due to the change of the religious line. You see, in our struggle against CBT, to rehumanize religion is an ambition we have to talk about.

This is the text of an intervention by Jacques-Alain Miller at the Psy-Forum entitled "For Desire, Against CBT" held on the occasion of the 3rd Congress of the New Lacanian School of Psychoanalysis, London, 21–22 May 2005. It was transcribed and edited by Natalie Wülfing and Bogdan Wolf.

Note

1. The *Accoyer* amendment sought to reserve the practice of psychotherapy to psychologists and medical doctors. Following the resistance of an alliance between the *Ecole de la Cause Freudienne* and a number of other 'psy' organizations, this amendment did not come into force. Around the same time, the INSERM (the French Institute for Medical Research) published a report on the relative efficacy of different psychotherapeutic approaches. It soon emerged that the authors of the report were associated with the cognitive-behavioral tradition. So, predictably, and measuring efficiency in terms of the disappearance of the symptom for which therapeutic support is sought, the report concluded that the most efficient approach was CBT (*ed. note*).

About the Contributors

Marie-Hélène Brousse is a practicing analyst in Paris. She is a member of the World Association of Psychoanalysis and *Ecole de la Cause Freudienne*. She teaches in the Department of Psychoanalysis at the University Paris VIII.

Jean-Louis Gault is a psychiatrist and practicing analyst in Nantes and Paris. He is a member of the World Association of Psychoanalysis and *Ecole de la Cause Freudienne*.

Pierre-Gilles Guéguen is a practicing analyst in Rennes and Paris. He is a member of the World Association of Psychoanalysis and *Ecole de la Cause Freudienne*. He teaches in the Department of Psychoanalysis at the University Paris VIII.

Gabriela van den Hoven is a chartered clinical psychologist and a practicing analyst in London. She is a member of the World Association of Psychoanalysis, New Lacanian School, and London Society of the NLS.

Richard Klein is a practicing analyst in London. He is a member of the World Association of Psychoanalysis, New Lacanian School, and London Society of the NLS.

Eric Laurent is a practicing analyst in Paris. He is currently the Delegate General of the World Association of Psychoanalysis and a member of the *Ecole de la Cause Freudienne*. He teaches in the Department of Psychoanalysis at the University Paris VIII.

Jacques-Alain Miller is a practicing analyst in Paris. He is the editor of Lacan's works and editor-in-chief of *Ornicar? Digital*. He is a member of the World Association of Psychoanalysis and *Ecole de la Cause Freudienne*. He teaches in, and is director of, the Department of Psychoanalysis at the University Paris VIII.

Alexandre Stevens is a psychiatrist and practicing analyst in Brussels. He is a member of the World Association of Psychoanalysis and *Ecole de la Cause Freudienne*. He is founder and Director of the *Courtil* clinic in Brussels and coordinator of the Brussels Clinical Section.

Esthela Solano-Suárez is a practicing analyst in Paris. She is a member of the World Association of Psychoanalysis and *Ecole de la Cause Freudienne*. She teaches at the University of Paris VIII Clinical Section.

Véronique Voruz is a practicing analyst in London. She is a member of the World Association of Psychoanalysis, New Lacanian School, and London Society of the NLS. She teaches at the University of Leicester and was the assistant editor of the *Psychoanalytical Notebooks* until 2005.

Herbert Wachsberger is a psychiatrist and practicing analyst in Paris. He is a member of the World Association of Psychoanalysis and *Ecole de la Cause Freudienne*. He teaches at the Paris-Ile-de-France Clinical Section.

Bogdan Wolf is a practicing analyst in London. He is a member of the World Association of Psychoanalysis, New Lacanian School, and London Society of the NLS. He was the editor-in-chief of the *Psychoanalytical Notebooks* until 2005.

Index